STRANGELY RHETORICAL

StRANGELY RHETORICaL

COMPOSING DIFFERENTLY WITH NOVELTY DEVICES

JiMMY BuTTS

UTAH STATE UNIVERSITY PRESS
Logan

Published by Utah State University Press
An imprint of University Press of Colorado
1624 Market Street, Suite 226
PMB 39883
Denver, Colorado 80202-1559

Printed in the United States of America

ASSOCIATION of UNIVERSITY PRESSES The University Press of Colorado is a proud member of the Association of University Presses.

The University Press of Colorado is a cooperative publishing enterprise supported, in part, by Adams State University, Colorado State University, Fort Lewis College, Metropolitan State University of Denver, University of Alaska Fairbanks, University of Colorado, University of Denver, University of Northern Colorado, University of Wyoming, Utah State University, and Western Colorado University.

∞ This paper meets the requirements of the ANSI/NISO Z39.48–1992 (Permanence of Paper).

ISBN: 978-1-64642-444-3 (hardcover)
ISBN: 978-1-64642-281-4 (paperback)
ISBN: 978-1-64642-282-1 (ebook)
https://doi.org/10.7330/9781646422821

Library of Congress Cataloging-in-Publication Data

Names: Butts, Jimmy (Professor of writing), author.
Title: Strangely rhetorical / by Jimmy Butts.
Description: Logan : Utah State University Press, [2022] | Title page title appears as "StRANGELY RHETORICaL." | Includes bibliographical references and index.
Identifiers: LCCN 2022019655 (print) | LCCN 2022019656 (ebook) | ISBN 9781646424443 (hardcover) | ISBN 9781646422814 (paperback) | ISBN 9781646422821 (ebook)
Subjects: LCSH: English language—Rhetoric—Study and teaching (Higher) | Figures of speech. | Literary style.
Classification: LCC PE1404 .B88 2022 (print) | LCC PE1404 (ebook) | DDC 808—dc23/eng/20220526
LC record available at https://lccn.loc.gov/2022019655
LC ebook record available at https://lccn.loc.gov/2022019656

Cover illustration by Scout Butts (age 6) and Selah Butts (age 9).

To those with whom I have not yet had the pleasure of sitting down and talking

(DIS)CONTENTS

STRANGELY RHETORICAL

NOTICE

Psst.

Hey there. Come here. You want some *strange*? Sure you do.

Listen up, heathens. I'm going to tell you what's up and give you the real low lowdown. The skinny without the dip. The medicine without the spoonful of sugar.

Let me lay it out for you real simple-like. Like a map.

So, spoiler alert. Strangeness is important. Like rhetoric, it's everywhere, and not just in the weird sci-fi show you watched last week. It's in weird texts like vacuum cleaner manuals—trippy stuff. And it's integrally related to rhetoric, because both are about relations.

Here's basically how it's going to go. We're going to begin together by riffing on what strangeness might be. We'll open with that kind of free association you can just sit back and relax with. Pour yourself a drink and enjoy the ride. Then we'll start easing in. We'll get our definitions down. So, step 1 is the *logos.* We'll talk about what a strange rhetoric is. And then, who talks about strangeness? Well, Aristotle for one, but also this Russian guy . . . Shklovsky, along with a lot of other folks whom we may or may not expect. And then we'll start a new chapter. And *that* chapter will be about why strangeness is important—its ethics. Surprise, surprise. Because strange rhetoric is involved in how we move and relate to each other as Others with capital Os. So, step 2 is the *pathos* with a bit of *ethos.* We have to talk about how strangeness makes us feel together, how it moves us, and how we identify as strangers. The third chapter gets into the how, the practical *praxis* of strangeness. How do we make strange rhetoric? Well, the secret is in the sauce—figures. And then we can safely (for the most part) move into a look into where strangeness lies (or floats). We already said it's everywhere, but it has containers, texts like this one and like the ones you make too. So, we talk about the W.A.V.E.S., the multimodal spaces where strangeness gets brewed and bottled, where it's made. Chapter 5 is perhaps the handiest one; it lays out Seven Strangers . . . seven figures that you can think about and use in your own strange creations. There are more than seven, of course, but this handy-dandy list will get you started. You can then begin to practice

https://doi.org/10.7330/9781646422821.c000

for yourselves, reading and composing strangeness all over the place. Go nuts. (Because, you see, the biggest antagonists to this whole shebang deal are the ones who warn you against going nuts—the ones who tell you to color inside the lines.) And then we're going to close with a consideration of strange networks, which, again, is just thinking about all of the complex relationships at work around strangers and their compositions. Those strange compositions move us. They make our world more or less strange along the way. We'll get to how strangeness is what really lets us all get together. And this is not some mere anti for the sake of anti. There's a reason that whatever might be considered normal is the real hitch, and what we see as strange are the real moments where we might just catch a glimpse of the really real relations going on. There is a brief coda . . . an epilogue or a short concluding idea that offers one last secret key. But you'll get there just fine if you stick with it.

It's not an easy journey. There are plenty of thorny detours. But strangeness requires a bit of ergodicity—the difficulty of travailing a winding, working path. Strange paths sort of buck straight lines. As in any exploration, we'll not deal with every linkage, not every diverging, forking alleyway, and so you will note your own connections, derivations, associations, and so on.

And what's with all this *we* stuff? Who is this we? Well, it's you and me, of course. It's just us weirdos in conversation together, thinking together. We're in this thing together. Strangers and rhetors never act alone; they don't exist in a vacuum. They need other people.

And who gave you permission to write this way? Well, nobody. That's not quite true. You can blame those who gave me permission—good teachers along the way. For their loose reins and encouragement, I'll always be thankful.

Put on some funky tunes, dear reader, maybe some wild ambient tracks, settle in, and let's go.

So, without any further ado . . . this way please . . . mind the gaps.

Buckle up. It's going to be a bumpy ride.

PART I

Understanding Strangeness

Chapter One
WHAT IS STRANGELY RHETORICAL?

There is no excellent beauty that hath not
some strangeness in the proportion.
—*The Essaies of Sr. Francis Bacon, Knight* (1613)

STRANGER RHETORS

You are strange. I am too. You are a stranger. That is your special power. And that is also the foundation of rhetoric in all its unique forms. This strangeness of ours offers us tricks for making potentially striking compositions. When we compose a text of any sort, we make something new, something slightly unfamiliar for a stranger, an other, our audience. We can tap into that novelty and make some *really* interesting things. As we make interesting things together, communicating endless novelties, we constantly practice being what we already are: stranger rhetors.

Let's riff or drift on this idea a bit and see where it takes us. Strangeness is apparent in the world around us. It might be rain while the sun is shining, spɹoʍ uʍop ǝpᴉsdn, axolotls, or it might be someone born with extra fingers, like me. Strangeness is natively mysterious because it means we are perceiving something that would normally be otherwise. Strangeness lies at the edges, across lines. This is strangeness's power. Strangeness sits outside of town, yet it is intrinsically political because it pulls away from whatever norms lie within the social structures at the center of a city, the pole that polices in the middle of our *polis.*

Here is the real crux of the matter. Our otherness can be imagined as being for others. It can be a gift. It can also be taken, co-opted, commodified. However, our otherness allows us to be rhetorical in our exchanges with one another, pushing and pulling in all of our suasive communicative acts. Our rhetorical strangeness doesn't exist for ourselves so much as how we are perceived. This is because it is often hard to see how we are viewed by others as strange beings in the world. Our strange being in the world exists as a fundamental aspect of our own realities. Our otherness is also sometimes *against* others. Our stranger-ness always

https://doi.org/10.7330/9781646422821.c001

exists as some part of our identity—but it's also always either somewhat off-putting or kind of attractive.

Strangeness and normativity considered through the various ways that we compose things in the world are particularly what the following pages explore. As Cynthia Haynes puzzles out with us in her essay "Writing Offshore," "Yet we know (don't we?) that writing should be strange, that we should feel alienated, removed, and detached from our *standard* habits of reading and thinking" (2003, 671). This tension and resistance regarding the strange and the standard continue to lie at the heart of theorizing and practicing composition and rhetoric. Plato too wrote, "Writing, you know, Phaedrus, has this strange quality about it" (1972, 69), because it remains a stranger and cannot speak back and become more familiar when questioned. Through this exploration, we will arrive at what I hope to be some potentially useful takeaways.

The attempt here is to arrive at a theory of strangeness to see what it entails and what it can do rhetorically. And while the theory can sometimes take us to complex and fraught sites of thinking, in many ways, this book exists simply in the hope that we can find more ways of getting folks to do more interesting things with their compositions. In essence, the gist of rhetorical strangeness is twofold: strangeness is important for rhetoric because we are always speaking as others to others. And second, as a lens, strangeness allows us to think about generating more interesting and engaging novel forms of rhetorical expression through invention, as opposed to those conventional, normative voices that don't often get heard.

WHAT STRANGENESS MAY BE

Definitions are slippery fish. Go on—try to define what a table is. Strangeness is especially difficult to define because it, by its very nature, sits outside what we can usually grasp or lay hold of. Still, we know what a table is when we see it. We also know strangeness when we see it. It sits there like an unexpected animal looking out at us from the woods. Can we find it? Can we really ever catch a true glimpse, and then sit there, with it staring back at us for a minute before it quickly and quietly scampers off? It stands out, is different—hair or fur strikingly distinct from the trees and leaves nearby. In her article "Listening to Strange Strangers, Modifying Dreams," Marilyn Cooper considers the rhetorical effect that results from the strange shock of a dragonfly zooming into her car window while she's driving (2016, 17). Dragonflies are strange creatures. What is the strangest creature you can think of? (Maybe that's not even a fair question, considering this new radical relativity.) And it is also important to remember that we're strange creatures too.

At the present time, our culture is invested in a constant hunt for novelty. We have become hunters and gatherers of strangenesses. Strangeness hunting is our new way of life as we scroll through media feeds, longing for a kick or a hit. So, what might it mean to consciously or thoughtfully practice strangeness hunting? Hunting a weird, wild beast, not to capture it but to have seen it, to have experienced its otherness: that is the contemporary condition.

For our purposes, strangeness is the measure of difference or distance between relations. Because relations exist at the heart of rhetorical situations, strangeness is the quality of any rhetorical object's distance from its most frequent formations—and often its audience. Strangeness is wrapped up in form. A strange table, for instance, might have 165 legs, be made of chocolate, and sit inverted. In any case, strangeness offers the potential of the not yet from the already. It offers similarities and differences, helps us perceive when things are more or less alike; it builds tension and creates attraction and repulsion.

Strangeness, though a noun, isn't exactly a solid thing, though it is a thing that can be felt, as with the adjectival *strange*. They are both qualities of things in more or less distant arrangement with other things. Strangers count as nouns, of course. Strangers offer unique singular beings that create tensions of difference and divergence. Strangenesses are naturally diverse, resisting old norms—found in places like normal schools and Normal, Illinois—and even resisting the oxymoron of the new normal. *Strange* seems to be something that we use to denote curious interest. As in, "Hmm . . . strange. That's out of the ordinary. . . ."

I do prefer the term strange to its most frequent synonym, weird, only because of etymology. Weird comes from the Old English *wyrd*, which essentially suggests a twist in fate—interesting, but not my main drive here, though strangeness is certainly connected to individuals experiencing twisting differences over time. The word *strange* comes from the Latin *extraneus*, meaning "from the outside." The first non-obsolete definition for "strange" in the *Oxford English Dictionary* is "Belonging to some other place or neighbourhood; unknown to the particular locality specified or implied. Of a place or locality: Other than one's own" (OED Online 2021). The otherness of strangeness is always called into question when any reader confronts a work or text—because a text is never one's own until it is taken in. How much does a composition fit within the nativity of one's experience, and will it be rejected upon this foundation? How do we compose when this strangeness always threatens or sweetens the success of our work? The thought as it pertains to composition is that it confronts the cultural value of *being-in*: plugged in, jacked in, in the know, in the mix, bask in, come on in. We oscillate then, perceptually, between media that draw us in and rhetorical moves that draw us outside of what we have come to accept as familiar.

We could try to define strangeness by the negative: it is the unconventional, the unordinary, the unusual, the outside, the non-normative, the irregular, the aberrant, the atypical; it is that which deviates. Strangers embrace their own eccentricities—out of center—peculiar and odd and queer, strikingly interesting and novel. Trying to get at what it is by considering what it is not is a little like trying to shine a light on a moving noise in the dark. In working outside and against the confines of the city, strangeness is to pagan as convention is to the polis.

OUR STRANGE WORLD IN CONTEXT

Who are you in this strange world of ours, fellow writing rhetor? What are your own peculiar rhetorical strangenesses? When I was little, I would sit in front of a light-blue box fan and speak into the blades. My voice would come back, chopped and foreign. I would do that for a while, enjoying my other voice, the speech that was mine but different, altered. I could turn the fan off, or move away, and my voice would be normal again, as it should be. But what *should* a voice be? Should it be normal at all? And what makes something normal in the first place? These are difficult questions but ones that are worth sitting with for a while. Rhetorical strangeness is an experience of oscillation, like spinning fan blades. In one moment, novelty can be breathtakingly exciting. Another, a strange move might be too off-putting to bear. When rhetorical strangeness has an affective quality (and it often does), when it moves us to curiosity, to pleasure, those are the most interesting moments, when strangeness offers some brief sway (and those moments rarely last long—strangeness doesn't stick around).

Let's consider just a few more strange things before we move on. What is the strangest thing you can think of? The duck-billed platypus is a classic example. Blue-tailed skinks. Vampire squids. Slime molds. Venus flytraps are particularly strange—sold at novelty stores. What makes these things so weird? What makes them feel so strikingly different? They are part of our world. They are not strange to themselves. A platypus isn't so strange to another platypus. But to us, they *feel* different. And what is more, nonhuman actants like butterflies don't even have the word *rhetoric* to think about what is going on among them. We interpret things in our own strange, human, culturally oriented terms.

10–66 is the NYPD radio code for an unusual incident, such as a building collapse. We know that the police are always on the lookout for the strange and unusual. The unusual creates policing. The kinds of things we are seeking here are works that dissent from the usual forms while still working within the rules set by an audience's imperative. The stranger rhetor learns to police itself for itself—to survive.

A bug in the house or a snake in the yard gives us a strange jolt. It feels different because there is a *should-not* about that sort of being in certain places. The house or the yard offers us a normative space. The classroom has its own norms and boundaries. Our own spaces—the ones that we claim to possess—seem safe and familiar. When something else enters, something unexpected, we feel the striking shock of strangeness. But we must and do allow the other to enter; we entertain difference. We too can elicit powerful shocks by being as wise as serpents. The welcome charm of the platypus is not the same otherness as the unexpected and uninvited snake. But both create affect. We can as well in our writing and our speaking with our own embodied gestures. With rhetorical strangeness, we shift attentions.

Our obsessions are a ripe place to look for our cultural strangeness. American football is a strange, complex set of cultural practices that—when looked at from a distance—can be perceived as jarringly unusual. But I might posit that everything works this way. Everything normal, with some distance, can be thought of as strange. You know what's strange? Vacuum cleaner manuals. And conversely, everything that is far off or weird, when made familiar with some time, becomes not so strange after all. Strangeness is everywhere. We only have to seek it out. We can hunt out a stranger any time we wish, something to occupy our strange little minds for a moment before moving on with our everyday lives.

Try this. Think about something you find to be particularly strange and what makes it so.

. . .

Strangers are things or beings. The strangeness between and upon things is an energy or force. As with any rhetorical missive, strange things can attract. Strange things can repel. It is in their nature to do so. Research in particle physics describes what are referred to as "strange attractors," as theorized by Edward Lorenz at MIT (Lorenz 1995; see also Gleick 1987). Physicists think of strangeness as a force—or a flavor, as a type of quark with certain unique qualities or properties. We might, after all, work with the quirkiness of our various quarks. Beyond that, of interest to rhetoricians, strangeness is paired or foiled with what physicists call charm, and both forces can be measured positively or negatively (see Anchordoqui and Halzen 2009, 6).

Rhetoricians have long understood conceptually how rhetoric itself is a force, at least since Aristotle outlined the term by saying, "Let rhetoric be an ability [or *dynamis*] to discern the available means of persuasion in any given situation" (2006, 37). Rhetoric is our dynamite. The dynamic power or ability involved in a unique rhetorical strategy may be thought of in similar terms to this emerging idea of strange attractors, chaotic formulas that make beautiful patterns. Beauty can appear in communication too. This examination of novelty in terms of rhetoric allows us to rethink what we mean when we talk about rhetoric at all. Still, with all the advances of the field, when I am asked to define rhetoric to the occasional new friend, I often spout out Aristotle's definition. Strangeness, too, offers available means for finding suasive ends within various forms. The ability to find strangeness, however, is a trick to be mastered, as with rhetoric. Being a good discoverer of means is like becoming an entrepreneur of language or a well-seasoned cook. The default is vanilla. So, we add sprinkles or spices. We have to learn to be savvy rhetors. A good, strange rhetor looks under rocks, behind trees, and through sheaves of paper to discover just the right means of grabbing listeners by their lapels.

The rhetor is a strange being in the world; he or she or it or they or xe is always already other. Strange composition strategies offer potentially effective sites of resistance for contemporary audiences who have been mediated in problematic ways by various procedural prisons; moreover, playful composing and reading strategies potentially free audiences from the forms, structures, conventions, and media that govern and anesthetize their everyday lives while offering them interesting new ones. I am arguing for novelty in the field of rhetoric and composition, or—I should say—a continuation of novel practices and their analysis. For some reason, I find that unless encouraged to do otherwise, students tend to create fairly conventional texts. Fun is at their fingertips. What we must be interested in doing, then, is helping us all find our unique voices within the boisterous contemporary public sphere by making use of the strangeness of various rhetorical devices. If we find strangeness provocative, then we are left with a question. Why is everything so boring?

A STRANGE SHKLOVSKIAN RHETORIC

In the field of rhetoric, to generate interesting connections, we can and often do create productive insights by simply considering the rhetoric of something. The rhetoric *of* X is a powerful tool that offers all sorts of paired potentialities (see Schiappa 2001, 269). We might consider the rhetoric of food, or the rhetoric of race, or the rhetoric of socks or snow globes. Here we have the rhetoric of strangeness, which gives us a lens and a framework with which to build. The way I got down this line of thought began with considering a Shklovskian rhetoric, which is to say, a rhetoric that pushes against familiarity.

As such, the central concept that I want us to explore in conjunction with rhetoric—defined broadly—is *defamiliarization* and its effects. Defamiliarization can help us think about creating potentially interesting rhetorical texts. To help us bridge this connection, we can begin with Viktor Borisovich Shklovsky, a Russian formalist and literary critic, who created the term **остранение** (transliterated *ostranenie*). Defamiliarization is just one translation of a word I am taking from Shklovsky. The word *ostranenie* has various contested translations: defamiliarization, estrangement, or enstrangment, along with simply making strange. Whatever the translation, Shklovsky's term has many connected theories beyond his own writing. Shklovsky remains a fringe figure in literary circles, but at the time he wrote during the early twentieth century, he was endangered and oppressed by the Soviet state as a dissenter, was interrogated, and barely made it out of the country with his life. That political outsider stance remains a serious aspect of his work, but it is also important in the present time for imagining an outsider rhetoric involving the composition of strangeness.

Defamiliarization still works as a rhetorical lens worth considering that functions across compositional media, especially within the buzz of media white noise. As a technique, defamiliarization is now more necessary than ever as our media ecologies become more familiar, and therefore more problematically captivating. Meanwhile, strangeness ebbs and flows within the tide of cultural novelties, from new digital spaces to new physical ones. In our mediatized world, a world that is increasingly fashioned for us, new forms—fashionably ahead of the trend—are the currency the contemporary rhetor must use to make his or her messages. We live in a flood—a media flood, an information flood, a world of bells and whistles, beeps and blips. And creating an argument that others will hear in a boisterous environment asks us to be increasingly interesting. In a world of media totalitarianism, one might do worse than return to a concept invented against totalitarianism: the avant-garde, defamiliarization.

The term *defamiliarization*, too, embodies this sense of something that was familiar but has deviated from that original form. According to translator Benjamin Sher, part of the Russian word *ostranenie*—*stranit*—signifies a homeland or state, but also "strange" (Sher 1991, xviii). This reinforces the tension-producing quality of strange rhetoric and its dynamism—which is to say that strange rhetorical moves unbalance a situation, putting the stability off balance. Sher suggests *enstrangement* to get at the strangeness of the word itself. I tend to use defamiliarization here because of the popularization of that translation. But the concept of making things strange in general is all we really need here.

Shklovsky's theories were developed in the Soviet Union under Stalin as a way of thinking about unique, complex work that resisted mass consumption. Yet it seems that strangeness may be pulled into the field of rhetorical criticism with some successful effects at the present time. And Shklovsky did not theorize novelty in a vacuum. He thought about the formal aspects of work alongside a group called the OPOJAZ (**ОПОЯЗ**), or ***Obščestvo izučenija POètičeskogo JAZyka***, the Society for the Study of Poetic Language. This group is similar in some ways to the popular French group the Oulipo, a group that was also committed to the experimentation of language and generated various textual experiments in order to make composition captivating in new ways. The Oulipo, or the *Ouvroir de littérature potentielle*, a working group investigating literature's potentials, represents another cohort that has explored the sorts of experiments on the surface of language that can make works interesting. The OPOJAZ, operating in Russia as the Soviet state mounted in political power, offers a different, politicized take. The work of collectives like these, seeing the text as textual, not *simply* as a lens to content, and yet viewing form and content as naturally interconnected, reveals the text—untexts the text, unmediates it—or unmediates it as remediation.

Defamiliarization, says Shklovsky, has the potential for working as an artistic device upon the audience. This unique term comes from Shklovsky's famous essay "Art as Device" from his book *Theory of Prose* (although I think it is a theory that applies to much more than prose). This insightful text has had a long influence; as Marjorie Perloff has said, it has "become a sort of bible to many of us" (2013, 15). In his writing, Shklovsky thoughtfully responds to a passage from Leo Tolstoy's diary where Tolstoy watches a man walking in the road bend down, pick up a stone, and sharpen his knife with it. The man is using the stone as a tool, but automatically, without thinking. Shklovsky recaps Tolstoy's story, then shares this insight. It is worthwhile to read the entire influential passage here:

> Objects are represented either by one single characteristic (for example, by number), or else by a formula that never even rises to the level of consciousness. Consider the following entry in Tolstoy's diary:

> As I was walking around dusting things off in my room, I came to the sofa. For the life of me, I couldn't recall whether I had already dusted it off or not. Since these movements are habitual and unconscious, I felt that it was already impossible to remember it. If I had in fact dusted the sofa and forgotten that I had done so, i.e., if I had acted unconsciously, then this is tantamount to not having done it at all. If someone had seen me doing this consciously, then it might have been possible to restore this in my mind. If, on the other hand, no one had been observing me or observing me only unconsciously, if the complex life of many people takes place entirely on the level of the unconscious, then it's as if this life had never been. (29 February [i.e., 1 March] 1897)
>
> And so, held accountable for nothing, life fades into nothingness. Automatization eats away at things, at clothes, at furniture, at our wives, and at our fear of war.
>
> If the complex life of many people takes place entirely on the level of the unconscious, then it's as if this life had never been.
>
> And so, in order to return sensation to our limbs, in order to make us feel objects, to make a stone feel stony, man has been given the tool of art. The purpose of art, then, is to lead us to a knowledge of a thing through the organ of sight instead of recognition. **By "enstranging" objects and complicating form, the device of art makes perception long and "laborious." The perceptual process in art has a purpose all its own and ought to be extended to the fullest.** *Art is a means of experiencing the process of creativity. The artifact itself is quite unimportant.* (Shklovsky 1991, 6, emphasis added)

The consideration of how much humans function on the level of the unconscious asks much of rhetoricians, who use their own artistic devices. Which devices awaken our senses? And when? And how? And are we unconscious now? If we dust our furniture unconsciously, as Shklovsky suggests through Tolstoy, then where or when does modern life actually find grounding? As Lauren Berlant and Kathleen Stewart poetically inure us: "Strangeness raises some dust" (2019, 5). Because of the tool of art, we have capability, agency in our compositions to feel out and find presence—phenomenologically and rhetorically. Shklovsky's focus on novels as his primary medium has kept current critics interested in new compositions across media from applying his concepts to the field of rhetoric.

Many have considered the relations of figures and strangeness, and that thinking remains useful even after over 100 years since Shklovsky first wrote about it. Defamiliarization functions rhetorically across different forms of composition and media. In other words, a stranged text will often become a suasive text. Shklovsky's exploration into the study of poetic language has been carefully examined by a host of scholars, but his theory of defamiliarization continues to haunt us as after modernism and strict theories of formalism have demurely gone upstairs. The ethics underlying Shklovsky's writing is intensely relevant for us today because it works against the flood of totalizing immersive media when ubiquitous media elicit only automatic or anesthetized responses from contemporary audiences.

The ability to bend forms and conventions after learning them, I would argue, is now one of the few ways that we have to jackhammer through the hazy apparatus of everyday life and get our audience's collective attentions in our overwhelmingly distracted mediatized culture. The introduction to Shklovsky's later book, *Bowstring*, contains a further elaboration and development of the idea of estrangement that may be connected back to this grounding found in the Greek consideration of the concept. The introduction tells us:

> Shklovsky redefines estrangement (*ostranenie*) as a device of the literary comparatists—the "person out of place," who has turned up in a period where he does not belong and who must search for meaning with a strained sensibility. The book's title comes from Heraclitus: "They do not understand how that which differs from itself is in agreement: harmony consists of opposing tension, like that of the bow and the lyre." Comparison, in this sense, does not involve the assimilation of someone else's "otherness"—rather, it catalyzes one's own "otherness" and the otherness of one's own language. (Avagyan 2011, x–xi)

A personalized language is distinct from an aberrant one, although it would almost depend upon taste to consider whether a composition differed too strongly, or—in the conceit of Heraclitus—pulled the bowstring too tautly.

Although he was much more interested in literary applications than strictly rhetorical ones, Shklovsky specifically mentions the one who first gave us a whole book on rhetoric, Aristotle. Their connection to one another often goes unnoticed, particularly in the field of rhetoric. Interestingly, Aristotle tentatively offers a similar program to Shklovsky's in his writing. His understanding of strangeness as an affective force exists in ancient Greece almost 2,300 years before Shklovsky's theory.

ARISTOTELIAN STRANGENESS

Strangeness may be thought of as a kind of applied poetics, and in Aristotle's book *Poetics*, we can see some early traces of strangeness for rhetorical effect. Because strange forms can be traced back so far, it is surprising that a more concerted effort has not been made to research the strange in terms of rhetorical practice. Aristotle suggests, "Every word is either current, or strange, or metaphorical, or ornamental, or newly-coined, or lengthened, or contracted, or altered" (1932, 3.21). The balance of both the current and the strange is figured in much of the Aristotelian rhetorical schemata, though one would not normally use those terms. Nevertheless, Aristotle does in fact use that terminology—precariously placing the strange at the limits of rhetoric, somehow simultaneously concerned by it and in awe of it.

Aristotle's thoughtful consideration of strangeness continues in *On Rhetoric.* Aristotle explains in book III, "One should make the language unfamiliar; for people are admirers of what is far off, and what is marvelous is sweet" (2006, 198), using here the term *xenen* for foreign-language use. He even quotes another writer, Aneschetos (whose name means "bearable"), who says, (and you'll have to forgive the old translation because I like it): "Thou must not be a stranger stranger than thou should'st." And here we must begin to feel our own alienation from Aristotle's paternal warning.

Aristotle's initial mention of "the strange" is dismissive, but he does seem to imply *indirectly* that strangeness is rhetorical despite his opinion that strange usage is a kind of abuse of rhetorical figuration. Elsewhere in book III of *Rhetoric,* Aristotle talks about misuse and "the employment of strange words" and inappropriate metaphors. "Strange words, compound words, and invented words must be used sparingly and on few occasions [*toutōn glōttais men kai diplois onomasi kai pepoiēmenois oligakis kai oligakhou khrēsteon*]: on what occasions we shall state later" (2006, 198) suggests a wary Aristotle. Aristotle carefully counsels against going over the edge, or going too far, but acknowledges the usefulness of strange style for rhetorical purposes, noting that such tactics must be used sparingly, warning that a balance must be struck, keeping the audience in mind. His anxiety about strangeness has persisted in Western ideals and traditions of thought that privilege a functional and acceptable conventionalism. An example Aristotle gives of this rhetorical abuse is Gorgias talking about "pale and bloodless doings" (2006, 204). Aristotle initially seems to dismiss this metaphor as signifying a gimmicky novelty, but then shifts into a section on the effective use of simile—there is a paradoxical approbation of the strange techniques he sees in different Greek writers, including Plato himself. Of course, Aristotle's work goes on to influence much of rhetorical theory, and many have taken up the impetus to consider and enact rhetorical strangeness. The fact that Father Aristotle feels he must give a hesitant, provisional permission to be strange in the first place only invites our own persistent resistance.

Taking Aristotle as a prime mover for rhetorical study will serve us less and less moving forward. He remains a grounding, but we can push off and find new frontiers, as many have done in problematizing a tack that takes Aristotle as origin story. We have to pave new paths.

A STRANGE NEW VIEW OF RHETORICAL COMPOSITION

All rhetoric is based on the quality of strangeness. The degree of difference is the key fulcrum upon which a claim is placed. An argument is always *other* in that it is not already accepted as given by the party being persuaded—or not. The level of affectability and desire elicited in the strange thoughts of others will eventually result in the acceptance or rejection of those thoughts. Too strange, and the argument is rejected. With the force of strangeness in a rhetorical act, we either estrange or enchant our audience. Too familiar, and there is no argument at all. We must necessarily be strange with our rhetorical moves. We cannot help but be strange, but we can shape how our own strangeness is deployed. *Wonderful* rhetoric, rhetoric that fills its audience with wonder, offers some promise in re-creating new avenues for thinking about inventive communicative strategies. If I could sum up my entire philosophy of composition in one brief and accessible catchphrase, I might steal Apple's "Think Different," with its brash nonstandard surface error and its appealing call. Thinking differently is precisely what all of us are always after, and it is what we are often doing. This analysis is then a critical framework for how to explore, analyze, weigh, and create strange composition within the long-tried tradition of rhetorical criticism and invention. Here we reskew rhetoric, and perhaps rescue it, from the tired ways in which we've come to view it.

All rhetorical moves are strange.

What is *strange*? Rhetoric is.

Richard E. Vatz writes that the sine qua non of rhetoric is "the art of linguistically or symbolically creating salience. After salience is created, the situation must be translated into meaning" (Vatz 1973, 160). The use of rhetorical strangeness to show a text's textness, to draw out its meaning by directing attention, is powerful. Then we twist the meaning through various kinds of strange shifts and redirect the text and our audience to create that salience.

Others have touched upon similar thoughts. Who has not thought about strangeness? In the interest of time and space, we can touch upon only a few instances here. For example, Freud's uncanny is of particular importance to defamiliarizing composition, especially to see how it affects the minds of its cooperative or resistant audiences. Freud explored the concept of the *unheimlich,* German for the not-at-home or the uncanny. Freud's discussion of the uncanny is also particularly interested in writing. Freud observes, "We laymen have always been greatly intrigued to know where the creative writer, that strange personality, finds his subjects . . . and how he contrives to enthrall us with them, to arouse in us emotions of which we might not even have thought ourselves capable" (2003, 25). I also want to note here that the distinction between creative writing and something else is often a faulty division. Freud explains in "The Uncanny," "*Unheimlich* is clearly the opposite of *heimlich, heimisch, vertraut,* and it seems obvious that something should be frightening precisely because it is unknown and unfamiliar. But of course the converse is not true: not everything new and unfamiliar is frightening. All one can say is that what is novel may well prove frightening and uncanny; some things that are novel are indeed frightening, but by no means all. Something must be added to the novel and the unfamiliar if it is to become uncanny" (124–25). The uncanny, employed in various modes of composition as a tactic, as a kind of *unheimlich maneuver,* rescues work from the banality of generalized media forms.

Moving from one German to another, we can connect how playwright and critic Bertolt Brecht, visiting Russia at some point in his career and coming across Shklovsky's work, translated the idea of ostranenie into the German word *Verfremdungseffekt,* which is often translated into English as alienation or distancing effect, but encapsulates some aspects of the same concept about which we have been talking (Bloch, Halley, and Suvin 1970, 121). The importance of consciousness for Brecht and Shklovsky means that a different kind of attention should be paid to form. Brecht mentions, "The effort to make the incidents represented appear strange to the public can be seen in a primitive form in the theatrical and pictorial displays at the old popular fairs" (Bloch, Halley, and Suvin 1970, 91). At the fair, Brecht relates, the emphatic peculiarity of carefully self-aware performances allows the audience a different, more thoughtful kind of experience.

Experiencing and coming to terms with difference is in order for recognition or rhetorical connections to occur. For one, Kenneth Burke has referred to a related concept he calls "perspective by incongruity" (1984b, 88). In a sense, the kind of composition sought here is really a Burkean "perspective by incongruity . . . established . . . by violating the 'proprieties' of the word in its previous linkages" (1984b, 90). Burke offers this tactic as a kind of resistance to what he terms elsewhere, in *Attitudes toward History,* as the "bureaucratization of the imaginative"

(1984a, 225). Playful composition—composition that violates its own proprieties—recalls to our mind the rules and structures of composition itself. Burke adds, "Perspective by Incongruity is both needed and extensively practiced" (1984b, 119). Burke also refers to this as "THE NIETZSCHEAN METHOD," which offers opportunity for invention: "Such a device quickly makes it possible to speak, let us say of Arabian Puritanism, thus extending the use of a term by taking it from the context in which it was habitually used and applying it to another" (1984b, 89). The result of finding strange combinations can help us overthrow habitual use through decontextualization and move toward a productive novelty. Beyond the novelty of novels, the need, the exigency, for this sort of playful structuralism continues into various compositional forms.

Burke also explored the concept of identification in *The Rhetoric of Motives.* He writes, "Identification is affirmed with earnestness precisely because there is division . . . If men were not apart from one another, there would be no need for the rhetorician to proclaim their unity" (1969b, 22). So, our rhetoric is naturally strange, but as we embrace a kind of connection to one another we create what Burke calls identification. We connect through (not just in spite of) our differences. We can find a way to identify when someone shares something unique with us. Here we can add another useful thought from Burke, who writes, "Rhetoric must lead us through the Scramble, the Wrangle of the Market Place, the flurries and flare-ups of the Human Barnyard" (1969b, 22). In our wild cacophony of difference, rhetoric allows us to connect and interact. In the introduction to *Landmark Essays on Rhetorics of Difference,* editors Damián Baca, Ellen Cushman, and Jonathan Osborne tap into the meaning and importance of studying alternative routes in rhetoric. They describe "difference" as "a descriptor for critically engaging multiplicitous, complex living experiences across assymmetrical [*sic,* but I like the typo] dimensions of power" (2019, 2). The influences of difference are inbuilt into the rhetorical system. And so, we can be thankful for our strange rhetorical identifications with each other and the world.

This concept of connecting across our otherness can also be found in the work of Diane Davis. Working in part from Burke's concept of identification and Emmanuel Lévinas's ethical consideration of the Other, Davis suggests a pre-originary connection that she refers to as rhetoricity, which is "an affectability or persuadability that is at work prior to and in excess of any shared meaning" (2010, 26). And so rhetoricity allows us to consider our affectability, the ways in which we are even able to be interested by interesting otherness in the first place. I am convinced now more than ever that rhetoric is the practice of attempting to reduce otherness by sharing our otherness with each other. That is, rhetoric is in its essence the creation of unique connections, about making ourselves strangers less and less.

And while the connection of strangers and stranged texts is one goal, it is also important to see strangeness as having the potential for intentional distancing, as queer theorist José Esteban Muñoz suggests with the counter-concept of disidentification. Muñoz explains it in this way: "Disidentification is about recycling and rethinking encoded meaning. The process of disidentification scrambles and reconstructs the encoded message of a cultural text in a fashion that both exposes the encoded message's universalizing and exclusionary machinations and recircuits its workings to account for, include, and empower minority identities and identifications. Thus, disidentification is a step further than cracking open the code of the majority; it proceeds to use this code as raw material for representing a disempowered politics or positionality that has been rendered unthinkable by the dominant culture" (1999, 31). Hence, this othered/othering stance is also itself productive. When strangeness creates too much distance, it is important for us to be able to allow rhetoric to fail. It offers the potential to agree to disagree when necessary and also to accept and allow our differences to exist at all. When we aren't all perfectly identified with each other (and we aren't), we maintain our aspects of difference because when we allow that space, it allows us to still be a little productively strange (and rhetorical) with each other.

Meanwhile, other colleagues in the field of rhetoric have begun to touch upon this term *strange* with different approaches. One significant connection may be found in Michele Kennerly who, with a rare nod toward Shklovsky, works with others in a collection on *alloiosis*, where she encourages us by explaining: "Wonder refreshes otherness" and then asks, "What resources of rhetoric feed the sort of wonder that nourishes strangeness?" (2015, 87). In asking how *alloio*-rhetorics might be practiced, we invite a distant other to be *inside* but not *requisite*, without gawking or requiring anything. Perhaps no other contemporary thinker of rhetoric has come closer to this project's orientation than Kennerly. Later, she uses the term *atopos* as a non-place, a strange place, from which an outsider struggles for voice or representation when they are out-of-place (2017). The term *atopos* is distinct from *xenos* because the odd one without a place is not necessarily coming from anywhere at all—or anywhere known to us. The not-at-home rhetoric is a kind of homeless rhetoric, a displaced rhetoric—and here we imagine a rhetoric of handmade cardboard signs where strangers ask something of an other.

Bradford Vivian, a philosopher of rhetoric, suggests that we are not merely creating strangeness as foreigners in the world, but that we are inherently strange, ontologically so. In his text *Being Made Strange*, which is one of the primary places where rhetoric and strangeness have been connected, he argues for moving to the boundaries of rhetoric and, by default, the will toward representation. There, he suggests, "between identity and difference, between past and present, between self and other, our being—once so transparent and familiar—suddenly appears strange. In the interstices of this strangeness, of this 'dispersion that we are,' rhetoric acquires an ethos no longer identical with representation" (2004, 192). For Vivian, exceptionally strange rhetors may not necessarily even care to be known or heard in their various eccentricities or idiosyncrasies. In his thorough study, Vivian calls both the subjectivity of the speaker and their associated ethos already a stranger, already an amalgamation of foreignness.

Finally, Kristie Fleckenstein and Anna Worm also outline a framework for thinking through an "other rhetoric" that we can look forward to in the future. They announce, "We choose *other* as our descriptor for this future vision of rhetoric to emphasize the reality of difference, the constraints imposed by difference, and the beauty of a temporary unity forged through and across difference" (2019, 35) and "Other rhetoric requires not just the acknowledgment of difference but acknowledgment of the value that difference has" (38). Difference has value. And as Fleckenstein and Worm suggest, that difference is available in the future, coming at us as we build our desire for it. Sameness has its own values as well, but little work is exerted to achieve the value of our comfortable and habitual daily lives.

As such, we can continue discovering the potential found in what we are and what we are to one another in the present. Then we can see how we might move forward toward something different in the future. The future is always strange. Normal doesn't come back to us. Normal is merely a memory. And sometimes a familiar form might remind us of it. But difference is on the horizon. It is evident that contemporaries in the field of rhetoric and composition are increasingly struggling to confront the tensions that bubble up with strangeness on the line. The foreignness of any rhetorical message is why, I would venture, rhetoric itself is so dependent upon an understanding of strangeness. Rhetoric is always already other, it grates against any prior identification, it calls one to change one's mind. Rhetoric is at its heart essentially and necessarily strange.

THE LIMITS OF RHETORICAL STRANGENESS AND ANTI-STRANGENESS: WHAT IS NOT STRANGE? WHAT IS NOT RHETORICAL?

One of my own conceptual limits of rhetoric revolves around when some kind of transaction of intentional meaning doesn't occur. So, where are the limits here? And what's at stake with this line? Too strange can elicit total dismissal. It is perhaps fairly important to note a pretty significant caveat here. *We need normalcy too.* Of course, certain norms are required within any rhetorical act—for example, I am writing in English, not some personal language. But the norms are simply the other side of the same coin that functions as the currency of rhetorical exchange. Rhetorical messages come from unfamiliar places, and they must be tempered with at least some degree of familiarity—finding the balance there is the key to becoming a successful rhetor. My detractors might object, "Rhetoric is not so strange." Of course, every rhetorical act is dependent upon following some conventions. So, we must sit with all the caveats, all the considerations and contradictions, all the other voices, that call and challenge practices of strangeness. There is a balance of familiar and strange within any rhetorical situation that either topples or finds harmony with its audience. Too normal can elicit total dismissal too.

Who is for anti-strangeness? Standardized tests and certain forms of grading and assessment and rubrics and core educational standards that ask for things like correctness *above* or *before* creativity seem to continue to stand against a valuing of rhetorical strangeness. Meanwhile, strangeness produces rhetorical effects. However, strangeness can also produce something of an anti-rhetoric by being potentially off-putting or aggravating. The existence of a strange object in the world does its own thing. Everything is naturally being strange, sitting in its own unique strangeness. And these strange beings, all beings, really, have the potential to draw in or put off. Considering this (or any) boundary of rhetoric is potentially polemical as rhetoric continues to grow ever bigger and encompass more territory. From this angle, we practice the ancient tradition of *dissoi logoi*, or arguing both sides: strangeness is attractive, and strangeness is distancing.

Every exchange is somewhat strange. Otherwise, a communicative act is not rhetorical—a non-strange communicative act is something else; it might be called preaching to the choir. I have been using choir-preaching to delineate an end of rhetoric that seems already evident. In other words, strange compositions are out of the ordinary; suasive work occurs only when the audience does not already have the message. For example, a churchgoer on Sunday hears once again that "Jesus saves."

The person either believes this completely or would need some persuading—though there is a spectrum of belief. However, I am arguing that the message is only rhetorical if the person does not already completely believe it, if there is a stasis to be overcome, if the message is something other than the worldview of the listener. Rhetoric in its essence often comes from some outside place, even if that otherness is in and of and for ourselves. Yet defamiliarization is rhetoric's power or *dynamis*—finding the strange availability out of the host of options. Some might argue that a familiar or habitual thought might reinforce a belief, but this function is only the case if the audience still does not quite completely and totally believe the thought already.

Strange is a stasis word, meaning it has a tension, it has a politics. It gives one pause. It makes us reel back. We are wary of strangers. Don't talk to strangers! Stasis, we know from rhetorical theory, is the space where two confrontational sides come to a head, a standstill. In its political origins, stasis signifies a civil war (see Berent 1998, 331; Agamben 2015, 1–18). Terms that have their own tensions embedded within them are stasis terms; they are inherently political in the broad sense of politics creating divisions and putting people at odds. Strangeness can potentially cause division, which is why it is so important to study its effects rhetorically. Because the exotic can also woo, sway, and win over.

And so, in every conversion, in every rhetorical moment, a strangeness quotient is reached, accepted, and consumed. The strangeness quotient of any rhetorical act asks us to measure how far the audience is being asked to step; in other words, how strange is the rhetorical invitation or provocation? The strangeness quotient of any rhetorical move is a measurement of its extremeness. After all, how far are you asking your listener to go? Are you persuading them to join you for lunch or to believe that you are god?

What is the most normal thing you can think of? Are baseboards strange? Strange or not strange might not be the question. Perhaps everything has strange potential.

WITH WHOM MIGHT WE DISAGREE? ANTI-AGON, AGAIN, I

Antigone was, in almost every respect, an outsider. Resistant to the state, she stood outside the bounds of law, responsive to something better. She resisted Creon (whose name means ruler) to remember her brother Polynices (Sophocles 2000). In Heidegger's translation and interpretation of the play, he notes the Chorus proclaiming, "Manifold is the uncanny, yet nothing uncannier than the human" (see Withy 2015, 108).

The status quo, resistant to deviation, is where we find our disagreement. And yet, who is against strangeness?! Most of our interlocutors here will inevitably come to our aid. Rarely will someone confess to hate otherness outright, especially in our collective written theory.

So, while it is difficult to find the Creons of theory, it is much easier, I believe, to discover the rulers of excision in spaces of praxis. In practice, we often find in the everyday schoolroom those who would squelch a Brown girl's handwritten "she ain't," which is in some ways, like Antigone's, a noncompliant expression of connection to home in a displaced and regulated space. Patricia Williams refers to this psychological attack upon minorities as "spirit murder" (1991, 55). It occurs in a variety of ways, some more subtle, such as microaggressions, but sometimes more explicit—in red ink.

Those who still practice rhetorics of exclusion, rhetorics of agonism and antagonism, rhetorics of gatekeeping, rhetorics of standardization: against these we stand—awkwardly. These rhetorics still proliferate. When rhetoric becomes closed off by gatekeeping or standardization or prescriptive rule-following, then—simply stated—certain prejudices have arisen in the situation. Now, in almost every rhetorical situation, certain expectations exist before the exchange occurs. But being open to the unexpected or the aberrant—which deviates from whatever has been predetermined in one's mind—allows real rhetorical change to occur.

And there is not only a psychological resistance to enacted difference, but also a careful resistance to pleasure and play. A *very normal* tension exists within ourselves as strange compositionists. Ira J. Allen points out this exact perceived tension within us as fantastic, imagined—the creator is also created, the ethos is crafted, and the stranger emerges. He explains, "Composition, in all its activity, centers and orients toward negotiation between senses of self, constraints internal and external to those (fantastical) selves, and the possibilities of enacting creative capacity in a shared world" (2018, 190). This negotiation between the behaving composer and the resistant one is something we figure out along with our texts themselves. But this is our great challenge and our great hope—that something is possible nonetheless.

We've straight-jacketed much of our compositional work in practice. And we can write that off to our fears of enjoyment. In an interesting twist, Lynn Worsham writes, "Make no mistake, I am not against pleasure (who could possibly be against pleasure?), but . . ." (1999, 717). Of course, who would be against pleasure? Who would admit to being against more interesting compositions? Yet Worsham adds that resounding "but." As have so many. Including myself, in weak moments.

Which leads me to my last antagonist—myself. I long for novelty. And yet there are my moments when I am squeamish about different iterations of strangeness, both in myself and around me. I pull back when it is too much. I walk this tenuous line between allowance and disavowal. And stylistic preferences are okay. But sometimes I recoil against the strange otherness that I find—even in me. This tension must remain—a constant working out toward opening up to whatever may come along and jar our senses. That's the potentiality in pushing our boundaries, or even stopping to consider why and where our different stopping points might exist in the first place.

STRANGENESS AS AN EXPERIMENTAL FRAMEWORK

Strangeness as a value system becomes an interesting point of reference for interrogating composed works regarding their interestingness or inventiveness. I know that I am asking for more than the standard here, to get us composing in a mode where we can begin to bend the conventions of composition practices toward productive new ends. It is important for us to always be considering the pros and cons of familiarity. In working along strange new paths, we buck various standards and conventions (often too male—too white—too straight) that we have come to normalize. As Vershawn Ashanti Young writes, "Standard language ideology is the belief that there is one set of dominant language rules that stem from a single dominant discourse (like standard English) that all writers and speakers of English must conform to in order to communicate effectively" (2010, 111). Seeing (or imagining) a single standard or only one way is prescriptive and restrictive. Young continues, "See, dont nobody all the time, nor do they in the same way subscribe to or follow standard modes of expression" (111). An idea about a standard persists, and yet we continue to wrestle against this tension. We must use something familiar, but we cannot let familiar forms hold us back.

A number of conventions within composition and rhetoric have become encrusted with stale traditions. We continue to follow the ruts we have worn in our paths of thinking and doing. Meanwhile, we continue to fear going off track and getting dirty in our compositional practices. If traditional methods such as formal grammar are dead in composition classrooms, they deserve some kind of autopsy. I hope we can interrogate what we perceive as a whitewashed sense of composition—pristine like a porcelain toilet placed in an art gallery. But not all good equates with cleanliness, of course, and not everything bad is dirty.

So, we want something within this framework or heuristic:

Table 1.1. A strange composition framework

	Alluring composition	Repulsive composition
Strange composition	X	
Plain composition		

What we really want is the top left quadrant: strange and alluring compositions. Plain and alluring compositions are okay. But we are interested in novel compositions that work upon us in engaging and positively productive ways. Of course, strangeness and plainness can work against an audience and be repulsive. Strange and terrible days like 9/11 are horrifyingly different from the normal humdrum of our everyday lives. Not every kind of strangeness is good, after all. For example, when Lady Gaga wore a meat dress, the effect was upsetting for some, too strange to be accepted for its novelty, although other aspects of her work have been strangely alluring and successful because she has been one of those rare purveyors of novelty. The boring and unengaging five-paragraph essay falls into the plain and repulsive category—uninteresting and drab and off-putting. (And we know that the problem with the five-paragraph essay isn't the number of paragraphs.) The problem is vomit, regurgitation, spitting back up what has already been given. One could argue that everything normal is strange, and vice versa. We play along these lines in our work as we create, potentially being engaging and off-putting along the way. It is all dangerous, I am reminded. We are playing games with our texts that can hit or miss.

Nevertheless, a strikingly real danger lies in designing, writing, and making for the sake of alienation. One may simply alienate one's audience. The potential to captivate or alienate, however, lies within every text, every work. In a sense, writing or designing in order to distract may be a kind of dissuasion rather than persuasion. The methodological approach of defamiliarizing forms achieves distraction from the everyday. This approach does not by any means seek to do away with conventions, habitualizations, or normalizations altogether—these provide a basis from which one can function and into which one might introduce form.

STRANGENESS? SO WHAT?

We are not merely interested in strangeness for strangeness's sake. Let us close here with a quick "Why?" that might help us transition to the next move in our line of thinking. First, it is worth simply acknowledging the power of strange communication strategies. There are still more connections to be made, as well as an outlining of the strategies or devices by which one may make a conscious effort to *strange* a rhetorical act. Theodor Adorno seems to emphasize the importance of this line of thought by stating in *Minima Moralia*, "The value of thought is measured by its distance from the continuity of the familiar" (2005, 80). Surely, all thinking is a moving away from what we already know, accept, and believe. All rhetoric helps us to shift our stance, rebalance our weight, and move into foreign territory. Let us then not be hostile to strangers or strange thoughts; let us learn to be hospitable to what will always be *other*. At the same time, we must learn as rhetoricians that we are strangers to our audiences, that we can make use of this peculiar status, and that if we fail to accept this role, we may never be heard at all.

Revolutionizing our attitude toward conventions is an approach that helps us to pierce through in our overwhelmingly televisual culture. Naturally, much of the world is already strange; it only has to be discovered as such. As critic David Crystal notes, "Linguistic strangeness is, in fact, a perfectly normal, everyday occurrence. That we are so used to it that we have learned to ignore it. That we forget to look for it, and therefore we do not see it" (1990, 13). So this is also a call for a critical reading of a strange world—and for always attempting to see it as novel.

Our modes of communication can move toward strange styles and forms, making waves like lights, sounds, and oceans do. What should we do to sound out our own barbaric yawps in a barbarously clamoring culture without being romantically invested in individuality, or even the powerfully divisive duality of stranging composition? Is it now time to reconsider a neoformalist—or at the very least, a conscientious informalist—view of composition strategies, one in which students are empowered by their ability to find, deploy, and bend rhetorical devices within the hum of the current media flood?

Prose stylist William Hazlitt wrote in a small article for the *London Magazine* in 1822, "It is not easy to write a familiar style" (Hazlitt 1822, 185). Of course, I would add that it is not easy to write an unfamiliar style either—partly because creativity is hard and partly because nonstandard forms are often considered culturally "uncalled for." Asao Inoue has taken a strong stance, for example, against a single monolithic STANDARD by which all compositions might be measured—calling such a standard racist because it comes out of a tradition decided by white men (2019). The endeavor here is to complicate expectations of standardization by seeing both potential and problems in normative and unusual compositions. Often in conflict with various ousted identity formations, norms in composition happen across forms. Defamiliarization in composition and rhetoric, then, is wrapped up in anti-sexist, anti-racist, anti-ableist, anti-classist, and other anti-categoricals that resist shunning. And also always we must resist our own individualistic narcissism that might tempt us to think that we are especially exceptional in some sense. We are each of us unique in our own ways.

Strangeness may be read and written in useful ways across our cultural landscape. It may be written in books, plastered on billboards, splayed across clothing, composed through cinema, or generated through other digital platforms. A look at strangeness offers insight to a variety of fields, including grammar, rhetoric, literary studies, visual arts, music, cinema, communications, game studies, web development, creative writing, advertising, and even soccer fields. How one composes, if one does it strangely, can be quite effective—there are simply questions left about why and how. Throughout this work, I intend to fluctuate between different forms of composition at will, although I am primarily a writing teacher. And while I am mainly exploring strange effects in written work, they appear in all sorts of creative rhetorical forms. Musicians and creative writers and painters and sculptors and graffiti artists and web designers and robotics manufacturers and makers of all sorts—everyone can make use of strangeness. The principles of rhetorical defamiliarization traverse across all the different forms or works that may be called composition, to the broadest degree. Rhetorical invention works across a variety of tropes through a variety of forms of composition.

If we do not learn to disfigure our writing and other creative work toward our own productive ends, we may never be heard. As Hunter S. Thompson wrote in *The Great Shark Hunt: Strange Tales from a Strange Time*, "When the going gets weird, the weird turn pro" (Thompson 2010, 49). Be unique, I say. Create something different, I say. With many students, I usually get five very long paragraphs on a subject rehearsing the same tired, old arguments. Much of the time we simply just have Normal People Writing. Normal People Writing embraces the safe everydayness of simplicity and regularity, which is sometimes nice. Homogeneity is after all the de facto move in much of our communication. In response, we can teach conventions, pattern recognition, and then encourage pattern breaking for effect.

A brief note on bad composition and learning the rules may be necessary here. This is punk writing and an advocacy of rule breaking. This knowing breaking is reminiscent of the idea that Picasso could draw a perfect circle but chose to paint distorted faces. The play that can arise from learning the rules in order to conscientiously move within them becomes notable for this approach pedagogically. But who owns the rules, and what are they exactly? Perhaps feeling it out and seeing what can be made regardless is always already legitimate in its own right. In this light, writing labs may truly become laboratories of writing. Imagine the students walking up as clients, the aides in their white coats (smudged up a bit, of course) gently helping them conduct strange experiments upon their own writing. A continued need for experimentation with language and other compositional practices can drive us onward. As the sciences move forward with funded experimentation and validated forms of inquiry, I suspect that some kind of formal understanding of language and forms might at least earn some interest from the humanities.

This call is a call for twists of style, an invention of argument by an invention of style. The trick, the joke, is that in order to make the text legible at all in a post-information society, you have to obliterate it. Explaining jokes away is no way to go about things, however. In what possible ways, we begin to think, could we go about making strangeness more accessible, or less strange? This isn't the goal at all. Instead, let's get to work. Seeing forms at the forefront of managing (or imagining) in*formation* becomes a means of outformation, moving toward the borders of composition into something interesting and engaging while also freeing and provocative.

Let us return to our first love, the reason we decided to start making—because we like when what we make is interesting or feels new. Meanwhile, I should add that one reason that this defamiliarizing move works is the presence of the rest of a composition as largely ready-to-hand, readable, or conventional. With art, I might compare it to all the work an art student puts into building her own frame, cutting and stretching the canvas, and gessoing it several times over in her studio space. The rest, the normative work, offers up a field for the surprising.

I'll close by offering a consideration of strange rhetorical moves as importantly *interesting*, which comes from the two Latin words *inter esse*, meaning "among" and "to be." Interestingness is ontological as the very fabric of our being. Interesting connects. Interesting work allows a composer to be among others, to be with them. This all makes me think about a triangle, one where interesting connection is key, the rhetorical triangle, where we see the relation between author, text, and audience. Yet strangeness places a tension between the audience and the other two points in this rhetorical situation, which often comes at great effort between the author and the text. How far can we stretch it? Is the rhetorical triangle equilateral, isosceles, or scalene? How sharp a point must we draw? We have to be safe to play, after all. Meanwhile, strangeness can seem dark and potentially dangerous. But strangeness has the potential to free us up too . . . it leads us through the dark. To what we can know . . . about each other and the world. Rhetoric might be stranger than we ever imagined.

Chapter Two
WHY STRANGENESS MATTERS

I was a stranger, and he took me in.
—*Narrative of the Life of Frederick Douglass* (1845), where Douglass is quoting Jesus from *The Book of Matthew*

WHY STRANGE?

So, why strange? Well, one answer from an old punch line is simply this: "To get to the other side." But let's get deeper into it. There are at least five (or 5 million) whys that make strangeness matter for us.

VIGNETTES FOR THINKING WHY

Reason one: Making interesting things

Hugo is an art student, a writer, a musician, a . . . He wants to make something new. He wants to do something different. He's in a rut. Inspiration feels like a joke. White pages lie before him. He wants to know what moves he can make. He picks up a book or takes a walk outside, and all of a sudden he sees it. It hits him. There is a way to make something novel. Now, he just has to do it.

This is why rhetorical strangeness is important. Or at least, it is the first reason.

Reason 2: Breaking out of banality

Now, I want you to imagine young people bored out of their minds. They are sitting in a classroom and the bell is about to ring, but they can hardly bear the wait. They close their eyes, feeling their bodies melting into their chairs. Someone is saying something unimportant at the front of the class. A lecture. The air-conditioner is whirring. They tap pencils or doodle just to do something. Their eyes feel like they going to fall out of their sockets. Powerpointlessness washes over them. They let out intermittent groans. They want to read the tweets of someone young and famous, not Jane Austen novels. School sucks. Life sucks. Everything is boring. They numbly head home tired at the end of the day. The roads

https://doi.org/10.7330/9781646422821.c002

lead the way. They stop at some generic store—the aisles mediating guides. They sit down on the couch and give in to some screen or other. They are watching MTV, HBO, FOX, NBC, CBS, YouTube, Netflix. It doesn't matter. They are drowning in mediation, mindless and dull. They scroll through endless content. They are watching, watching, watching for hours—a generation bound up in the tethers of flickering signifiers—anesthetized zombies, unthinking subjects, docile bodies. They just want to see something interesting on the screen during the break from the drudgery before they drift off, but the screen shows pretty much the same thing today as it did yesterday, as it will tomorrow. They wake up again to do the same thing. They must not pass go. They must move along now. They have the right to remain silent.

Reason tres: Have fun

As soon as the bell dings, she rockets out of her chair, gets to her car, cranks the radio on to something loud, lights a cigarette, and slams on the gas. She drives dangerously fast. She just wants to feel something good. She wants to drink and dance and get high and orgasm. She's got plans for another tattoo or piercing. She's got plans for cliff jumping or skydiving. She's got plans to travel to Malta or Belize. She's getting on another plane tomorrow. She buys and wears the newest, brightest colors. She tastes everything on the menu. She loves fireworks and neon signs. She wants to experience some sort of pleasure so that she doesn't blow her brains out. She wants to have fun, fun, fun, fun, fun.

Hedonists seem to get it. Strangeness is just a hit of something different.

Reason D: Have a voice in the crowd

A child is crying. She is sitting at the border with lots of other children who are also crying. They do not speak the language. They just want some food, some safety, clean clothes, some hope. The guards have seen it all before. They are unflinching, unmoved. The droning cry of little children has ceased to affect them. They are jaded. Nothing happens. Politicians also don't do much because they need to run for the same offices in the same parties as they did before. Nothing changes because no one has a unique voice to speak into this big structure, this looming apparatus. It's the same flow on every media stream. With a billion voices all saying pretty much the same things over and over, it's hard to get a word in edgewise. Democracies are the congealed voices of multitudes, so how do we sound a roar in the midst of a steady hum? Somewhere, a mohawked teenager begins to write a protest sign in bright pink.

Do you see it yet? Let's add another.

Reason V: Hospitality

A group of men is standing together on the street. A woman wearing a hijab walks by. The men yell things. They have forgotten how to be nice, or maybe they never were. They have forgotten that their ancestors too came from some foreign place. She runs off, and another woman waves her into her little shop off of the street. She welcomes her in, gives her a seat and some water. It was hot outside. She has some nice music playing in the store that the woman has never heard before. She invites her to a party later that week where a group of nice strangers will get together at someone's house.

These and more are why strangeness is important.

WHO CARES? STRANGE NEGOTIATIONS

Here let us delve into the whys of strangeness, its purpose. Exploring a number of justifications for why strangeness is important ethically, politically, and culturally justifies the thoroughness of the weight it carries here. As such, we are able to see and unpack the outcomes, both positive and negative, that a kind of rhetorical strangeness provides. The weirdness of composing in divergent patterns allows us to resist hateful segregations and (sub)standardizations. As such, we may find strange negotations that allow us to make some new connections.

Why is strangeness our value? Because it values life, certain kinds of life, ours and others' otherness, and a life that is filled with excitement rather than boredom. Why have we not cared more about it? The tension of strangeness and its opposition sets up a potential prison. In the prison problem, we face endless constructs of conventions from which it is difficult or even problematic to escape. It is uncomfortable to get out, to push for freedoms. Ruts are easier to follow. As such, too, we confront what Nietzsche calls our inescapable "prison-house of language" (quoted in Jameson 1972), which allows and constrains inventive thought. In this metaphor and others, we see the regularity and regulation that occur with our routine use of language and rhetoric. Because rhetorical acts are regular, many become white noise, a blur, a fog.

The haze of everyday life functions as a kind of walling in for us as actants in the world. The regularity of daily living has habituated us into living as automatons or robots, derived from the Czech word работя (*roboti*), signifying slavery. As such, regularity and convention become for us a kind of obligation that we are forced to labor toward, to enact a kind of decorous servitude. As such, various kinds of compulsory or requisite compositional attitudes have crept into education, assessment, and even governmental systems. For example, plainlanguage.gov was created after the passage of the 2010 Plain Writing Act, which requires a certain style. As Nietzsche writes in *Die fröhliche Wissenschaft,* "Laws do not betray what a people is but rather what appears to it as foreign, strange, uncanny, outlandish" (Nietzsche 2010, 58). College testing and other norming practices often obliterate differences among student expression. In the push/drive toward performance, excellence, and efficiency, we stigmatize anything but conformity.

THE FIVE WHYS EXPLAINED

The main reasons that strangeness is significant for contemporary thinking in rhetoric and composition follow two interrelated axes—the interestingness axis and the interchange axis. The first axis suggests that strangeness allows us to make interesting things and read for interesting things. In this first sense, strangeness allows us to escape banality. It gives us a way of emerging from media overload and the anesthetization of our everyday lives, which was Shklovsky's primary concern regarding defamiliarization in "Art as Device." Interesting materials release us from our collective stupor, the repetitive prisons of our daily habits, and help us to wake up. Strangeness allows us to see and bend conventions—and to have fun doing so. Strangeness invites a hedonistic approach to the pleasurable response to and generation of divergent texts. The other major reasoning for strangeness follows a second significant axis of interchange: being heard and being open. It allows us to speak out and stand out—to be heard in a noisy, boisterous public sphere. In the middle of these two axes, we find the intersection, or the punctum, the point of influence. It makes me think of a fly on a television set tuned to no channel, or a speck standing out among the white noise or the snow. In that strange spot, we find affect and meaning and conveyance. If we begin with the premise that strangeness helps us to create rhetorical interest and affect, everything else falls into place, and we create interesting interchanges and strange exchanges.

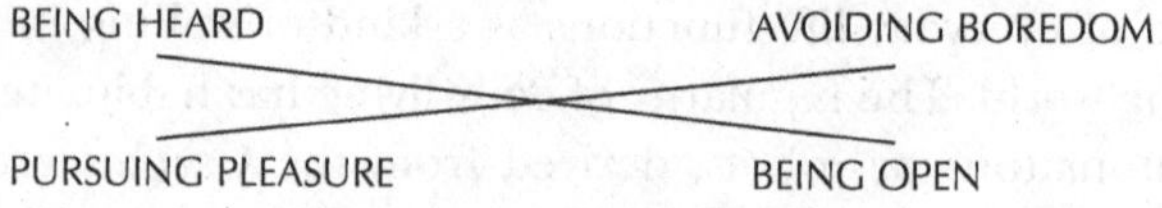

Once we have these two axes, we can then pinpoint at least five reasons why strangeness is important for us. The first is that strangeness helps us compose interesting rhetorical work; it really lies at the heart of the two axes and is the main drive for everything we're after here.

Second, strangeness allows us to have fun. Third, and as a counter, it allows us to resist boredom. Fourth, strangeness allows us to have a unique voice in the public sphere—to be heard. And fifth, strangeness gives us a lens that allows us to be more open to the Other. So, as a recapitulation: (1) *Make and look for interesting stuff*; (2) *Have fun. Live it up. Be weird*; (3) *Break free from boredom*; (4) *Find your own voice so that others can hear it*; and (5) *Be as nice as you can to strangers.* These are our five whys. There may be others. And before we move on, we might list them out like so:

I. Making Strange and Reading Weird: To Create Novelty
To practice rhetorical strangeness by considering purposeful production

II. Convention and Contravention: To Become Hedonists
To practice recreation by considering pleasure/pain

III. Immersion and Emergence: To Escape Banality
To practice resistance/repentance by considering political and procedural prisons

IV. Speak Out and Stand Out: To Be Heard
To practice responding by considering public participation

V. Hostility and Hospitality: To Invite Others
To practice relationships by considering perpetual peace

MAKING STRANGE: THE MOMENTARILY EPIPHANIC ROLE OF RHETORIC

Strangeness wakes us up. Making with strangeness or reading for it offers different sites of possibility. RuPaul said it best, "Be the strange you want to see in the world" (2016). A unique style may not immediately overhaul the world. A flutter of style, however, can offer rhetorical repentance in an age of media baptism. Why repent from baptism? The word *repent* comes from Latin and means to "turn again" or "turn around." But the Greek word is *metanoia*, which essentially means to "meta-consider" or "to think about your thinking," which seems much less threatening. This term, secularized, is precisely what I hope to achieve in the creative compositional work that I ask from my students and myself. We repent, then, from complete immersion, from bad baptism in bad structures. And what are bad structures? Structures that prevent the turn of metanoia and only encourage automatic responses.

If we can't get out of the media flood in which we're stewing, then we should at least critically engage it—reconsider it—metanoia it—if only for a moment. In other words, if we are unable to flip the switch off with media, it may at least be possible to flip the Gestalt switch within media. Conversion is the hopeful result of good strange rhetoric. Surprising composition can help our students be priests in a Quixote culture—a zombie culture—a YouTube culture—a slavish culture—a sleeping culture. Surprising composition can function rhetorically to salvage our culture from being lulled to sleep by various media.

Good rhetorical moves can create what we might call an epiphanic moment, a term borrowed from Northrop Frye (1971) and also out of the work of James Joyce that connotes a brief experience of awareness, an epiphany. And it is satisfying to allow these moments of small, strange effects to be momentary, but also to build on one other and gain momentum. Defamiliarization has chronological parameters. The epiphanic moment is what the strange can achieve, a brief encounter with something novel—however fleeting. Incongruity plays with breaking from expectation, and delivers the payoff in a moment. Strange and novel work can wake people up, even if only momentarily, and even if they go back to sleep. Strange composition can create *satori*, a Buddhist word for a moment of enlightenment. Roland Barthes writes of this very experience in *Camera Lucida*, reflecting, "This *something* has triggered me, has provoked a tiny shock, a *satori*" and follows up by calling it "a strange thing" (1982, 49). I'm not proposing utopian ideals with strange composition; I am, however, offering some u-chronian ones, or well-used kairotic moments. Kairos almost always offers incongruity because it offers sight, taking advantage of a novel seeing. Strange rhetorical moves may not change the world, but they might elicit an emotion—a tear or a guffaw, however brief. Persuasion is not necessarily permanent and unidirectional. We rarely change minds forever. Minds and bodies are always changing, always in flux. We only engage in *rhetorical butterfly effects,* a release of neurotransmitters, little changes here that will, perhaps one day, cause hurricanes off the coast of Kenya.

I am tired. And I am bored. And I want something more.

THE INTERESTINGNESS AXIS: BOREDOM AND PLEASURE

In some sense, what we are wanting above all else is a *pedagogy or practice of creativity in composition.* Strangeness not only helps us to make interesting things; it helps us to make things interesting. There is a subtle difference there. Can you remember an especially good meal or book or film? What makes one stand out among all the rest? If you think of any feed—a news feed or an image feed—what stops you and grabs your attention? The flow of rhetorica—the bulk and flux of rhetorical matter constantly streaming at us—requires willful ignorance, disregard. As such, we are constantly looking for what stands out among the blur.

The need for newness is nothing new. George Campbell writes that there are four ends of rhetoric. "All the ends of speaking are reducible to four; every speech being intended to enlighten the understanding, to please the imagination, to move the passions, or to influence the will" (1988, 1). And there is certainly overlap between his list and ours: imagination and passion. These things are in concert with one another. He continues shortly after to explain how the quality of strangeness plays a part in reaching these aims: "It is the design of wit to excite in the mind an agreeable surprise, and that arising, not from any thing marvellous in the subject, but solely from the imagery she employs, or the strange assemblage of related ideas presented to the mind" (8). As we compose strange assemblages for others' minds, we can excite the other, even with the most banal subjects. This arousing quality of rhetorical strangeness permits us to influence and sway. These are the ends of our strange utterances in practice from day to day.

In the classroom, there is potential to cultivate or suppress this potential. bell hooks writes helpfully about a pedagogy of transgression, asking us to boldly move toward unconventional places with our students. Working out of her inspiration from Paulo Friere's resistance to a banking model of education, she shares with us, "Throughout my years as student and professor, I have been most inspired by those teachers who have had the courage to transgress those boundaries that would confine each pupil to a rote, assembly-line approach to learning" (1994, 13). Unfortunately, composition has too often been seen as an assembly-line space rather than a less regulated assemblage of processes. As Marcia Tate has explained in countless workshops and in her research, " 'Sit and get' won't grow dendrites" (2004, xxi). Of course, something beyond a mere transactional approach is precisely what a stranger composition pedagogy would aim to achieve. Making strange is about making, poetics, fabrication, and re-creation, even with something as simple and pleasurable as an interesting turn of phrase. This is not about transgressing for transgression's sake, a pointless maneuver, but transgressing when the greater good may be experienced with the greatest pleasure.

Our axis aligns with the axis of pleasure and pain. That which helps us generate novelty also helps us escape the painfully humdrum. Pleasure may be found as the goal of rhetoric as far back, at least, as Plato's diatribe against it in *Gorgias.* There, questioning whether rhetoric is art or knack, Socrates stumbles upon one of rhetoric's purposes:

POLUS: So you think oratory's a knack?

SOCRATES: Yes, I do, unless you say it's something else.

POLUS: A knack for what?

SOCRATES: For producing a certain gratification and pleasure. (2009, 462c)

With Polus as an interlocutor, Socrates reveals one thing that rhetoric does. It gives pleasure. And like some drug, or enticing young boy, the rhetorical is dangerous in that it offers strange and enticing claims and (as he says later in the *Phaedrus*) strange flesh. In Plato's *Sophist*, the Stranger appears, whom Victor Vitanza has informally referred to as the Strang(l)er and St.Ranger, and attempts to define the slippery sophist in various ways and by differing categories. The Stranger finally concludes that sophistic rhetoric is a productive art.

Aristotle too acknowledges the pleasure-giving quality of rhetoric. In book I of *On Rhetoric*, Aristotle devotes an entire section (11) to the rhetorical quality of pleasure. Nevertheless, Aristotle's views on what gives pleasure diverge from our own. Aristotle begins, "We may lay it down that Pleasure is a movement, a movement by which the soul as a whole is consciously brought into its normal state of being; and that Pain is the opposite" and continues, "It must therefore be pleasant as a rule to move towards a natural state of being" and finally adds, "Habits also are pleasant; for as soon as a thing has become habitual, it is virtually natural" (2006, I.11.1370.). Aristotle's inability to accept that which is unhabitual, or strange, as pleasurable comes from his more conservative views on "the good," which pervade his writings. He strongly emphasizes that what is normal brings pleasure—a claim distinct from the argument being made here. And while we certainly can see how, yes, watching the evening news at the same time every evening with the same anchorman brings some degree of comfort, that kind of pleasure seems pale in comparison to escape from the couch, to the lone beautiful evening decadently wasted in some unfamiliar place.

T. R. Johnson's book *A Rhetoric of Pleasure* begins with an essay called "School Sucks," originally published in *College Composition and Communication*, that explores what teachers of composition "might do to make the pleasures of writing more available" to students (2001, 624). And then Johnson shifts into this wonderfully vivid description of what he sees as successful composition in the classroom, an experience that is filled with pleasure:

> After all, learning to write is by no means always a dreadful experience. On innumerable occasions, when I've halted class discussion and asked

> the students to scribble down their thoughts or begin drafting an essay, I've invariably seen at least a few of them, after a minute or two or five, register that strange, highly positive surge of energy—and their pens begin to wiggle across the page more quickly than a moment before, their heads lower a notch, and they emanate a whole new kind of intensity, all of which signals that they have entered "the zone." And, intuitively, I sense that the stuff they write while in this experiential mode is more engaged and engaging than the other stuff. (624)

The fact that Johnson sees pleasurable writing as more engaging and more successful is not necessarily surprising—unless we have ourselves experienced the boring, rote, programmatic, and sometimes lifeless experience of writing yet another dull essay, what Johnson calls "the other stuff."

Another enthusiastic English teacher, Lex Runciman, once asked us why we aren't having more fun writing. "Fun?" he exclaims. "Well, why not?" He also laments, "We don't talk much about enjoyment, about the rewards of thinking and writing well. Maybe we do discuss such things within the informal confines of our classrooms, but we don't write articles about enjoyment nor do many textbooks mention it" (1991, 158). If fun is one goal of writing, then how do we get there—why can't we seem to get there? What powers prevent the pleasures of strange composition?

For one, we teach too cheaply when we teach the structure of the five-paragraph essay and place that as the goal for college entrance examinations. It would be akin to handing out a stack of coloring books to college freshmen taking art classes. So, how can we make composition sexy, novel, amazing, and wonderful? Pleasure as a motive for embracing strangeness allows us to briefly return to the initial problem of banality as a foil. Pleasure works against the dullness of the everyday. Again, we may return to Shklovsky to elucidate this problem:

> If we examine the general laws of perception, we see that as it becomes habitual, it also becomes automatic. So eventually all of our skills and experiences function unconsciously—automatically. If someone were to compare the sensation of holding a pen in his hand or speaking a foreign tongue for the very first time with the sensation of performing the same operation for the ten thousandth time, then he would no doubt agree with us.
>
> After being perceived several times, objects acquire the status of "recognition." An object appears before us. We know it's there but we do not see it, and, for that reason, we can say nothing about it. The removal of this object from the sphere of automatized perception is accomplished in art by a variety of means. (1991, 6)

Because most of the experiences of our lives are neither pleasurable nor painful, but just automatic, unconscious, or regular, an opportunity exists to offer moments of release, of gratification through rhetoric, or art, as Shklovsky explains, *by a variety of means.* The focus on objects in particular here at the end is also interesting from a rhetorics of materiality perspective. Where can we take this?

In some sense, we're trying to get outside. Michel Foucault in *Abnormal* (and to some degree in *The Uses of Pleasure*) suggested that the cognitive desire to fix—primarily for him arising from the realm of psychiatry—*introduces* or creates the normal or normative figure, "the principle of conformity opposed to irregularity, disorder, strangeness, eccentricity, unevenness, and deviation" (Foucault, 162). Conformity and disciplinarity arise in opposition to otherness, needing to be corrected either sexually or criminally using an apparatus, or *dispositif*, of power, such as the prison or education system. The playful poststructuralism of continental thinkers such as Foucault allows us to keep tracing this antidisestablishmentarianism of thinking and composing as it has progressed.

In Foucault's *The Archaeology of Knowledge*, the chapter "The Regular and the Original" explores how the familiar and the unfamiliar depend upon one another; they are two sides of the same coin. Foucault excavates these perspectives held in tension, reflecting, "In general, the history of ideas deals with the field of discourses as a domain with two values; any element located there may be characterized as old or new; traditional or original; conforming to an average type or deviant" (2012, 141). The potential within deviance gives us new ideas, new thoughts, new things. In terms of Foucault's investigations into the history of madness, for example, we discover the powers of normativity; however, in "The Discourse on Language," Foucault tells us that that madman's "words were credited with *strange* powers, of revealing some hidden truth" (2012, 217; emphasis added). The strange qualities of mad, non-normative discursive practices are avenues for invention, practices for generating novel ideas. Foucault goes further, "One can distinguish between two categories of formulation: those that are highly valued and relatively rare, which appear for the first time, which have no similar antecedents, which may serve as models for others, and which to this extent deserve to be regarded as creations; and those, ordinary, everyday, solid, that are not responsible for themselves" (2012, 141). Here Foucault clearly distinguishes between these two categories, and so we too may draw a distinction between the rare and the ordinary.

If tensions between individualization and sociality are hard to tease out, deciding what a norm is in the first place might be even more difficult. Yet because of the association with illness, neuroatypical behaviors are seen as abject (see Yergeau 2017). Norms force us to rethink what rhetoric is and does—how it functions. Deviance and eccentricity are merely dots along a spectrum of unique differences. As Oscar Wilde said, "To define is to limit" (1993, 144), or to cut, or to excise, or to other. So, who or what is normal?

Roland Barthes calls this potential power the "pleasure of the text" and refers to the *plaisir*, or pleasure, that comes when the reader is completely immersed in the text (which may or may not be happening to you now, dear reader). Barthes separates readerly and writerly texts; the writerly offers distinct *jouissance*, or bliss (Barthes 1975a, 20), which requires the reader to not be immersed but to enjoy the cognition and recognition of himself as a reading subject with a writerly text (1975b, 5). Barthes asks, "Why is the writerly our value? Because the goal of literary work (of literature as work) is to make the reader no longer a consumer, but a producer of the text" (1975b, 4). In this sense, Barthes—concerned and critical—argues that the reader solely as passive recipient of the text is a problem. He values the writerly. The writerly operates in a way that allows the audience to not just receive numbly. There is a mindlessness associated with the solely readerly text. Barthes is concerned, as I am, about texts that do not offer pleasure—that is, works in which *jouissance* is absent:

> This reader is thereby plunged into a kind of idleness—he is intransitive; he is, in short *serious*: instead of functioning himself, instead of gaining access to the magic of the signifier, to the pleasure of writing, he is left with no more than the poor freedom to either accept or reject the text: reading is nothing more than a *referendum*. Opposite the writerly text, then, is its countervalue, its negative, reactive value: what can be read, but not written: the *readerly*. (1975b, 4)

Note the plunging of the reader into the text, which jibes with our metaphor of immersion. Barthes's statement here also corroborates the fears of many texts being created for the austere, sober, and slack-faced audience.

Richard Lanham also suggests that "we play for pleasure, too. Such a scheme is galvanized by the Gorgian prime mover, ἡδονή, pleasure. Purposeful striving is invigorated by frequent dips back into the pleasurable resources of pure play" (2004, 5). Lanham too outlines two kinds of approaches to life: *homo seriosus* and *homo rhetoricus*; the latter is a pure player filled with . . . oh! let us say *jouissance!!* The former is that stilted composer taking themselves and the world too seriously. He explains, "*Homo rhetoricus* cannot, to sum up, be *serious* . . . He is not, like the serious man, alienated from his own language" and furthermore, he knows that he "not only may *think* differently, but may *be* differently" (5). This being different in the world appears in our writing, our gestures, our voicings, and other expressions. As educator John Dewey said, "To be playful and serious at the same time is possible, and it defines the ideal mental condition" (1997, 218). Serious play is good work.

Author Saul Bellow reinforces this very same value in "The Distracted Public" in *It All Adds Up*.

> If the remission of pain is happiness, then the emergence from distraction is aesthetic bliss. I use these terms loosely, for I am not making an argument but rather attempting to describe the pleasure that comes from recognition or rediscovery of certain essences permanently associated with human life. These essences are restored to our consciousness by persons who are described as artists . . .
>
> Such a writer has power over distraction and fragmentation, and out of distressing unrest, even from the edge of chaos, he can bring unity and carry us into a state of intransitive attention. People hunger for this.
>
> But this is why the artist competes with other claimants to attention. He cannot compete in the athletic sense of the word, as if his objects were to drive his rivals from the field. He will never win a clear victory. Nothing will ever be clear; the elements are too mixed for that. The opposing powers are too great to overcome. They are the powers of an electrified world and of a transformation of human life the outcome of which cannot be foreseen. (1995, 168)

I quote this at length because it is good writing. But it is also true. The writer or artist has a power over attention that comes through aesthetic bliss. All of this exists in the midst of an *electrified world*. It is not an accident that purveyors of literature are some of the ones most sensitive to this technological distraction, dissociation, and disorientation. And while some literary texts pierce through by creating pleasurably strange moves, those moves are yet possible in other compositional spaces as well.

THE INTERCHANGE AXIS: BEING OPEN AND BEING HEARD

The second axis is the interchange axis. It involves the sociality of strange rhetoric's various interactions or interfaces. Thus, the strangeness of rhetoric helps us be heard as a unique voice in the crowd, and it helps us be open and hospitable to rhetorical others. Strangeness helps us to listen first, and then be heard. Strangeness as a lens helps us to be more hospitable. As Nietzsche reminds us, "One must learn to love: We are always rewarded in the end for our good will, our patience, our fair-mindedness and gentleness with what is strange, as it gradually casts off its veil and presents itself as a new and indescribable beauty. That is its thanks for our hospitality" (2010, 186). A rhetorical view toward the strange stranger is inviting—and perhaps even rooted in learning to love the other. And there is a view of rhetoric as love. As Jim Corder taught us, "Rhetoric is love, and it must speak a commodious language, creating a world full of space and time that will hold our diversities" (1985, 31). Strangeness not only allows us to read for and create new rhetorical texts, it allows us to connect to each other in new ways as well.

If we can begin to open ourselves to the stranger, then rhetoric is possible. As G. K. Chesterton wrote, "How much larger your life would be if your self could become smaller in it; if you could really look at other men with common curiosity and pleasure . . . You would break out of this tiny and tawdry theatre in which your own little plot is always being played, and you would find yourself under a freer sky, in a street full of splendid strangers" (2017, 183). Splendid strangers allow us to broaden our connections, to resist the closed-offness that prevents change and exchange.

This orientation also opens us up to different kinds of diversities. Race, sex, class, and other qualities of selves can show up in composed spaces as other-than-the-norm. This diversity valuing makes us think of Clifford Geertz's "The Uses of Diversity,"[1] where he describes the job of ethnographic study, arts, and other narratives as to "refocus our attention" with narratives, "not, however, ones that render us acceptable to ourselves by representing others as gathered into worlds we don't want and can't arrive at, but ones which make us visible to ourselves by representing us and everyone else as cast into the midst of a world full of irremovable strangenesses we can't keep clear of" (2012, 84). This powerful stance of orienting ourselves toward an attempt at comprehending our collective strangenesses is the core of a generative rhetorical strangeness.

Homi K. Bhabha takes up Geertz's call in "On the Irremovable Strangeness of Being Different," noting, "The anxiety of displacement that troubles national rootedness transforms ethnicity or cultural difference into an ethical relation that serves as a subtle corrective to valiant attempts to achieve representativeness and moral equivalence in the matter of minorities" (1998, 34). This anxiety over our natural proximity to one another requires an ethics transfer, a consideration for what has not been considered. And what are the uses of diversity now? When we write off a strange voice, reject it outright, the stranger faces inhospitality. To rhetoric our strangers is to love them, to care enough to change their minds, or at least to acknowledge their perspectives. Practicing hospitality is a core facet of rhetorical engagement, of course.

1. It is worth noting that G. K. Chesterton and Jonathan Kozol have also used the title "The Uses of Diversity" in their own interesting and generative ways.

Who is the rhetorical composing stranger to whom we must be open? What foreign inscriptions might the figure of the stranger really offer? Georg Simmel, a sociologist from the early twentieth century, penned a short essay entitled "Der Fremde," or "The Stranger," in which he explores the social role of this figure and its impact on cultural relations. Simmel formulates the stranger as being part of the group, and adds: "As such, the stranger is near and far *at the same time*" (1950, 407). Hence, the stranger has to be known, recognized. Simmel explains that any inhabitants around Sirius, a distant star, would not be strangers because they are completely unknown to us. This paradox of the stranger being both foreign and familiar or strange and already known challenges us. The stranger is, by definition, paranormal.

Who is my neighbor, my stranger? We have the valuable work of thinking through our complex, multilayered, multifaceted intersectional identity formations. Gloria Anzaldúa suggests, "Woman is the stranger, the other. She is man's recognized nightmarish pieces, his Shadow-Beast. The sight of her sends him into a frenzy of anger and fear" (1987, 17). And, of course, the stranger is always coming from the margins or, as Anzaldúa would write, from the borderlands. What kinds of compositions are regularly marginalized? Sexual differences, skin differences, language differences only multiply the possibilities of composition. The Other is a blessing. Cynthia Ozick suggests that we can perhaps only imagine the other, be acquainted with the other through language, writing, "Without the metaphor of memory and history, we cannot imagine the life of the Other. We cannot imagine what it is to be someone else. Metaphor is the reciprocal agent, the universalizing force: it makes possible the power to envision the stranger's heart" (quoted in Atkins 1994, 632). Envisioning what may reside within the Other allows us to generate productive rhetorical connective tissue, compositionally. As Stacey Waite writes in *Teaching Queer: Radical Possibilities for Writing and Knowing*, "It's our civic duty to think in queerer ways, to come up with queer kinds of knowledge-making so that we might know truths that are non-normative, and contradictory, and strange" (2017, 187).

But watch out! You may be hated for your strangeness. Jamaica Kincaid warns us, "It will never occur to you that the people who inhabit the place in which you have just paused cannot stand you, that behind their closed doors they laugh at your strangeness (you do not look the way they look); the physical sight of you does not please them" (Kincaid 2000, 17). But whom are we trying to please? It's worth noting the way Kincaid ends this little piece about them not liking you: "They envy your ability to leave your own banality and boredom, they envy your ability to turn their banality and boredom into a source of pleasure for yourself" (19). And this is just it. Are we not writing and playing for the pleasure of it—to be our own selves, not obligated to those who only see error in difference?

The sheer variety of others is encompassed under the big, broad umbrella of strangeness, which shelters the foreign, the feminine, the neuroatypical, the queer, and all sorts of different bodies that compose differently. How far can we go in listening to these various others? I want to say that we will always go all the way—listening long, and not shutting up the potential of the other by our own interjections. Cheryl Glenn teaches us that "our capacity to know ourselves, make sense of the world, and know and learn from Others is further enhanced when we realize how the power of our social location (that is, our individual and collective cultural identity) regulates our ability to know things, to make insights, and to speak and listen to Others with respect and sensitivity" (2018, 47–48). To listen to Others is the challenge of rhetorically complex identities that are strange to one another. She adds that "given that our identity can be constructed or realized only in the presences of Others (regardless of our positionality), our identity automatically equals a comparison and contrast about our own social, physical, economic, intellectual, cultural—that is, rhetorical—position vis-à-vis that of Others" (47) and that "identity is always created in the presence of complex Others—and, largely, through speech, action, and, often, skin" (48). The issue of identities always already being strange to one another creates the potential for a pre-rhetorical hostility, which is precisely the reason for rhetorical action.

Perhaps one of the central voices that calls us to listen is Krista Ratcliffe's. She suggests that "rhetorical listening may be imagined, generally, as a trope for interpretive invention" but also allows us "to hear discursive intersections of gender and race/ethnicity" (1999, 196). So, if we think about what is at stake in this project of clamoring for strangeness, we are forced to contend with the extent of our own willingness to practice hospitality. And we consider how people are and are not read and misread, written and rewritten. Stephanie L. Kerschbaum responds to this same ethics, trying to find practical applications: "Markers of difference can provide a new set of tools for tracing and analyzing patterns in how we might understand one another" (Kerschbaum 2014, 7). This is because difference offers potential in composing, and finding out where we misunderstand, or where we try to co-opt and understand on our own terms.

As we find these boundary lines, we continue exploring together a rhetoric of borders. Lisa Flores has begun thinking about the stoppage of immigrants at borders as a kind of rhetorical stoppage and a practice of inhospitality wrapped up in languaging and procedural practices (2019, 1–2). Elsewhere, Flores relies upon a text, *Unwelcome Strangers*, which offers a historical account of American hostility toward outsiders—a change from early narratives built around new frontiers (2003, 368–69). It is up to us, then, to open doors and not stand in the way—here our open hands are an intimate choice, rather than the rhetoric of the fist. As Edward Corbett noted of the rhetoric of the closed fist, it is more "coercive than persuasive" (1969, 293) and it is "non-conciliatory" (294). He concludes that "the closed fist just prompts another closed fist to be raised" (295). We can find better ways.

The Other is too often punished, ousted. Gayatri Spivak offers a thoughtful investigation into the subaltern and alterity, famously concluding, "The subaltern cannot speak" (1988, 308) because of the harsh resistance that arises to speaking otherwise. She is offering a particular use of this word, a particular other. Edward Said, too, is part of Spivak's heritage. His book *Orientalism* is certainly foundational when it comes to alternative voices. Said writes, "For Orientalism was ultimately a political vision of reality whose structure promoted the difference between the familiar (Europe, the West, 'us') and the strange (the Orient, the East, 'them')" (1979, 210). Hence, sides and distinctions have always been there. It's an old war.

As Kenneth Burke writes in *A Rhetoric of Motives*, the purpose of rhetoric is *ad bellum purificandum*, or toward the purification of war (1969b, 319). Burke calls the connection made possible via rhetoric alternatively consubstantiality or identification. Burke explains, "A is not identical with his colleague, B. But insofar as their interests are joined, A is identified with B" (20). So, of course we already know that in rhetorical situations there is a difference between the two parties—a separation or strangeness. Lloyd Bitzer explains in "The Rhetorical Situation," "Any exigence is an imperfection marked by urgency; it is a defect, an obstacle, something waiting to be done, a thing which is other than it should be. In almost any sort of context, there will be numerous exigences, but not all are elements of a rhetorical situation—not all are rhetorical exigences. An exigence which cannot be modified is not rhetorical" (1968, 6). As such, one might posit that any situation or object that cannot be unstranged might be arhetorical. Unchangeable or unmalleable strangeness may fall outside the bounds or purview of rhetorical action.

But Burke adds that rhetoric exists because of this lack of familiarity between parties. So, the rhetorician could be seen as eliminating strangeness, although he or she may employ it in the process. Additionally,

Burke suggests that with pure identification or consubstantiality there is no need for rhetoric, but there would also be no war. He explains, "In pure identification there would be no strife. Likewise, there would be no strife in absolute separateness, since opponents can join battle only through mediatory ground that makes their communication possible" (1969b, 25). Complete strangeness would dissolve strife the other way, by making communication impossible. However, the ethical move sought here would be to be accepting of strangeness—to allow it without judging, without damning, without excommunicating. Meanwhile, we have to acknowledge the integral, interwoven, inseparable nature of communication with consubstantiality, as Burke explains: "So, there is no chance of our keeping apart the meanings of persuasion, identification ('consubstantiality'), and communication (the nature of rhetoric as 'addressed')" (46). The connection between strangers and rhetoric is fundamental; strangers allow rhetoric to take place.

There is the desire to be and also to oust the other. Is everyone an other? In being at odds, we face the very site of rhetoric. We have to be careful about moving in this direction because it can discount the countless violences that have been done to various specific historical others; yet in some variations of degrees, we're always already strangers in a host of different ways. Deborah Britzman explains the value of welcoming the queer subaltern into the learning space in "Queer Pedagogy and Its Strange Techniques": "Exploring how experiences of those deemed subaltern are imagined, then, means taking a second look at the everyday normative and rethinking the normative as producing the grounds of estrangement and new forms of ignorance" (2012, 299). The practices of others composing as others in and outside of classrooms is increasingly being brought to the fore. These oriented emplacements certainly haunt strange writing.

We can also turn to Jean-François Lyotard, who explicitly explores the ethical relationship to the stranger as other in *The Differend*. He teaches: "The obligation is immediate, prior to any intellection, it resides in the 'welcoming of the stranger,' in the address to me, which does more than reverse a preexisting relation, which institutes a new universe. This upheaval precedes any commentary upon the nature of the other, of the request, of my freedom" (1989, 111). Here, we return to our obligation to the other; as addresser and addressee meet, we are *immediately* faced with an ethic that calls for a welcoming. Because we do not *know* the stranger, we cannot call her or him enemy, and whom can we ever fully know, even ourselves? Hence, in this sense, we are obligated to always be hospitable, to lose some of "my freedom," as if we ever owned much.

Sara Ahmed cautions us about how we take up the strange figure in *Strange Encounters*. She worries us: "I suggest that we can only avoid stranger fetishism—that is, avoid welcoming or expelling the stranger" as an "effect of processes of inclusion and exclusion" (2000, 6). Ahmed says that we see the stranger, noting, "The stranger has already come too close" (21), and it must be recognized as such. It is not invisible. And yet . . . there is power in invisibility as well—to blend in and be unnoticed. But that is not the stranger rhetor's power. Stranger rhetors are seen as present but out of place. In a stranger rhetor's paradoxical belonging-out-of-place, we accept and resist simultaneously—creating rhetorical pressure to shift and open or push back.

Is it not evident that strangeness as a lens allows us a kind of hospitality to others—to become more open to forms and voices that we might otherwise reject? In helping us think about responding hospitably to strangers as rhetors, we also see our own roles as strangers in the world. Xenophobia and xenophilia, as another view, always threaten to present themselves in the face of the uncanny. Loving and fearing others, when we seek to exploit the homogeneity of everyday life with strange composition, audiences will react with things with which they are unfamiliar. This continues to present itself today in the forms of various kinds of hatred in reaction to whatever may threaten the stabilizing, normative structures of our everyday culture. Xenophobia has led our cultural critiques to respond to ways of defending what is seen as other. Julia Kristeva's consideration of both abjection and strangeness are immediately relevant here. Kristeva reads Freud's sense of the uncanny as something that we must deal with in ourselves in order to respond appropriately to otherness in others in *Strangers to Ourselves*. She wonders, "In the fascinated rejection that the foreigner arouses in us, there is a share of uncanny strangeness in the sense of the depersonalization that Freud discovered in it, and which takes up again our infantile desires and fears of the other" (1994, 191). Kristeva outlines a wonderful history of thinkers dealing with strangeness in the self and in the other, and how it pertains to a politics and philosophy regarding subaltern statuses, including feminism. Xenoglossia, as a methodology, may offer ways of surprising and affecting audiences that have been lulled into canniness, knowability, and boredom, but also an inability to read otherness.

The premise of hospitality is almost always already agreed upon or dismissed beforehand. Kant's treatise on the subject, *Perpetual Peace*, argues for the aspects we are treasuring. In its simplest terms— naively, perhaps—the treatise asks us to be nice to others. Kant's third premise in order to concoct perpetual peace reads:

> THIRD DEFINITIVE ARTICLE FOR A PERPETUAL PEACE
> "The Law of World Citizenship Shall Be Limited to Conditions of Universal Hospitality"
>
> Here, as in the preceding articles, it is not a question of philanthropy but of right. Hospitality means the right of a stranger not to be treated as an enemy when he arrives in the land of another. One may refuse to receive him when this can be done without causing his destruction; but, so long as he peacefully occupies his place, one may not treat him with hostility. (1903, 20)

Because Kant introduces this proposition as a question of rightness in certain cases, we can never completely know exactly how hospitality should be carried out in every case. However, to not be hostile, to not cause destruction, to keep the peace is what can happen if we allow ourselves to be hospitable to the other, the stranger, the foreigner. Personally, I would almost prefer, however, that Kant allow the injunction to be based upon philanthropy rather than right—on the love of humankind rather than upon some a priori right. But if we are not expected to be kind to the Other, who will make us do so? Certainly not the Other himself, quiet and afraid?!

Derrida picks up this theme of protecting the strange in *Of Hospitality*. Troubling the Host/Hostage dichotomy in the ancient law of hospitality, Derrida tells us:

> Absolute hospitality requires that I open up my home and that I give not only to the foreigner (provided with a family name, with the social status of being a foreigner, etc.), but to the absolute, unknown, anonymous other, and that I *give place* to them, that I let them come, that I let them arrive, and take place in the place I offer them, without asking of them either reciprocity (entering into a pact) or even their names. (Derrida and Dufourmantelle 2000, 25)

Tell me your name. Then I can *know* who you are. To be able to accept a stranger's strangeness, we must allow ourselves to be open, vulnerable, and unasking. Derrida notes the impossibility of privacy in the information age—technology floodingly connects us to everyone and everything else. This difficult, perhaps impossible, position asks us how willing we are to allow the stranger to be strange to us as an endlessly exposed audience. And yet, we also always long for the stranger to appear, for the reasons we have cited above. Derrida later adds, affirmatively: "Let us say yes *to who or what turns up*, before any determination, before any anticipation, before any *identification*, whether or not it has to do with a foreigner, an immigrant, an invited guest, or an unexpected visitor, whether or not the new arrival is the citizen of another country, a human, animal, or divine creature, a living or dead thing, male or female" (Derrida and Dufourmantelle 2000, 77). And yet, to say yes to a monster? To hateful strangeness? To the rapist? This last stranger is, troublingly, how Derrida closes his interrogation into the matter of hospitality through the story of Lot, who gives his daughters to the rapists at his door in order to spare his angelic guests.

A true advocate of the monstrosity of the other can be discovered in Slavoj Žižek's warning that our neighbor, the one we're supposed to take care of, like good Samaritans, may be "the bearer of monstrous otherness" (2013, 162). The difficulty is to avoid romanticizing loving your neighbor. That makes our task more difficult, but more important. The neighbor is not necessarily kind, and is dangerously inestimable, yet we must attempt the impossible injunction to practice hospitality—in the face of the most difficult Others. Eric Detweiler, in a small piece called "The Rhetoric of Weirdness, the Weirdness of Rhetoric," empoweringly suggests that in the face of monstrous otherness our most effective response might be "to be earnestly, carefully, weirdly incoherent rhetors" (2018). Still, my argument is that by exploring strangeness, we are given a means through which we can learn to practice radical hospitality—to be as hospitable as possible. In spite of the difficulty, I want to be something like a *good* welcoming person. I am a do-gooder. I want to be nice or kind. And so, I have faith that hospitality is yet possible. We continue to believe in the ineffable task of making the stranger welcome. And yet, as a good host, must I always be second-guessing what strangers I'm letting in, and considering the difficulty?

I'd like to share a startling and wonderful little personal essay written by Toni Morrison titled "Strangers." Morrison describes meeting a woman who is a kind of charming stranger. After her encounter, Morrison considers what it means to be a stranger and to confront one. She wisely asks, "Isn't that the kind of thing that we fear strangers will do? Disturb. Betray. Prove they are not like us. That is why it is so hard to know what to do with them" (2017, 34). And perhaps it is the tendency toward distrusting *first* that we are attempting to undermine. She continues, "Why would we want to know a stranger when it is easier to estrange another?" (38). This question also allows us to ask another, if we take a step further. Why would we practice rhetoric at all? Why convince and coax and trouble ourselves to find available means of persuasion? Why argue? Perhaps it is for the sake of creating community with other strangers. Or maybe, as Morrison concludes, "that there are no strangers" (38). She continues with a meditation on the self:

> There are only versions of ourselves, many of which we have not embraced, most of which we wish to protect ourselves from. For the stranger is not foreign, she is random, not alien but remembered; and it is the randomness of the encounter with our already known—although unacknowledged—selves that summons a ripple of alarm. That makes us reject the figure and the emotions it provokes—especially when these emotions are profound. It is also what makes us want to own, govern, administrate the Other. To romance her, if we can, back into our own mirrors. In either instance (of alarm or false reverence), we deny her personhood, the specific individuality we insist upon for ourselves. (38–39)

Morrison reveals how strangers present an opportunity for us. They allow us to face something foreign and acknowledge its being, just as we desire others to do for us. It is something like the Golden Rule. Elsewhere, Morrison writes, "The ability of writers to imagine what is not the self, to familiarize the strange and mystify the familiar, is the test of their power" (1993, 15). If the practice of recognition, of seeing by not capturing and holding in place, of letting pass, is possible in the guardianship of various compositional front lines, then the hope of new forms is possible.

Jean Baudrillard's *Radical Alterity* notes the singularity of the stranger in helping one create for oneself. Culturally we adopt and manipulate strangers for our own purposes, and hence create what Baudrillard calls "artificial strangeness" (Baudrillard 2008, 26–27). In this, we capture and control the other for our own ends under our own devising, which is why Baudrillard calls for a more radical alterity, or otherness, which may allow us to escape inscription or detection or capture. This positionality is true for the students in our classrooms as well. To not be bored, to be interested and interesting, full of delight, and to be heard and to hear all: that is, in effect, the reward of great strangeness.

And so we may be left to wonder again at the relationship between the stranger and strangeness. When strangers do things or create inscriptions that at first seem strange to us, we are in our own ways obligated to read the stranger. I am thinking of the difference between a welcome other and one that makes us feel uncomfortable. The terms I might use are *verging* and *converging*. When we are pushed or pulled outward, we lean or veer out—perhaps slightly off balance—in order to take in an unsettling other. This is different from the safety of convergence—where familiar others recognize each other and join up. This leaning, on the verge, is the call to really push to the outside, to see if we can take in that which feels especially divergent to our selves. As Emmanuel Lévinas ponders looking into the face of *l'autre,* we too must consider our own divers(e) interactions with *l'autre, l'etranger,* the Other, the Stranger. Lévinas writes, "Meaning is the face of the Other, and all recourse to words takes place already within the primordial face to face of language" (1969, 206). *L'autre* is perhaps different than *l'etranger*, but Derrida uses *l'etranger* in his lecture on hospitality, noting of his earliest example from *Oedipus Rex*: "We hear him, this foreigner, this stranger, uttering his complaint strangely" (Derrida and Dufourmantelle 2000, 103). And so, here at the end we remember *Zeus Xenios*, the deity who presides over hospitality, who offers us a lens for early rhetorical thinking that ends up making its way into current conceptualizations regarding unfamiliar Others. Do strangers reflect us? The linkages are certainly there. We recall Maya Angelou's poetic suggestion: "We are more alike, my friends, than we are unalike" (1990, 5). We can only offer this limited gesture, a wave hello, and perhaps—if we are brave—a waving in.

STRANGE VOICES IN PUBLIC

Only when we have listened long to others should we even begin to think about speaking and practicing our own strange rhetorical interventions. Then, and only then, should we allow our own strangeness to be heard. That unique rhetorical voice allows us to be heard as opposed to bleating out and being drowned out by the herd. Strangeness offers a voicing—nay, plural, our variegated voicings.

In order to communicate, to be heard, we have to hyperbolize, to express ourselves with difference. What do I mean by that exactly? Well, something simple. Perhaps we might take a rule of grammar, any grammar—written, oral, cinematic, and so on. Breaking it creates a voicing that stands out in some way. Let us take the sentence fragment. For one, Edgar A. Schuster concludes, "Writing a fragment/minor sentence rather than a grammatically complete one (major sentence) is a grammatical choice and . . . that choice can have positive, powerful rhetorical effects" (2006, 83). Many potent texts contain sentence fragments. Yet they are eschewed, despised, and rejected when we teach formal composition. And yet. The sentence fragment. Has power. Has uniqueness. Has voice. And fragments are just one of many options. To perform such moves, to stand out within the public sphere offers a different kind of relationship to the thing we call democracy. And this differing relationship is something we—as good educators and admonishers—should attempt to encourage for all of our students, such that part of the end of education would be participation, an enabling, a voicing. There is always room for divergent forms that exist to break free from traditional, normative patterns of language and thought—expressive communicative acts.

Here I want to consider Jürgen Habermas's establishment of the public sphere concept. Strangeness helps individuals find their voice in democratic spaces. Novel forms are not just interesting; they are political. The public sphere, as defined by Habermas, is "a realm of our social life in which something approaching public opinion can be formed. Access is guaranteed to all citizens" (1974, 49). But there has not been access for all who wish to participate. And now, with various networked apparatuses—such as Twitter—functioning as part of the public sphere many voices blend to create "the democratic voice." Still, this approach to politics simply means that everyone merely voices together, and our political system is the average or the mean of all the other voices. For the most part, democracy works exceptionally well; this is not an anti-democratic stance. However, with this politics, a distinct voice is increasingly difficult to hear; there are only averages and means, a blur of thoughts—something far afield from any singular rhetoric, one might suggest.

Alternatively, some have rejected Habermas's claims, arguing that not all have been able to participate in the bourgeois public sphere, in part because it is bourgeois. Nancy Fraser famously challenges Habermas's assumptions—that there is equality, that all have the ability participate within the public sphere. She counters Habermas's construction of the public sphere, suggesting other minor spheres of interaction. She explains, "Even the language people use as they reason together usually favors one way of seeing things and discourages others. Subordinate groups sometimes cannot find the right voice or words to express their thoughts, and when they do, they discover they are not heard" (1990, 64). Fraser encourages subaltern voices as a good thing. Furthermore, she espouses an egalitarian view that all should be able to participate in discursive spaces on their own terms—even if they are not necessarily virtuous. Not being heard *because of* alterity means, then, inventing not only new forms but new platforms. Fraser warns, however, "Let me not be misunderstood. I do not mean to suggest that subaltern counter-publics are always necessarily virtuous" (67). There are all sorts of strange ideas out there taking on all sorts of shapes. Strange is not necessarily good in terms of morality, but Fraser does offer that it creates a widening of views, voices, and participation, which is good in a different sense in that it values diversity, multiplicity, and hearing various differences of opinion, different voicings.

After Fraser, Michael Warner further examines the paradox of publics with a deep consideration of strangers and counter-publics—where the outed strange typically hang out. Warner challenges the concept of a public: "A public . . . must be more than a list of one's friends. It must include strangers . . . A public is a relation among strangers" (2005, 55). In this sense, Warner counters that the stranger is a part of our everyday—unremarkable, not so exotic, but normal and natural. Strangers are the people in front of you at the checkout counter or the drivers cutting you off in traffic. This integrated view of the stranger allows him to assert, "Reaching strangers is public discourse's primary orientation" (76). As such, we can only agree with Warner that "my world must be one of strangers" (87). In this sense, counter-publics are merely sanctioned publics that allow strangers to be both in and outside simultaneously—what writings or rhetorical works can say the same?

BRASS TACKS AND THE REAL POLITICS OF STRANGENESS

So, we have this beginning to an ethics on strangeness—this manifold answer. Although strangeness isn't necessarily an answer, or an ethic, but a *lens*. Strangeness is deeply political. As Robert Hariman asserts, "To the extent that politics is an art, matters of style must be crucial to its practice" (1995, 3). When I first began to see strangeness as such, it took me by surprise. I did not, I confess, initially expect a politics of strangeness. Now I can't imagine thinking about strangeness or politics without each other.

The state is merely a drawn boundary line. Outside of that line lie strangers. When we walk into a new or different place and call it weird, dismissing or writing it off, we act only in our ignorance of our own isolated otherness. This perspective makes Shklovsky's Russian term *ostranenie* a political term, because the word also connotes being outside the structure of the state. This second reason for exploring strangeness has grown out of thinking about how experimental forms of communication have a lot to do with how to offer a unique voice within a democracy, where many voices are present and can tend to drown one another out. Eric King Watts has considered when and how voice and voiceless occur in rhetorical studies, concluding that voice "is the enunciation and the acknowledgement of the obligations and anxieties of living in community with others" (2001, 180). So, defamiliarizing composition is one way to pierce through the crowd, but also to be a part of it. Jacques Rancière argues that consensus is the end of politics; where there is agreement there is no need for politics. Dissensus, then, is the way to participate within a political space. Rancière puts it so: "The essence of politics is *dissensus*. Dissensus is not a confrontation between interests or opinions. It is the demonstration (*manifestation*) of a gap in the sensible itself. Political demonstration makes visible that which had no reason to be seen; it places one world in another" (2010, 38). Here the distribution of the sensible, in politics as in art, offers a reorienting for an audience, whether that audience is a reader, a viewer, a politician, or another citizen. And as Terry Eagleton writes in *Trouble with Strangers*, "Political matters such as justice and equality apply to the relations between oneself and the Other just as much as they hold between strangers" (2008, 324). There is an ethics between whatever might want to be called the non-stranger and strangers, who also have a politics and ethics among themselves, but it is no different. Dissent occurs not only in the content of a political message but also within its very form, making aesthetics particularly significant.

In compositional spaces, abnormality is similarly rejected. As Deleuze suggests in *Difference and Repetition*, concepts awaken new possibilities: "the claws of a strangeness or an enmity which alone would awaken thought from its natural stupor or eternal possibility" (1995, 139). The ferocity of strangeness shakes us up. I must, alas, at least touch upon a Deleuzean politics here, for mine have come up to the edge of nomadic war machines, in the case of the ever-new, the ever-strange. While it may seem that a strange politics would be one grounded in anarchism, I am afraid to push my politics that far. (I would be happy with some slight change—more inclusive policies on immigration reform.) In *Nomadology*, Deleuze and Guattari shriek, "To place thought in an immediate relation with the outside, with the forces of the outside, in short to make thought a war machine, is a strange undertaking" (1986, 38). The odd couple expresses the need to move beyond the boundary lines of the state, without ceasing. While this seems close to what is being argued for here, I am loath to embrace the violence of this angle. And while Deleuze would balk at my fear, I have to say that I am hoping for a more comic frame—one that causes more laughter than suffering. In some ways, yes, this too is a call for a multiplicity of forms.

Finally, associations may be made here to Hannah Arendt's concept of freedom; she does indeed connect this concept to poetics and aesthetics, even using the idea of "the strange" and "estrangement from the world" experienced as inner freedom (2006, 145). Let us turn to her to further explore the possibilities of this connection. Arendt writes, "Freedom needed, in addition to mere liberation, the company of other men who were in the same state, and it needed a common public space to meet them—a politically organized world, in other words, into which each of free men could insert himself by word or deed" (147). And so, in order to participate within the public sphere, we need freedom and others, which require certain preconditions (including, at times, according to Arendt, some people being without freedom). We need platforms, even those fraught ones like YouTube and Twitter, and we need strangers to interact with. But we also need a means of inserting ourselves, a way of functioning as singularities within a collective society. Arendt adds, "We are inclined to believe that freedom begins where politics ends" (147). So, while dissensus for Rancière is the practice of politics, leading to the end of politics in consensus, Arendt suggests that the end of politics is freedom. And yet freedom and consensus are not necessarily consubstantial; in some cases, they *nevertheless* work together.

To return to Derrida's consideration of hospitality, it may be that the stranger functions as a savior. He writes, "Strange logic, but so enlightening for us, that of an impatient master awaiting his guest as a liberator, his emancipator. It is as if the stranger or foreigner held the keys. This is always the situation of the foreigner, in politics too . . . —as if, then, the stranger could save the master and liberate the power of his host; it's as if the master, qua master, were prisoner of his place and his power" (Derrida and Dufourmantelle 2000, 123). We may be waiting, after all, on our own strange otherness and the otherness of others to save us from everything that's gone before—tradition and convention—in our practices of composing rhetorically.

A stranger rhetoric is generally a more ethical one. This is primarily because it is more inclusive rather than exclusive. And it might tie better into what some call for with regard to empathy. Lisa Blankenship, in her epilogue to *Changing the Subject*, offers a theory of rhetorical empathy: "Rhetoric never is isolated, and rhetorical empathy increases the possibilities for less toxic, more effective ways of connecting across difference in sustained ways" (2019, 120). This expanded view of listening and opening up to difference, rather than dismissing it or squelching it, gives us a more promising liberatory horizon to look toward.

Another relevant and helpful view of rhetorical empathy appears in Sharon Yam's *Inconvenient Strangers*. I'd like to quote her at length here because of how she teases out two separate views of empathy. She explains it this way:

> To effectively address the tendency to dehumanize the Other, therefore, we must take a simultaneously affective and deliberative approach, rather than relying only on either one of them. While deliberative empathy entails critical reflection on the shared material contexts and interests between mainstream audiences and marginalized subjects, it is also an affective response that opens the possibilities for bodies to affect and be affected by others in ways that are not predetermined. Different from affective empathy, which often promotes identification and misrecognition, deliberative empathy prompts the more dominant interlocutor to

> engage in two layers of deliberation as they experience empathy that draws them closer to the Other: First, they consider the structural and material causes that lead to the suffering of others, and second, they reflect on how they are implicated in the same structures that entrap others and engage in an internal deliberation on how their relations with others ought to shift. Deliberative empathy invites interlocutors across power difference to move toward each other affectively, while always keeping in the foreground the structural, political, and material factors that simultaneously bind them together and separate them. (2019, 192)

In this sense, we can see here how there is a kind of empathy that can still be colonizing or manipulative. And yet a complex, nuanced view of rhetorical empathy can—and does, in fact—allow us to move toward the other in a conscientious and cooperative way. Recognizing our complicity in anti-strange rhetorical practices can help us change our behaviors for the sake of each other as we communicate more broadly together.

Rhetorical strangeness is a way of being more empathetic to different kinds of rhetors. The strange view involves an alternative way of seeing, of shaping, of resisting, of experiencing, of speaking, of writing, of reading, of making. Rhetorical strangeness allows us to move toward new things, strange things, and to try to be open to them. If we, at least, use the strange as a premise when we are talking about rhetoric, composition, the arts, and varying forms of communication, we are lent a rationale for thinking more kindly, more openly, to see where that leads. Once we begin seeing this way, this lens, it seems, tends to prompt us toward caring for the other, being vulnerable, and cherishing the pleasure this brings. And yet there is still a reservation from the margins because of a collective woundedness—and why should we open up? Forcing kindness or kinship is a potentially harmful obligation, but more openness can allow compositional movement. On top of this, we know from experience that the strangest moments of our lives are the most memorable, and perhaps the most rhetorical in the ways they have shaped who we are and who we will become after having tasted the strangeness of the world. If we begin to see the interrelated inner workings of strangeness, we also begin to see its effects and its purpose. Meanwhile, artists, writers, and other creative types will continue to reach out and tickle the consciousnesses of those who dare to entertain them or be entertained by them. As Francis Bacon said of rhetoric, imagination has reason applied to it "for the better moving of the will" (2008, 238). Strangeness moves. It moves in the spaces within and across normative composition.

So, where are we with this potentially useful rhetorical strangeness? It pivots rhetoric on hospitality in a time of interest and public policy on borders and excommunication, as well as a time of an endless desire for novelty. As Walt Whitman once confessed in "To a Stranger," "Passing stranger! you do not know how longingly I look upon you" (1867, 135). This connection is wrapped up in desire. The rhetor and the auditor both arrive as strangers, and they remain strangers if they cannot find identification with one another. We should continually pursue this strangeness, but not necessarily let strangeness remain outside. So, where are we? Strangeness is an integral part of rhetoric, and it has been all along. I do think that much of our work has been and continues to be about the stranger's positionality in the world.

Chapter Threee

HOW STRANGENESS WORKS

Reforming norms, or figuration and disfiguration, is the primary means to achieving strangeness. If strangeness is the goal, then figures are how we do it. Rhetorical figures have long offered the potential to shock audiences to attention. Christopher Tindale explains, "Rhetorical figures are devices that use words to make some striking effects on an audience" (2004, 60). These are devices that deviate. Whether we are referring to figures in the form of tropes (deviant meanings) or schemes (deviant patterns), they grab us and help us take notice by making language or forms strange. And they are everywhere. Style is deviation. We dis/figure strangeness out (of our selves). We never really figure strangeness out, but we figure it, we form and shape it, out of our selves, expressively. As Jean-François Lyotard considers the work of Freud in *Discourse, Figure*, the way we refigure our lives in dreams also occurs in representations of the world in language. That is, weird dreams and colorful language are rewritings, disfigurements, or "*sich entstellen*, to disfigure oneself; *die Sprache entstellen*, to do violence to language" (2019, 236). Interesting, then, that not too dissimilar is the Einstellung Effect, which is essentially the opposite: a set way of doing something (see Blessing and Dronek 2006). How do we get outside of the same old, same old?

COMPOSING IN TECHNICOLOR

The rhetorical figures always seem to return, but now we can see them in Technicolor. Technicolor offers something dreamt, something promising. The rainbow is a sign of something better. Michele Kennerly, for one, attunes us to the possibility of rainbows and the long history of them as a metaphor for welcoming difference (2015). And Technicolor composition is our way to craft strange, novel, and engaging texts that are potentially rhetorically affective. We now have more media than ever before to house different figures. We've got hyperbole on every channel. The dream of Technicolor composition is not new. One call for its

https://doi.org/10.7330/9781646422821.c003

instigation can be traced to Winston Weathers, an advocate of defamiliarizing composition practices. He exhorts us:

> I think we should confirm for our students that style has something to do with better communication, adding as it does a certain technicolor to otherwise black-and-white language. But going beyond this "better communication" approach, we should also say that style is the proof of a human being's individuality; that style is a writer's revelation of himself; that through style, attitudes and values are communicated; that indeed our manner is a part of our message. We can remind students of Aristotle's observation, "character is the making of choices," and point out that since style, by its very nature, is the art of selection, how we choose says something about who we are. (1970, 144)

There is nothing new under the sun. But finding new ways of conveying the old is what we have to continue educating for generation after generation. Weathers encourages a Technicolor composition and urges us to view style as offering selection, significance, and personality. This history of a colorful style lingers with us, perhaps straining back to Horace's acknowledgment of *purple passages.* As such, we begin with this injunction: All hail Roy G. Biv, full of grace. And yet there are more than seven colors in the rainbow; the possibilities are endless.

STRANGE STYLE AS METHOD

Strangeness is made possible by imagining and crafting new forms and figures in different modes and media. Go figure. In investigating both style and invention, it seems that style, at least, is the productive core of this investigation, although the two are integrally intertwined. While a host of studies have been conducted into both stylistic considerations of rhetoric and reviewing Shklovsky's concept of defamiliarization, there have been no thorough studies of defamiliarization connected to rhetorical considerations of style as a means of methodically composing strange work for rhetorical effect. Through this generative (rather than limiting) heuristic, compositionists may be able to find new patterns by recombining various tropes to new effects without the process becoming stale or trite.

Shklovsky explains the nature of these helpful devices without laying them out one by one. In *Theory of Prose,* he focuses upon an overarching sense of the effects of figures, writing: "A poetic image is one of the means by which a poet delivers his greatest impact. Its role is equal to other poetic devices, equal to parallelism, both simple and negative, equal to the simile, to repetition, to symmetry, to hyperbole, equal, generally speaking, to any other figure of speech, equal to all these means of intensifying the sensation of things" (1991, 3). And here we return to using these poetic devices for impact. But Shklovsky sees a use for these devices beyond mere poetics, for rhetorical effect as well, although Shklovsky himself never embraces rhetoric as a field, opting instead for the literary. He concludes, "This is indeed a form of thinking, but it has nothing to do with poetry" (3). Moving alongside poetics gives rhetorical figures an end where the figures themselves function as a means.

The forms we use in compositions are not only a means for creating standards; they are also a means for understanding how to challenge them. A return to formalism, or structuralism, through defamiliarization allows us to work with students to get them to deautomatize their writing and other practices of *poesis.* Why is deautomatization our value? Here we see the potential for text to move beyond the mass production line. As Wendy Bishop writes along with her coauthor David Starkey, "We believe all writing—even the one-minute, uncorrected e-mail—involves some creativity, some thinking, some imagination. In this belief, we have not always been in accord with some of our academic colleagues" (2006, 71). Creativity happens in everyday word choices and syntactical decisions. Strange texts call for productive engineering, moving from passivity toward an increasingly active role in meaning making.

We might reconsider what commas can do in sentences, and then we could start to fool around with those commas in the back seats of cars. We can experiment with language once we consider what can go in this beaker, and what this contraption does, and so on. We can interrogate structures critically. This involvement can be aided by using the concept of defamiliarization within our compositional practices. Defamiliarization is essentially the employment of various rhetorical strategies so that the new composition may be perceived. Defamiliarization, then, might always involve a kind of editing. And editing, coming from the Latin *edere* (to bring forth), like polishing a gem out of a rough rock, is always a fundamental principle of making or composing.

In the "Weird Content" section of *Weird Realism,* Graham Harman says, "We cannot support formalism" (2012, 253), which is to say that we cannot support a mere formalism that rejects the content and context of any work. But rhetoric has always had this conflict of form and content, where effects can be used ethically or unethically. Still, a strictly formalist regard for strangeness is not what we're after, since we are also valuing the stranger—the often-marginalized voice. Mere or strict formalism would reject the meaningfulness of experienced difference. Harman also explains that because of the weirdness of the world and language, "nothing can be paraphrased" (251). In other words, for example, because a whale is strange in its own right, it cannot be recounted in the mere word *whale*, or even in a rich description of it. The world is too removed, too strange—so too, then, are our inscriptions of the world, in language or by other means. These inscriptions are performed, acting as strange mirrors—not reproducing, but bending reality into new light. And finally, we know that form and content are not really such strangers from one another.

Formalism is dead. Long live formalism.

A return to style and grammar can help us move forward. Adding spice, then, eventually becomes a means of re-pro-grammaring. So, we write with spice. As Nietzsche imagines, "When one lets rhythm permeate speech," that force "reorders all the atoms of the sentence, bids one choose one's words with care, and gives one's thoughts a new colour, making them darker, stranger, and more remote" (2010, 84). As hopeful as we are for something more, I also want to emphasize that I am *not* attempting to offer a clean-cut apparatus. As Burke does in *A Grammar of Motives* (1969a), I hope to deconstruct any apparatus as it is being unfurled. We want no tyrants here. Strange writing is always on the move. It is nomadic. It doesn't bureaucratize the imagination, as Burke says. Strange moves, while sometimes creating cultural capital, sometimes undermine capitals. Strange writing doesn't capitalize by setting up a capital building; it doesn't even always capitalize its sentences or its own name. It resists authority, so it can't become the authority. Still, innovative or stranged rhetorical forms can be used to acquire capital and authority, as with advertising and politics. The internal conflict remains. Yet strangeness is infinite and on the move. It's what we already know that has stale, static, authoritarian boundaries.

ANCIENT FIGURES AND NOVELTY DEVICES

In 1910, one Herman Schwartz applied for a patent for what he called a Novelty Device. The device was just this: a horn or a walking stick with a flag attached at the end that could be swung around. So, patent 978,943 stands. Inventors like Schwartz are walking around us all the time creating novelty devices. We are asking you to be creative as well. Be childlike in your compositional practices. Invent a squiggle. Find new artistic or aesthetic practices that may be fit for use. These figurations and inventions are the stuff that rhetorical strangeness is made of.

Where did the first rhetorical figures come from, anyway? If figuration, or disfiguration, becomes a means of making strange, then we should consider the origins of how rhetorical figuration has been thought of. The first collection of rhetorical figures we know of comes from Gorgias himself, who lived from 483 to 375 BC. However, since we only have fragments of his writing beyond *The Encomium to Helen*, we must turn to later writers who took up what was before and added to it. And while Gorgias is one of the oldest extant sources for the naming of figures, we may also look back to earlier works, to Homer's own language, full of stylistic devices that were later named, categorized, and put back to work. Any attempt at a history or a catalog of the use of figures from the Greeks on is almost always going to be a clunky, unwieldy, and perhaps a silly endeavor. But ah, well. The gist here is that so many have tried to pin down the figures that they bleed and ebb and overlap in strange, sometimes unmanageable, ways.

From later in the third century, Aristotle's *Rhetoric* obviously touches upon various figures systematically, but in a different manner than the usual places we turn to for developed outlines of figures. Aristotle gestures toward figures, but often resists recommending them in case they become barbarisms. In the third book, Aristotle focuses on *lexis*, or stylistic moves possible at the sentence level. Later, we find that *The Rhetoric to Herennius*, once attributed to Cicero, contains a careful outline of various figures that we still employ today. Cicero's *De Inventione* (1949) is a valuable resource for considering the figures. Also, Quintilian's *Institutio Oratoria* works along a similar framework, carefully delineating various formations and their effects.

Cicero acknowledges unique forms when discussing language that stands apart. Cicero writes in *De Oratore*, "These are the figures, and others like these, or there may even be more, which adorn [*inluminent*] language by peculiarities [*conformationibus*] in thought or structure of style" (1860, 254). And Cicero writes in his section on figures: "Hence it happens, that all the virtue and merit of single words consists in three particulars: if a word be antique, but such, however, as usage will tolerate; if it be formed by composition, or newly invented [*novitate*], where regard is to be paid to the judgment of the ear and to custom; or if it be used metaphorically; peculiarities which eminently distinguish and brighten language, as with so many stars" (1860, 242). The stars of figural peculiarities make texts shine—and that shining work of novel forms is useful. The forms take all shapes and sizes. Cicero uses alliteration and assonance in *De Inventione*, and Quintilian accepts catachresis, or misuse, as a rhetorical figure. These uses offer significant potential for contemporary composition, but they are not often thought of in contemporary composition and rhetorical practices. Quintilian writes off Seneca's rhetoric as being dangerous because it is too unconventional, in spite of the fact that he describes the rhetorical figures as artful deviation from normal usage (1922, 9.2.1). And for Quintilian, there are rhetorical vices, such as *battalogia*—or excessive repetition—that are not admitted into the list of valid rhetorical moves. More broadly, Quintilian considers the value of these deviations of language, and admittedly focuses on them, confessing, "I purpose to treat only of those figures of thought which deviate from common modes of expression" (1922, 9.2.1). Quintilian too suggests a similar value: "As salt, too, mixed with food rather liberally, but not so as to be in excess, gives it a certain peculiar relish, so salt in language has a certain charm, which creates in us a thirst, as it were, for hearing more" (1922, 6.3.19). Strangeness offers rhetorical attention, adding measured salt and style, often through the use of figures, of which there are hundreds and hundreds.

Aristotle had also previously outlined several topoi, such as looking for contradictions or similarity and difference. Carolyn Miller insightfully reads the Aristotelian topoi, or commonplaces, as possible sites of generative novelty, suggesting that what "this approach to invention emphasizes is the generative potential of the familiar, the possibility of novelty within the commonplace" (2000, 134). Familiar moves like repetition or addition offer the possibility of multiplying new forms. And yet Aristotle disallowed, for example, the pun as one of the valid topoi for logical composition. However, Paul Butler gives a nice account of Aristotle's understanding of unusual style connected to figuration in his excellent text *Out of Style*:

> Aristotle discusses contrasting "faults" or "bad taste in language" that results from violating the principles of clarity and appropriateness in word choice, suggesting his effort to restrain style as a general principle. According to Aristotle, the faults consist of the misuse of compound words (e.g., "many-visaged heaven"); the use of "strange words" (e.g., Alcidamas's discussion of "the witlessness of nature"); inappropriate epithets (meaning "long, unseasonable or frequent"; e.g., Alcidamas's use of "the laws that are monarchs of states" instead of "laws"); and "inappropriate"—far-fetched or grand and theatrical—metaphors (e.g., Gorgias's "events that are green and full of sap") . . . It is clear that these "faults" indicate a way in which Aristotle essentially contains style by narrowing the notion of appropriate discourse. Aristotle's specific examples suggest his critique of more expansive techniques employed by some of the Sophists. (2008, 35)

The question of who and how and how much one gets to twist a word or phrase using various tropes and schemes seems to rely on a sense of permission. And who will give permission? As Butler adds, "The very name of 'bad taste in language' indicates the need to control, balance, and find a mean" (35) and so on in the context of our larger senses of language and rhetorical usage. The acceptability of strange style has influence, and whoever stands against those unique forms is typically advocating for something more familiar that has gone before.

For his part, Shklovsky presents Aristotle's own claim that poetic language should be strange. These values are echoed elsewhere, as in Horace's "Ars Poetica," or "The Art of Poetry," which begins by explaining how we have to be careful about mixing things like a horse with feathers or a woman's body and the body of a fish. These chimeras, he says, make us laugh because they cross the bounds of propriety. In Horace's text, the young writer receives a warning against too strange, or too incongruous, an image. It begins:

> Suppose you'd been asked to come for a private view
> Of a painting wherein the artist had chosen to join
> To a human head the neck of a horse, and gone on
> To collect some odds and ends of arms and legs
> And plaster the surface with feathers of differing colors,
> So that what began as a lovely woman at the top
> Tapered off into a slimy, discolored fish—
> Could you keep from laughing, my friends? (2002, 271)

Certainly, this long opening sentence seems like a warning against too strong instances of what is called a purple passage—a colorful passage that stands out, a term that comes from Horace himself. However, it is Horace's own strange invention—some kind of mermaid—that makes this work so enticing from its introduction. The incongruity of certain pairings, however, we know from Horace's own example, can be thoroughly useful, especially if it can make our audiences cackle.

Quintilian, coming on the heels of Horace historically, briefly touches upon similar connections in the effectiveness of certain rhetorical abuses. In attempting to pin down the complicated definition of rhetoric, he observes that there is something twisted built into the art of persuasion. In *The Institutes of Oratory*, he owns this particular nature of rhetoric, writing, "Of those who separate the talent of speaking from the greater and more desirable praise of a good life, some have called rhetoric merely a power; some a science but not a virtue; some a habit, some an art, but having nothing in common with science and virtue; some even an abuse of art, that is, a *κακοτεχνία*" (1922, 2.15.2). κακοτεχνία is such an interesting term; it means something like poor workmanship or botchery, but more literally something like a shit technics. It is bad form. But badness and goodness always work along a scale—there are good/bad things, like punk. Literally, punk is performing in bad form. Punk composition is κακοτεχνία; it's a shit technics. Later Quintilian asserts, "Hence, what is called *catachresis*, the abuse of words, becomes necessary" (1922, 8.2.6), laying out a theory of perspicuity pertaining to rhetorical acts. However, he allows that complete clarity is not the preferred rhetorical choice in every situation, despite what writers like Joseph M. Williams say. What Williams says in particular is this: "It's good to write clearly, and anyone can" (1999, 4). What he implies is that everyone should. The problem is that an obsession with clarity generally leads to a smattering of essays that look very, very similar—along with the need for a full pot of coffee for those teachers condemned to read those stale artifacts.

Beyond the Greeks and the Romans, various Middle Ages and Enlightenment texts attempted to catalog or rework classical themes and tropes. Of note is Erasmus (1999), whose *De Copia* is much more enthusiastic and hyperbolic than some other works. George Puttenham's (2007) sixteenth-century text *The Arte of English Poesy* offers a fairly thorough overview of rhetorical devices cataloged as various tactics. More contemporarily, we have Richard Lanham's (2012) *A Handlist of Rhetorical Terms* or even sad little self-published books like Ian McKenzie's (2015) *Sixty-Nine Tools: Sixty-Nine Useful Rhetorical Devices Which Will Assist in Vastly Improving Your Presentations and Writing*, which sold for $6 on Amazon .com. The idea persists that these texts offer something of worth and contain some mysterious key to unlock secret doors. The need to continue cataloging these frameworks has allowed scholars of rhetoric to look backward while pushing forward into new territory, always with a renewed interest in figuration.

Within the past century, we have seen a number of scholars return to the schema and figures found in rhetorical handbooks. Chaïm Perelman and Lucie Olbrechts-Tyteca outline a set of non-formal arguments in *The New Rhetoric*, first published in 1969. Perelman and Olbrechts-Tyteca (1971) reinstated a classical rhetoric using logical forms. They explored structures and schema that lay beyond traditional reasoning, moving toward more fluid scenarios based upon the particular case or the audience. This articulated set of moves is always established within a context. Similarly, Group μ from Brussels outlined a program for working through rhetorical schemes using a "general theory of the figures of language" in *A General Rhetoric*, first published in 1970, only a year after *The New Rhetoric*. Their book analyzes different expressions under four moves: Suppression, Addition, Suppression-Addition, and Permutations (1981).

We have fun when we talk about the uses and abuses of English. A consideration of rhetorical effects lies at the heart of these offerings. These are not stifling maxims, but recommendations that lead younger writers down promising paths into new territory. The likes of E. B. White and William Strunk (2007), who gave us the pinnacle of precision in *The*

Elements of Style, are central to this discussion. What was originally only Strunk's little book, which I both cherish and strive with, has this final rule: **21.** ***Prefer the standard to the offbeat.*** Rule 21 must be contended with at every step in the composition classroom, with some degree of balance and dignity. But many have moved on. We have experienced postmodernity. As Steven Pinker writes in his book *The Sense of Style,* "Much advice on style is stern and censorious" (2015, 12). Unfortunately, we agree, despite his easy dismissal. He continues, "The classic manuals, written by starchy Englishmen and rock-ribbed Yankees, try to take all the fun out of writing, grimly adjuring the writer to avoid offbeat words, figures of speech, and playful alliteration" (12). While Strunk and White do actually have their fun moments, our students are not often encouraged to branch out and explore the unbeaten path. Playful figures are taboo. Standards are old hat. Yes. But.

Aside from the desire for cleanliness, the many models continue to rely upon coming up with the next new thing. *Purple Cow: Transform Your Business by Being Remarkable* by Seth Godin takes up the defamiliarization cause and capitalizes upon it. The stranger has often been caught up in capital; the Venetian gondolier is paid €100 to sing gladly to the smiling American couple. Godin encourages out-of-the-box thinking. He urges, "Something **remarkable** is worth talking about. Worth noticing. Exceptional. New. Interesting. It's a Purple Cow. Boring stuff is invisible. It's a brown cow" (2007, 3). We want purple cows; we want to make all things new, and see what interesting things we can build with language and other materials we can find ready to hand, but often first with language.

A rhetorical view of grammar, structure, and form still has some gas left in its tank. While there are calls for plain language in variously appropriate spaces, strangeness is catching sway. The possibilities of forms and figures have been richly covered by Martha Kolln's (2006) *Rhetorical Grammar,* Ed Corbett and Bob Connors's (1998) *Classical Rhetoric for the Modern Student,* and Jeanne Fahnestock's (2011) *Rhetorical Style: The Uses of Language in Persuasion.* There have been other more progressive books published on these matters—interesting little tomes that explore rare examples of grammatical uniqueness through the quirks of our language. Books like Lynne Truss's (2006) *Eats, Shoots & Leaves,* June Casagrande's (2010) *It Was the Best of Sentences, It Was the Worst of Sentences,* Patricia T. O'Conner's (2019) *Woe Is I,* Karen Elizabeth Gordon's (1993) *The Deluxe Transitive Vampire,* and Bill Walsh's (2004) *The Elephants of Style* each offer a nod toward grammatical values, but seem to be more like coffee-table books than anything we might generally take up in practice. Grammar continues to be a niche market.

THE PROBLEM WITH STANDARDIZED STYLE

It is not that we have too formulaic a view of composition; it is that we have too few formulas to work with and expand upon. The five-paragraph essay has offered a singular form—a powerful form, though generating innovative forms by only being able to work from one is hard. If we think of jazz musicians being able to riff from a collection of formulas, scales of various kinds, chromatic, achromatic, octaves, pentads, and such, then writing as composition actually has left us fairly bereft of patterns to work from and diverge from. We mainly have the five-paragraph essay. That's pretty much the extent of it for many.

This is not the old schoolmarm teaching grammar to correct you from being wrong. This is the new media world calling you to innovate using what you know. And if you don't know language and its workings, why, then how might you begin to work with it in some engaging ways? Thinking of defamiliarization in the composition classroom is largely unheard of. An examination of the current textbooks shows things like how to write a clear thesis statement using a carefully chosen collection of unique essays. The figures are simply not there, and even books that outline the figures can be drab.

As Jonathan Alexander reminds us in one of his explications of queer theory and pedagogy, Henry Giroux himself famously called for a "pedagogy of difference" (2008, 101). This difference can be queer itself, or associationally so. Lillian Bridwell-Bowles has also been an advocate for this kind of textual differentiation: "When one attempts to write outside the dominant discourse, one often has to begin by naming the new thing. I have used various terms for our experiments, including 'alternative' and 'feminist,' but recently we have been using the term 'diverse discourse'" (1992, 350). Lilly invites without pushing too hard, noting, "If [students] are not attempting to write outside established conventions, I invite them to consider how others might feel the need to do so" (350). When we then are welcomed not just to compose differently but to read for others' divergence, the interchange of our otherness becomes possible.

Winston Weathers was one composition scholar who allowed for something beyond Standard English in what he called "Grammar B." Weathers, a clever stylist himself, embraced strange and broken grammatical structures. He encouraged the use of forms like fragments and labyrinthine sentences. He suggested the use of these alongside Grammar A, or Standard English. Weathers words it this way in *An Alternate Style*: "In today's classroom we keep all our stylistic options within the confines of one grammar only—a grammar that has no particular name (we can call it the 'traditional' grammar of style/or for my purposes Grammar A) but has the characteristics of continuity, order, reasonable progression and sequence, consistency, unity, etc. We are all familiar with these characteristics" (1980, 6). The familiarity of standardized grammar, then, gives us a rhetorical opportunity, found in defamiliarizing grammatical forms.

Yet now our students find the expectations of written language insurmountable. And still they might try playing with language, seeing what it can do. The future of writing is not a singular standardized writing, one hopes. I talk to non-English majors about their interests and they light up like firecrackers. When I ask them if they would like to write about those various interesting interests, they say sadly, "I can't write." It is the *can't* that closes off the play space of composition, a *cant* that we hear too often.

A TECHNE OF STRANGENESS; OR, HOW TO BREAK THE RULES

So, we might venture to conclude that one vanguard approach for a method for making strange can be found in the rhetorical figures. And while we have recounted various sets, catalogs, and employments of the figures deployed over the course of history, we are now in a media environment that calls for a revisionary approach to figuration rooted in both old and new methods. Using a revised set of updated rhetorical figures, I have seen success in considering unique moves based in rhetorical choices within a number of diverse compositions. This strategy offers an approach to teaching and reading for interesting moves across media, a heuristic for exploring and crafting strangeness. As Jonathan Culler suggests, we reduce a text's "strangeness by reading" (2002, 171). We expose ourselves to new conventions and naturalize ourselves to them as we go.

So, what do we do? We create new forms or words like Viktor Shklovsky with ostranenie or Johannes Göransson (2020) with his little piece "To Vibrebrate: In Defense of Strangeness." New words that we create for an occasion, like *vibrebrate*, have their own unique meanings, and the sense is there. Or we learn from creatives of all kinds of media, such as painter Jackson Pollock, who says in one interview: "I happen to find ways that are different from the usual techniques, which seems a little strange at the moment, but I don't think there's anything very different about it. I paint on the floor and this isn't unusual," acknowledging that some art in Asia was done on the floor as well (quoted in Ross 1991, 142). While we do not have to work on the floor (though we could), we might think of practices from elsewhere broadly as potentially generative (being careful about remaining authentic to our own practices and processes without gliding into cultural appropriation). Strangeness helps us embrace the hedonism of novelty and creativity across our vast media ecology. If we conceive of productively wrangled language or forms in media, we can begin to stir up the stream.

As a caveat, I also want to be wary of solely promoting a romantic thinking subject who makes meaning. I should make clear that I do struggle against the naive belief that we are able to spout out perfectly beautiful compositions. Conceptual artist Sol Lewitt says, "When an artist learns his craft too well he makes slick art" (1999, 107). Lewitt saw the iterability of an idea as providing a literally endless framework within which to work. But, to avoid the slickness of a programmatic approach to composition practices, I hope to instead offer a heuristic that offers endless iterations, a path-making approach rather than a set of paths. I agree with Victor Vitanza's critique of the traditional heuristic model for composition, where he notes "the differences between heuristics (the old economy) and aleatory procedures (the ever new economy)" (2000, 187). Aleatory procedures, such as randomized text generation, can be found in combining and recombining different tropes, and can create more interesting interactions via chance operations. There are traditional heuristics, and ones that can produce a kind of recombinant strangeness. On the one hand, I can see how this exegesis would err on the side of starry-eyed idealism. And yet I expect that strange formalism offers a method to something new—not always great, but often affective.

So, a set of strange figures, useful for invention, has a special value. A catalog of strangers, a list of outsiders can break through the plaque of the strictures of composition. Such a set becomes a means to many ends. A strange techne can be a fruitful resource. As Heidegger himself says of techne in "Building, Dwelling, Thinking": "The Greek for 'to bring forth or to produce' is *tikto.* The word *techne,* technique, belongs to the verb's root *tec.* To the Greeks *techne* means neither art nor handicraft but rather: to make something appear, within what is present, as this or that, in this way or that way. The Greeks conceive of *techne,* producing, in terms of letting appear" (2013, 157). And a techne of strangeness (as we have already said and shown in the work of Shklovsky) is a means of letting things appear, a means of crafting epiphanies.

On a related note, I have recently wondered about the connection between topoi and *atopos.* Strange tropes are still often rhetorical commonplaces, which in some ways makes them *unstrange.* Hyperbole, for example, is a common trope, but can make things seem strange by blowing them out of proportion. Does this make hyperbole a commonplace or an uncommonplace? In order to lay out and examine my own solution briefly, I'd like to outline some thoughts on the applications of rhetorical figures. The balance for what functions as an acceptable figure has complex, often self-contradicting perspectives. In any case, our own set of updated figures might be connected to Cicero's sixteen topoi, Quintilian's figures, Ramus's divisions, loci, and topoi, Burke's four master tropes and his pentad, Jungian archetypes, Greek mythology, and mathematical operators, as you will see.

There are a number of simplified configurations worth covering here. Quintilian's schema from *The Institutes of Oratory* involves different groupings, but most saliently what is known as the four rhetorical operations, or the *quadripartita ratio.* We only get a few lines from Quintilian on the group:

> For the present I will define barbarism as an offence occurring in connection with single words. Some of my readers may object that such a topic is beneath the dignity of so ambitious a work. But who does not know that some barbarisms occur in writing, others in speaking? For although what is incorrect in writing will also be incorrect in speech, the converse is not necessarily true, inasmuch as mistakes in writing are caused by addition or omission, substitution or transposition. (1922, 1.5.4–7)

So, from Quintilian, we have addition, omission, substitution, and transposition, and he calls them barbarisms—disfigurations. They are sometimes considered as four categories of change, as a kind of morphology of how forms are transformed into other forms. In Latin they are *adiectio, detraction, transmutation,* and *immutatio.* In Greek they are πλεονασμός (addition), ἔνδεια (omission), μετάθεσις (transposition), and ἐναλλαγή (permutation), or alternatively grouped as addition (πρόσθεσις), subtraction (ἀφαίρεσις), transposition (μετάθεσις), and transmutation (ἀλλοίωσις). When I am attempting a quick lesson with students, these four basic figures work pretty well. They are handy and can do enough surgery to awaken some deadness. We might take an opening or closing sentence, or a thesis, or perhaps an image and add something, take something away, move something around, and replace something to generate some productive new thoughts or forms.

Different figural groupings are useful and helpful. But I have also found them cumbersome at times and disconnected from contemporary life and contemporary media. Indeed, some forms of strangeness are particularly strange because they are unaccountable, although this is not always the case. It is both enthusing and intimidating to consider that there are hundreds of figures and combinations possible—which would lead to endless invention, and has led to a horde of inventions already. Here, for example, is every figure from the online database *Silva Rhetoricae* (2016):

-A-
abating
abbaser
abecedarian
abcisio
ablatio
abode, figure of
abominatio
abuse
abusio
abusion
acoloutha
accismus
accumulatio
accusatio adversa
accusatio
acervatio
acrostic
acyrologia
acyron
adage
adagium
addubitatio
adhortatio
adianoeta
adjectio
adjournment
adjudicatio
adjunct
adjunctio
admonitio
adnexio
adnominatio
adynata
adynaton
aeschrologia
aetiologia
affirmatio
affirmation
aganactesis
agnominatio
agnomination
aischrologia
allegory
alleotheta
alliteration
amara irrisio
ambage, figure of
ambiguitas
ambiguous
amphibologia
ampliatio
anacephalaeosis
anacoenosis
anacoloutha
anacoluthon
anadiplosis
anamnesis
anangeon
anaphora
anapodoton
anastrophe
anemographia
anesis
antanaclasis
antanagoge
antenantiosis
anthimeria
anthropopatheia
anthypophora
anticategoria
anticipation
antilogy
antimetabole
antimetathesis
antipersonification
antiphrasis
antiprosopopoeia
antiptosis
antirrhesis
antisagoge
antistasis
antisthecon
antistrophe
antithesis
antitheton
antonomasia
apagoresis
aphaeresis
aphorismus
apocarteresis
apocope
apodioxis
apodixis
apologue
apophasis
apoplanesis
aporia
aposiopesis
apostrophe
apothegm
apparent refusal
appositio
apposition
ara
articulus
aschematismus
aschematiston
asphalia
assonance
assumptio
assumption
avancer, the
asteismus
astrothesia
asyndeton
auxesis
aversio

-B-
barbarism
battologia
bdelygmia
benedictio
bomphiologia
brachiepia
brachylogia
broad floute, the

-C-
cacemphaton
cacophonia
cacosyntheton
cacozelia
casus pro casu
catachresis
catacosmesis
cataphasis
cataplexis
categoria
cause shown
change of name
characterismus
charientismus
chiasmus
chorographia
chreia
chronographia
circumlocutio
civille jest, the
clause
climax
coenotes
colon
combined repetition
comma
common cause
commoratio
communicatio
commutatio
comparatio
compensatio
complexio
compositum ex contrariis
comprobatio
conceit
concessio
conciliatio
conclusio
condescensio
condescension
conduplicatio
congeries
conjunctio
consonance
contencion
contentio
continued metaphor
contractio
contrarium
contrast
conversio
correctio
counterchange, the
counterfait in person
counterfait place
counterfeit time, the
counter turne
cutted comma, the
cutting from the end

-D-
deesis
dehortatio
dendrographia
deprecatio
descriptio
diacope
diaeresis
dialogismus
dialysis
dialyton
dianoea
diaphora
diaporesis
diaskeue
diastole
diasyrmus
diazeugma
dicaeologia
digressio
dilemma
dirimens copulatio
distinctio
distributio
doubtfull, the

-E-
ecphonesis
ecphrasis
ecthlipsis
effictio
elenchus
ellipsis
emphasis
enallage
enantiosis
energia
encomium
energia
enigma
ennoia
enthymeme
enumeration
epanalepsis
epanodos
epanorthosis
epenthesis
epergesis
epexegesis
epicrisis
epilogus
epimone
epiphonema
epiplexis
epistrophe
epitasis
epitheton
episynaloephe
epitrochasmus
epitrope
epizeugma
epizeuxis
erotema
ethopoeia
eucharistia
euche
eulogia
euphemismus
eustathia
eutrepismus
example
excitatio
exclamatio
excursus
exergasia
exouthenismos
expeditio
expolitio
exuscitatio

-F-
frequentatio

-G-
geographia
gnome
graecismus

-H-
hendiadys
heterogenium
homiologia
homoeoprophoron
homoeosis
homoioptoton
homoioteleuton
horismus
hydrographia
hypallage
hyperbaton
hyperbole
hypophora
hypotyposis
hypozeugma
hypozeuxis
hysterologia
hysteron proteron

-I-
icon
indignatio
inopinaturm
insinuatio
interrogatio
inter se pugnantia
intimation
irony
isocolon

-L-
litotes

-M-
macrologia
martyria
maxim
medela
meiosis
membrum
mempsis
merismus
mesarchia
mesodiplosis
mesozeugma
metabasis
metalepsis
metallage
metaphor
metaplasm
metastasis
metathesis
metonymy
mimesis
mycterismus

-N-
noema

-O-
oeonismus
ominatio
onedismus
onomatopoeia
optatio
orcos
oxymoron

-P-
paenismus
palilogia
parabola
paradiastole
paradiegesis
paradigma
paradox
paraenesis
paragoge
paralipsis
parallelism
paramythia
parathesis
parecbasis
paregmenon
parelcon
parembole
parenthesis
pareuresis
paroemia
paroemion
paromoiosis
paromologia
paronomasia
parrhesia
pathopoeia
perclusio
periergia
period
periphrasis
perissologia
peristasis
permutatio
personification
philophronesis
pleonasm
ploce
polyptoton
polysyndeton
pragmatographia
procatalepsis
proclees
prodiorthosis
proecthesis
prolepsis
prosapodosis
proslepsis
prosonomasia
prosopographia
prosopopoeia
prosphonesis
protherapeia
prothesis
protrope
proverb
prozeugma
pysma

-R-
ratiocinatio
repetitio
repotia
restrictio
rhetorical question

-S-
sarcasmus
scesis onomaton
schematismus
scheme
scurra
skotison
sententia
sermocinatio
simile
solecismus
soraismus
sorites
subjectio
sustentatio
syllepsis
syllogismus
symperasma
symploce
synaeresis
synaloepha
synathroesmus
syncatabasis
syncategorema
synchoresis
synchysis
syncope
syncrisis
synecdoche
synoeciosis
synonymia
synthesis
syntheton
synzeugma
systole
systrophe

-T-
tapinosis
tasis
tautologia
taxis
thaumasmus
tmesis
topographia
topothesia
traductio
transitio
transplacement
tricolon

-V-
verborum bombus

-Z-
zeugma

The significance of such a collection is perhaps untapped and unthought. And yet . . . I am saddened when I think of the high school student forced to memorize the meaning of *anaphora* and *anadiplosis* and *asyndeton* and *antimetabole.* What a waste!! Who needs to know those things? How about just repetition?! How about just repetition?! *Chiasmus* is sometimes nice, and *zeugma* is fun to say, but consider the value of thinking about real terms to describe the forms we see in the texts and items from our everyday encounters. However, again, we must consider a more manageable way. From Chaucer to Kanye to Banksy to your mother, everyone uses rhetorical figures, because we are all always shaping our texts. Rhetorical figures have sway everywhere: in art, media, culture, and language. The effects possible through figuration are boundless, and the places one may discover these rhetorical moves are as well. The figures have effects, and they elicit various, perhaps endless, senses of affects from us.

SEXY AND INTOXICATING

And those who dare can willfully leap toward the sexy and intoxicating qualities that may be found in the composing process. Some of what we're after is really in line with the unholy trinity: sex, drugs, and rock and roll. Strangeness is sexy. The erotic, blindfolded stranger is rhetorical in the most libidinal ways. Each composition, each rhetorical act, now competes with a milieu of exotic pleasures. The contemporary rhetor has to be sexier than the competition. And sexual desire lies at the heart of rhetorical action and inaction. As Jonathan Alexander and Jacqueline Rhodes have asked, "What's Sexual about Rhetoric, What's Rhetorical about Sex?" (2016, 1). *Stranger,* after all, is also used as a word to mean an unfamiliar sexual partner; these terms combine our meanings, as with the word *punk,* as with the word *queer.* The sexual politics of strangeness are not to be ignored.

Imagine two lovers. One desires the other. And yet one is tired, or afraid, or angry, or resistant to lovemaking. There is a stasis, a point where the difference of opinion regarding the evening's activities reaches stalemate. This sexual metaphor gives us the opportunity of seeing difference as strangeness, but also the strangeness of the other's desires—strange in that they are not *my* desires. Hence, strangeness, the unique move of a good lover, will conquer the strangeness of difference between the two. It is an interesting paradox. As Michael Warner considers this tension between normalcy and sex, he ponders, "To be fully normal is, strictly speaking, impossible. Everyone deviates from the norm in some way. Even if one belongs to the statistical majority in age group, race, height, weight, frequency of orgasm, gender of sexual partners, and annual income, then simply by virtue of this unlikely combination of normalcies one's profile would already depart from the norm. Then, too, the idea of normal is especially strange in the realm of sex. In one sense, nothing could be more normal than sex" (1999, 54–55). Formalizing defamiliarization, then, might be seen as an invitation—*perhaps a late-night message*—to confront the glamour of grammar's etymological history, the strange paradox involved with being both persuasively appealing and unique, in other words to be exotic without being disorienting or distant.

From sex to drugs, strange effects may be delivered chemically too. Strangeness can enter your veins, take you over, enter your bloodstream. Strange brews can intoxicate. We can dope up on strangeness—taken intravenously, injected, or taken orally, swallowed down whole, drumming up mind-altering hallucinations, delusions, illusions. It can come in the form of uppers or downers. And if there is an opiate of the masses still lingering about, strange intoxication can also *demystify* the masses, wake them up with a rush of norepinephrine. Two drugs are used in the case of an overdose of an opiate: Naloxone and Revivon. Revivon is too strong for humans. It's used on tranquilized rhinos and elephants. It wakes them up, removes stupor, allows them to feel again. Opiates remove pain sensation. So, there is also a potential violence to making someone else feel something that they don't want to feel.

William Burroughs used drugs to make things, but we don't have to; we have language itself. But he was at least aware of their strange effects—how to mix, to cut up, to drift, all toward constructive ends. Answering the question "Why did you start taking drugs?" in a 1965 interview with the *Paris Review*, Burroughs replies, "Well, I was just bored." And then adds, "I think drugs are interesting principally as chemical means of altering metabolism and thereby altering what we call reality, which I would define as a more or less constant scanning pattern." However, Burroughs has been high enough to stop taking drugs, to not be romantic about being high, and to warn, "The hallucinogens produce visionary states, sort of, but morphine and its derivatives decrease awareness of inner processes, thoughts and feelings. They are pain killers; pure and simple. They are absolutely contraindicated for creative work, and I include in the lot alcohol, morphine, barbiturates, tranquilizers—the whole spectrum of sedative drugs" (quoted in Knickerbocker 1965). Again, drugs move the mind, although not always toward elation, creation, or revelation.

Ronan Hallowell argues that drugs function as perceptually affective media. He explains, "Speaking, writing, printing, and electronic media are four communication media that scholars recognize as having had revolutionary impact on the development of consciousness, society, knowledge discovery, and culture" (2011, 237). He also looks at issues of consciousness and how media affect the human mind. He suggests, "Chemical media and drugs should also be included in the natural history of human media" (237). New drugs, new technologies, new grips we make for the world are all wrapped up in various packages—the forms of media.

What we are talking about here is *poesis*, a poetics that can grab the audience's attention in the midst (the mist) of information overload. Chad Scoville writes in a *Wired Magazine* article: "Higher levels of automation, media and communication equate to progressive levels of information. Humanity has surpassed the point of inundation; levels of information constitute an obsolescence" (2010). Defamiliarization—at the present time—is more necessary than ever. Strangeness, that which can't speed past the senses, provides new opportunities for attention in the (post)information society. Scoville adds, "When perception is no longer able to detect the sensible event" we become "electronically stoned" (2010). Techne is our drug—atechne is the *pharmakon*. Derrida explores the double meaning of this term in "Plato's Pharmacy," where the term suggests both poison and remedy. Derrida urges, "Contrary to life, writing—or, if you will, the *pharmakon*—can only *displace* or even *aggravate* the ill" (1983, 100). And we will aggravate here as well, with the drug of defamiliarization as our rhetorical methodology across media.

I might add just one more delivery system, a medium that affects people deeply: music. I want to explore what makes certain music strange, and thereby valuable in a particular way. Alternative music embraces the abrogation of laws. I can remember walking into a smoky punk club called Ground Zero when I was sixteen years old. A mannequin's legs are sticking out of the wall wearing fishnet tights. There are people dressed in tight clothes, and some dressed in baggy clothes. Bad Brains was playing that night. I may have bobbed while they chanted "Miss Freedom," though I can't recall the set list now. Punk literally means bad. Three chords. Unsophisticated. And so, while I could reference many punk classics, "Anarchy in the UK" may be a representative track here. The jarring actions that we can get into with our rhetorical bodies are there for resisting our own non-rhetorical soporific existences. What do rhetoricians *make* with sex, drugs, and rock and roll? That's the rollicking, roiling fun of composition in the first place. The strange rhetor makes interestingness with strangeness. That's all any of us ever do. What's the takeaway? We can think of becoming more enticing with our compositions.

TEACHING AND LEARNING NEW FIGURES FOR OURSELVES

A pedagogy or practice that employs strange figurations may inhere in the natural functions of rhetoric. If you are a composer yourself or if you are teaching composers, we have to begin thinking, then, of what ways we might use to generate specific strangenesses in order to do new things and construct new meanings, and thereby garner increased attention in and toward our texts.

If figures are merely names for describing what we perceive as different, then our options are only limited by language and observation. What is possible to dis-figure out of our selves and the infinite textualities around us? What have we got? Forms. Figures. Novelty Devices.

There are easily visible shapes that we can begin to name, using our own language. The Greeks did this with their own terms like *amphibologia.* The Russian formalists too began coming up with some of their own terms, such as **пустота** (*pustota,* or emptiness) and **сдвиг** (*sdvig,* or shift, break, displacement) (Esanu 2013, 73). These Russian **прибор** (*priemy,* or devices, methods, or techniques) offered early modernist poets and artists like Aleksei Kruchyonykh their own language to talk about the moves they were making (Esanu 2013, 73).

But we don't have to use those terms. We have to begin to think about what we can see or notice ourselves. What shapes and forms are discernable or describable to us today? We can think of immediate forms, things like repetition and doubling. For one, Mark Fisher writes in *The Weird and The Eerie*: "The form that is perhaps most appropriate to the weird is montage—the conjoining of *two or more things which do not belong together.* Hence the predilection within surrealism for the weird, which understood the unconscious as a montage-machine, a generator of weird juxtapositions" (2017, 11). He also negotiates and teases out the differences among our terms a bit further: "There is certainly something that the weird, the eerie and the *unheimlich* share. They are all affects, but they are also modes: modes of film and fiction, modes of perception, ultimately, you might even say, modes of being" (9). Thinking about the unique meaningful affects of different forms and gestures forces us to combine form and content. In "Our Aesthetic Categories: Zany, Cute, Interesting," Sianne Ngai invites us to reconsider our investments in certain kinds of forms that appear in contemporary culture and have real meaning. For Ngai, zaniness, for example, is a quality that is specifically tied to selling commodities within contemporary capitalism (2015, 948). This perspective forces us to consider how and whether certain forms are innocent, devoid of any particular meaning until they are filled with content, or whether they have their own inherent meanings tied to their specific shapes. What do we draw, for instance, from strangely used hyperbole and repetition? The value that any particular form can offer by generating interest is only somewhat innocent of its own affects. Inversions, for example, can be good or bad, but what connotations do we think of with things being inverted? There is the vertigo, the unsettling of ungrounded abandon. Inversion is its own type of thing.

There are other ways of making strange as well—perhaps infinitely so. So, let us begin to examine and imagine our own revisionary grouping of figures that may be employed to various effects in a number of different media. Figural impropriety offers a host of inventive strategies as the core of many rhetorical actions—including new possibilities to be found in old and new media. The natures of strange forms present themselves all around us. The iterations of strangeness are infinite. Meanwhile, the number of norms will always be finite and countable. This is why invention relies on strange forms. Refiguring our compositional frameworks rhetorically allows us to generate endless variations that each produce novel effects.

PART II

Using Strangeness

Chapter 4
WHERE IS STRANGENESS?

The roar of wind and waves produce such a tumult that one must shout aloud to make himself heard a few feet away.

—Example of an incorrect sentence in Abraham Howry Espenshade, *The Essentials of Composition and Rhetoric* (1904)

NEW WINE / NEW VESSELS: THE WAVES WHERE STRANGENESS LIES

If we are going to think about how strangeness works, we should also think about where it works. Where is our weirdness? Where does strangeness lie? It works in you and me, but it also sits or lies in its various containers—an intriguing film or a jarring book. If you can think about a specific container for some strangeness you have encountered, you can begin to think about its form and shape. Even strangeness needs containing. It doesn't float independently but is always tied to something. Strangeness doesn't have complete independence; nothing does. Still, we experience unique forms across genres, literacies, media, and modes of communication. These various vessels of strangeness form our surrounding media ecology—ever weirder as we journey into wilder woods or embark into deeper waters. In explaining what media ecology is, Neil Postman uses the analogy of a Petri dish: "A medium was defined as a substance within which a culture grows" (2000, 10). He suggests, "If you replace the word 'substance' with the word 'technology,' the definition would stand as a fundamental principle of media ecology: A medium is a technology within which a culture grows; that is to say, it gives form to a culture's politics, social organization, and habitual ways of thinking" (10). Hence, we strange up our ecologies, with our thinking in tow, as things in the world are modified, tweaked, and resurfaced—and the strange world shimmers back. The modes, media, and genres employing different literacies are precisely where strangeness is found. The relations of figural forms to the containers in which they sit are strange negotiations, and of course there are always other strange relations to negotiate and tease out along the way.

https://doi.org/10.7330/9781646422821.c004

WAVES AND MEANS

Oh, the waves!

Virginia Woolf knew (1987). There is always another shore of composition and the safety at shore. Out there among the waves though, things can get treacherous, but not much happens if you stay at shore. The shore is what you know. When we try to connect from afar, we might offer a few waves, arm gesticulating with an appended "Hello, over there!!" In the midst of a media flood, we can see what interesting things wash ashore from the waves. Water, water, everywhere, and we have to drink it all. Suasion is everywhere. So is water. So are electrons. So is rhetoric. The waves help bring out interesting things from a faraway place, strange detritus that we might find intriguing from some distant, unknown locale. We reconsider the possibility of going offshore as Cynthia Haynes invites us in "Writing Offshore" to ponder what she calls "the disappearing coastline of composition theory" (2003, 667). We are looking for the new wave, all the while awash in media, in an attempt to clean away the aridity of a bare life. As Victor Vitanza writes in "Abandoned to Writing," "The teaching of writing—is passing *awayves*, just as the Ptolemaic system passed away. The waves are climbing higher and higher until they reach so far beyond the horizon that they fall up and *awayves*. And 'we,' with them. Up and *awayves*" (2003). These alternate wayves are a way forward—a flowing circulations of paths for us. To this end, we continue seeing rhetorical possibility with sense and affect and novel forms across different media carriers.

Rhetorical strangeness can be projected through the air with light or sound or with other vessels. These are the ways and means of composing strangeness. In "The Available Means of Persuasion: Mapping a Theory and Pedagogy of Multimodal Public Rhetoric," David M. Sheridan, Jim Ridolfo, and Anthony J. Michel consider the material conditions afforded to rhetors, asking, "What modes and media are both within our means and are best suited to our audience and purpose?" (2005, 814) and "What material limitations and affordances must I take into account?" (818). As such, we are seeking what we might call a medium uniquely suited, but for particular strangenesses. What modes and media are best suited to the kinds of strange changes I am trying to effect within my intended audience and purpose? As Kati Fargo Ahern writes, "Only when students can appreciate all available forms of writing may they feel more comfortable negotiating unfamiliar reading situations, and potentially moving back and forth between different communities and practices of reading" (2013, 83). When we think of rhetorical means, or the affordances available to us, we can see what's possible. As Jonathan Alexander and Jacqueline Rhodes explain in *On Multimodality*, "We need to ask about other possibilities for expression, for representation, for communicating meaning, for making knowledge. We need to ask about possibilities that may exceed those of the letter, the text-based, the author, the *composed*" (2014, 20). They encourage us all to consider further "how rhetorical affordances of media might help us challenge ourselves to teach composing more robustly, with greater awareness of how to use different media effectively. We challenge ourselves and the field to think as critically as possible about the available means of persuasion at our disposal" (20). In short, we have to ask what holds this version of weirdness best. Working in and along these means is a little like composing like alien life forms in alien environments. We're adrift, and that means that everything is full of potential.

THE TERRIBLE FARCE OF MULTIMODALITY

If we want to begin seeing rhetorical strangeness across the different possible expressions, then we need to reconsider those expressions, lay them out on the table, and see what our options really are. When we consider multimodality, what have we meant—and what is a mode, exactly? In composition pedagogy today, the term *multimodal* has lost its theoretical ground to generally refer to composing in different media. It is evident that many teachers really mean *multimedial*, I suppose, but that hasn't tracked well. When we hear talk of composing in different media, from film to the printed page, we lose the primary modes that exist before the medium. For the New London Group, there were five modes: visual, aural, gestural, spatial, and linguistic (1996).

Cheryl Ball and Colin Charlton, in "All Writing Is Multimodal" from *Naming What We Know*, write simply, "Multimodal means multiple + mode. In contemporary writing studies, a mode refers to a way of meaning-making or communicating. The New London Group (NLG) . . . outlines five modes through which meaning is made: Linguistic, Aural, Visual, Gestural, and Spatial. Any combination of modes makes a multimodal text, and all texts—every piece of communication that a human composes—use more than one mode. Thus, all writing is multimodal" (2015, 42). And of course, it is. All rhetoric. All strangeness. All traces. All of these things exist in multiple dimensions and are perceived as such.

The complex interweaving of textual possibility in different spaces is always multilayered. Complicated factors go into the negotiation of a text coming into existence. In *Remixing Composition*, Jason Palmeri has acknowledged the complex and nuanced nature of multimodal composition as both intrinsically tied to expressivist values and, more than that, also tied to other lineages and anchors in the process. He writes, "The study and teaching of multimodal composing must necessarily be an interdisciplinary endeavor" (2012, 155). That interdisciplinarity acknowledges that there are many, many facets to composing and expression. Palmeri continues at length,

> For example, scholars of graphic design, visual culture, and architecture have much to teach us about ways that images and built environments can be employed to persuade audiences; cognitive scientists have much to teach us about the similarities and differences in the creative processes of writers, visual artists, and scientific innovators; visual anthropologists and sociologists have much to teach us about the political and ethical implications of employing photography as a research tool; our colleagues in speech and communication departments have much to teach us about the persuasive effects of live oratory; and, of course, musicians, actors, painters, sculptors, performance poets, dancers, animators, filmmakers, and other artists have much to teach us about understanding and practicing composing as a complex, recursive process of making meaning. (155)

So, where does strange meaning making occur? Everywhere. This realization is useful because it allows us to see that all of us have access to these varying possibilities in composition.

The sad joke or farce is that we can't completely get ahold of media. They are more complicated and blurry or squishy (or blurrier, squishier, and complicated-er) than we can imagine. We can't pin down every mode. And often, we don't even know exactly what we mean by multimodality. Why is composing in video so important? And don't visual artists get *better* training in composing that way than whatever visual amateurisms might arise in a college composition class? We are always already writing multimodally. There's really nothing we *need* to do. But there are things we *can* do and consider. And we're also always working in and out of the box. These are all tensions to hold together.

And it is worthwhile to consider our containers. Let's reflect: What is the significance of a white 8½ × 11-inch piece of paper? It might be good to remember the effects of the unseen graphite mines for our pencils or that we used to kill sheep and skin them to get something to write on. What unique things have happened on Twitter or with a hashtag that have never happened before? Computers as writing instruments might force us to consider simply what effects using Microsoft Word has upon the essay. Like Nietzsche writing on a typewriter, honing shorter forms of writing like the aphorism (see Kittler 1999, 206; Carr 2008), we need to be aware of the media in use as well as how forms get deployed within them—strangely or conventionally.

Modes contain media, of course. While some might call expressing in different media multimodal composition, we might consider what we're really after. Multimodality itself has become customary—non-novel. But when we are thinking about novel possibilities, we need to see all of the options—strangeness in visual, written, aural, and other formatted expressions. As Adam Banks writes, "The most important issue in this particular convergence of digital, networked technologies and writing or composition is the fact that composing in everyday and academic contexts is far more multimedia and multimodal than it has been at other times in our history (although rhetoric and composition's history has many reminders that notions of the oral and visual have always been a part of our conceptions of writing on some level)" (2011, 154). This expansion of our playing field offers more options. *Composition*, we know, is preferable to the term *writing* because it suggests something broader—we can compose a poem or a song or a painting. We see this in writing across the curriculum or communication across the curriculum structures. Multimodality, by nature, begins as an amateur approach because it requires trying out different containers for texts.

CONTAINERS FOR STRANGE SOLUTIONS: PAPER, PICTURES, TANKS, VESSELS, JARS, AND SACKS

When we strange a container, how does its shape change? From billboards to airplanes writing in the sky, if we want to really reimagine what texts can do in different iterations, we have to reconfront what we have talked about with multimodal composing. As such, we must see the different ways of arranging texts, and some of those modes or media involve written texts, aural texts, visual texts, electrate or electronic texts, and spatial texts. Finally, back to my major point, we can see all sorts of strange figurations within different modes of composing. Johanna Drucker explains for us in her book *Graphesis* on visual production, "New modes need not replace older ones in a media ecology, but the novelty by which we recognize innovation crosses quickly into familiar habit" (2014, 185). If we think to the rhetorical figures first oriented toward public speaking, we can always reconsider the forms to look for examples, such as visual or aural paralepsis in a film or a song. We can then also consider our own other figures, like addition or negation across different communicative containers. We can think of compositional modes as waves of sound and light. Media are like sacks that hold differently shaped iterations of strangeness. Genres are like jars, holding the fluids of novelty that push against the walls and help define the shape of different fluid expressions. Media as containers for strangeness wash over us, and stranged media *jar* us.

In short, I think the waves are nice. We can use WAVES as a nice mnemonic: we can see strangeness in written, aural, visual, electrate, and spatial texts. I ~~see hear feel~~ notice them everywhere reverberating around us. The waves, to me, are simpler and more accessible, and conceptually more memorable than linguistic, aural, visual, spatial, and gestural—although those are fine too. It is helpful to pull out and highlight digital media for contemporary compositionists, despite overlaps and connections. Digital media might have images, text, and sound. As with rhetorical devices, we need an update that works for contemporary students. Still, we won't ever create a perfect list of modes or figures as such. We certainly leave out taste and smell—which have their own rhetorical grammars—in this list. There are certainly strange smells and strange tastes that take their own affective forms. I have smelled something strange. There are yet other sensations that humans have and some we don't. Nevertheless, we can think about several modes of communication set out here, what we might get at with this grounding set of containers, and finally consider further how different modes work.

I like the idea that each of the figures might be likened to a jar (or a sack, or a beaker, or a jug, or a perfume bottle), which can be combined to create noxious or potent mixtures and effects. The image of each container is striking and elicits the diversity possible through figuration. As such it allows us to pay attention to the slash that lies in form/content, both joining and dividing. *Text* is a broad enough term to encompass different kinds of rhetorical works. Signifying something woven together—in the same way many threads weave together to compose a multicolored textile—the meaning is always multilayered, composite.

As Friedrich Kittler explains in *Gramophone, Film, Typewriter*, as media ecologies grow and morph, they take over—and they lead to a kind of erasure of differentiation, meaning, and distinction. He unpacks it in this way: "The general digitization of channels and information erases the differences among individual media. Sound and image, voice and text are reduced to surface effects, known to consumers as interface. Sense and the senses turn into eyewash" (1999, 1). Beyond this, we push toward novelties and twisting media for different effects.

As multimodal as strangeness is, it is also then associatively interdisciplinary. Hence, there are other ways of thinking about strangeness's containers, such as another mnemonic I have used: LACE, or literature, arts, cinema, and electronic media. Or we might consider different specific objects, such as books, films, and music albums. We might also consider different genres, like comedy, tragedy, history, fantasy, and sci-fi, or in music punk, folk, and hip-hop.

MODE BAGGAGE

It is interesting to think through the baggage that different modes of composition have. Frequently with new students and teachers of writing, there is an assumption that essays are boring and videos or podcasts are fun. But there are, of course, some fun essays out there along with some pretty dismal videos. This brings to mind Marshall McLuhan's consideration of hot and cool media. While often confusing, McLuhan does suggest that "any hot medium allows of less participation than a cool one" (1964, 25). The engagement of various kinds of media, from paint and canvases to alphabetic letters to headphones, offers different interactions and hence different shapes and forms for rhetorical strangeness to take on. Painters and writers and musicians and different media shapers can create strangeness in their own unique ways. But you have to love your own medium. As Annie Dillard suggests of writers in "Write till You Drop" you kind of have to love sentences the way a painter loves paint. The story goes like this:

> A well-known writer got collared by a university student who asked, "Do you think I could be a writer?"
>
> "Well," the writer said, "I don't know. . . . Do you like sentences?"
>
> The writer could see the student's amazement. Sentences? Do I like sentences? I am 20 years old and do I like sentences? If he had liked sentences, of course, he could begin, like a joyful painter I knew. I asked him how he came to be a painter. He said, "I liked the smell of the paint." (1989)

In this way, we find what fits with different modes. We *accommodate.* We find the most suitable or appropriate manner for our message. We tend to handwrite love notes rather than email them. We find the right wave for the job. 🌊👋

When we think about strange media, or we think about strange genres, we typically think of them in terms of examples. That was a weird movie. Or that was a weird book. Or that was a weird essay. The converse is a typical movie or book or essay. And these things run along that spectrum. But they also run along a spectrum of whether we liked it or not. That was a weird song, and I liked it. Or that was a pretty typical song, and/but I hated/loved it. As Jacques Derrida writes in "The Law of Genre," "as soon as genre announces itself, one must respect a norm, one must not cross a line of demarcation, one must not risk impurity, anomaly or monstrosity" (1980, 57). Genres offer us lines to work within and also to cross. Yet encouraging risk in compositional spaces is exactly how we generate productively novel and strange forms—which, admittedly sometimes fail. But sometimes they don't. We therefore respect and disrespect our strange containers and see when and how we can push or squeeze.

Joseph Kosuth's (1965) art piece, *One in Three Chairs,* conceptually expresses the variations of media, and pertains to the concept of ekphrasis or expression in an alternate media. In his work, Kosuth asks us to see the difference in forms, as a chair is shifted from one medium to the next—first physical, then a two-dimensional photographic representation of a chair, and finally a textual definition of a chair. The title asks us to consider the connection between different iterations of the shift, being both many and singular.

The newness of new media at the surface seems to offer the potential for generative strangeness. As David Bowie once claimed, the internet is something of "an alien life form" (quoted in Sydell 2016). But we know that image and text are old bedfellows from medieval manuscripts and hieroglyphics. In their introductory piece on "The Newness of New Media," Ilana Gershon and Joshua A. Bell write, "Today the media technologies that are understood as new—the Internet, mobile phones and social networking sites—provide another venue for innovation and continuity, as well as a means to reflect on how newness is constituted" (2013, 259). Newness has the potential for novelty, but as Gershon and Bell suggest, "Newness without context, be it the newness of a medium or a social practice, is not meaningful" (261). So, how can we find something truly generative in new media formats? What limits exist with clay or paint or writing or voice or video?

WHO SPLASHES IN WAVES?

So, who has laid the groundwork for thinking modes and media for us? Who are our wavers? Our media surfers? Daniel Anderson from UNC–Chapel Hill is one person in rhetoric and composition who consistently pushes experimental boundaries to see what's possible. In one video piece entitled *Waves (Response to a Blog Post),* he brings up several layers and video and text that overlap to create a non-normative response. At times using a generated autocomplete script, he writes,

"We seek transformation. We seek to be several things and we want to make things. There are more than enough of the old things in place. This is the place where we make scholarly where are the waves? We seek waves. We have found them!!!! We feel them flowing through the screen" (2012). The gist is what we've been reveling in. Anderson is a waver. Cynthia Selfe too writes, "By broadening the choice of composing modalities we expand the field of play" (2009, 644). Play is what we're after—all over the place. And Kathleen Blake Yancey's now well-known speech, "Made Not Only in Words: Composition in a New Key" suggests that multimodality is now *de rigueur.* To our own point, she explains, "You can only invent inside what an arrangement permits—and different media permit different arrangements" (2004, 317). Difference begets difference. What happens when we make an argument in writing and then shift into sound as the primary mode? What stays the same and what gets weirder? Consider how Anne Wysocki challenges us in her experimental piece "awaywithwords":

> Under what conditions would you accept a paper handwritten in crayon on colored construction paper?
>
> If you can imagine no conditions whatsoever, then for you color of paper and technologies of print typography are like water or stones: things whose natural properties (seem to) necessarily constrain how we can use them.
>
> But.
>
> If how we conceive of water is unseparable from place and time, how can our communication materials, for which we can make no similar claim to naturalness as we can with water, be otherwise? (2005, 56)

She pursues the water metaphor for media, "As with water, constraints of communication materials are often social and historical; to ask after the constraints as we teach or compose can help us understand how material choices in producing communications articulate to social practices we may not otherwise wish to reproduce" (2005, 56), and also concluding, "By focusing on the human shaping of material, and on the ties of material to human practices, we might be in better positions to ask after the consequences not only of how we use water but also of how we use paper, ink, and pixels to shape—for better or worse—the actions of others" (2005, 59). The question is, what continues to hold us back or hold us up? What sorts of strangeness are possible only visually, or only in film? Or, alternatively, what is better placed in sound than sight? Beyond these initial limitations, can we begin thinking that moves like hyperbole or inversion can generally apply to all media? Why can't we wade out further into the waves?

Jody Shipka, for one, taps into the language of Shklovsky, suggesting defamiliarizing the familiar across different compositional media as a strategy. However, she also encourages us to "work to make the seemingly strange or unfamiliar aspects of multimodal texts and strategies appear less strange and unfamiliar" (2011, 134). The goal of this is to make strangeness acceptable in practice. Shipka encourages novel multimodal compositions that often make use of physical artifacts and sometimes even food. Steph Ceraso too vociferously waves multimodal composition in the direction of sound studies, also making use of Shklovsky's language of defamiliarization. She says, "Just as poets and writers use defamiliarization techniques to heighten readers' awareness of language, teachers must plan occasions that give listeners a chance to experience sound in new and surprising ways. The heightened awareness gained from multimodal listening practices can help students become more savvy consumers and composers of sound" (2018, 40). Working with Ceraso on the "communicative and affective aspects of sound in a variety of texts, genres, objects, environments, and experiences," some composers have noted that for them "sound was a new, strange endeavor," with some being "initially resistant and confused" (56). She pings sound, attuning us to this stance: "To teach multimodal listening involves creating assignments that encourage the kind of heightened awareness that enables students to learn and grow with every new sonic experience. Students need to unlearn listening practices that they have become accustomed to in their everyday lives, and so teachers must find ways to defamiliarize these habitual practices to make them strange again" (40). She acknowledges, "In a way, then, multimodal listening pedagogy is similar to the defamiliarization strategies that are used in textual composition" (40). Of course, because forms have always permeated different modes of discourse, from writing to sound, we can learn to see and hear strangeness in all its forms throughout compositional history.

Also sounding the depths of aural composition, Eric Detweiler speculates what is possible in "The Weird Possibilities of Academic Podcasting." His several insights include that "Rhetoric is, arguably, the art of inventing discursive conventions. A strange tension, perhaps: the invention of conventions. Aristotle's notion of topoi suggests there are certain conventional places we can visit when we desire to invent new arguments" (2019). Detweiler sees potential in the aurality of podcasting and other sound-based media, but cautions, "Their present weirdness and creativity, which does not necessarily equal newness, will generate its own conventions, and that will make it harder to imagine other ways of doing things." As such, he questions whether we may forget that these media are "multimodal and full of strange possibilities, just as we so often and easily forget these things about the all-too-familiar medium of writing." Defamiliarization is key, and familiarity haunts every medium as it gets used and used up.

Roland Barthes suggests in *Image-Music-Text*, "Rhetorics inevitably vary by their substance (here articulated sound, there image, gesture or whatever) not necessarily by their form" (1978, 49). Thus, the rhetoric of the image or any particular mode is specific. Barthes considers, for example, how three images in a coffee advertisement suggest asyndeton, and that different traits within different media hold different connotations (50). He sees it. He concludes that linguistic principles *are* often broader semiotic principles. The structures overlap and intertwine.

We could do worse than including the words of *Star Wars* creator George Lucas: "If students aren't taught the language of sound and images, shouldn't they be considered as illiterate as if they left college without being able to read and write?" (quoted in Daly 2004). He memorably continues, "We must teach communication comprehensively, in all its forms. Today we work with the written or spoken word as the primary form of communication. But we also need to understand the importance of graphics, music, and cinema, which are just as powerful and in some ways more deeply intertwined with young people's culture. We live and work in a visually sophisticated world, so we must be sophisticated in using all the forms of communication, not just the written word." The point is that we need all of it. We need every wave, every means necessary, to do our own unique rhetorics in the world. This allows us to tap into every kind of audience across all abilities. There are no lossless media, so we need all of our faculties.

Electrate or electronic texts are inherently composed of visual and aural and written components, but they are inevitably distinctive when they are born digital. When the electron is required of the text (and what text exists without the hum of electrons?!), or rather when the flow of electricity, of ones and zeros of digital media, of computationally derived new media is inherent, there arises a separate new interest. In some sense here, we might have to think of the previous kinds of compositions combinatorially. And furthermore, we have to consider how computational code or algorithms can generate specifically strange texts that require processing and electrate mediation (see Brock 2019). Through hyperlinking, we surf the net, channel surf. Electricity flows through us and all around us.

The embodied experience of rhetoric physically laid out in the universe is something else altogether. Of course, we see space, but here we move into 3D. The gestural is a kind of spatial communication. So, touch, space, gestures, physicality . . . these modes can contain their own forms of strangeness. We see figural strangeness in sculpture and in geographies. We see it in different rooms with different décor—the difference of a motel versus a hotel.

We might distinguish between what is written or aural or visual or electronic or spatial, and how they differ or overlap. Sound waves, waves of light and seeing and color and patterns, radio waves that carry Wi-Fi signals bouncing off and passing through walls and more, surround us. Separating lightning from thunder can be difficult, but we notice the buzz of a bee even when it's not in our line of sight. Our eyes look for the source when we hear a strange creak or crack in the next room or a cell phone going off.

IN AND OUT OF BODIES

When we think about what we can do and where it happens, we are invited then to also think about how our own different bodies play a role in strange composition practices. In *Bridging the Multimodal Gap,* the host of authors collectively composes a manifesto to introduce the text. They write, "Unlike many 'traditional' texts, multimodal compositions afford composers the ability to engage all the senses, and thus embodiment is a necessary consideration when engaging in multimodal composing. Not only do our bodies react to the spaces and interfaces—digital and physical—in which we compose, but we have the opportunity to engage readers/viewers aesthetically and materially with our compositions" (Khadka and Lee 2018, 23). Here, we can think of aesthetics as actually touching the body in different ways—colors and shapes lighting the eye or tones tickling the ear and so on. They continue in their manifesto: "Multimodal composing requires that we interrogate and negotiate different tools, technologies, langauges, and interfaces and that we also use them, experiment with them, make with them, and reimagine them. Making meaning requires taking chances, and taking chances requires the risk of failure" (21). The risk of failure is not very well embraced in composition; we think we must perfect. But with all of the tools and possibilities, we create all kinds of dishes, some tantalizing, others less so, depending on taste. Novelty requires throwing off some constraints. The manifesto refers to a line from Bump Halbritter, who explains it this way, "With the yoke of language, *per se,* lifted, *writing* may not only be and do the new work, it may live and breathe in scenes of symbolic action that we may not have been recognizing as scenes of writing" (2012, 8). There may be places or forms or spaces that we have not even recognized yet. I want to go as far as to say that there are absolutely strange rhetorical forms that we have not even begun to imagine. Yet they will come.

Another way to conceptualize the body's role in placing compositions in the world is to think about it being corrected against its natural condition. Jay Dolmage provides a helpful overview in thinking about the body's abilities in "Writing against Normal," which expresses this tension in this way:

> When I use this word—norm—I refer to a complex social and cultural force. Norms can be 'passive': a name for an ideal or standard; or the unexamined and privileged subject position of the supposedly (or temporarily) able-bodied individual. Norms are also very active: normalcy is used to control bodies; our normate culture continuously re-inscribes the centrality, naturality, neutrality and unquestionability of the normate position; our culture also marks out and marginalizes those bodies and minds that do not conform. (2012, 115)

The nonconformity of writing bodies creates unexpected rhetorics that squish and slide out in between spaces and find what harbors they can. Dolmage explains that certain normative writing seems "profoundly and impossibly unmarked" and "error-free, straight and logical," concluding that grammar and usage rules "are the conventions of written language that allow [people] to discriminate against one another" where "we see normalcy imposed multitudinously through 'surface features'" (116). We live in a world of imposition of obligation; rhetoric requires some; some is unnecessarily alienating. After all, the alienation of the marked stranger doesn't come from the stranger.

Finally, Dolmage nods to Trinh T. Minh-ha, who discusses writing this way, first noting how we are warned off: "Do not choose the offbeat at the cost of clarity. Obscurity is an imposition to the reader. True, but beware when you cross the railroad tracks for one train may hide another train. Clarity is a means of subjection, a quality both of official, taught language and of correct writing, two old mates of power: together they flow, together they flower, vertically, to impose an order" (1989, 16–17). She alerts us to how certain people "continue to preach conformity to the norms of well-behaved writing: principles of composition, style, genre, correction, and improvement. To write 'clearly,' one must incessantly prune, eliminate, forbid, purge, purify; in other words, practice what may be called an 'ablution of languge'" (17). Here at the end Minh-ha loosely refers to Roland Barthes. I trace this murky set of connections because they are so engaging, they discuss our point, but also they are difficult to quote, to parse out, because they are interconnected and easily become muddled in conversation with each other. This complex interlinking forces me then to reconsider this clarity of language, of reference. It is like the desire for clarity in water. We filter it obsessively, but something always remains. The impossibility of it, the impossibility of purity, the inability of something to lack taint reminds me of Nathaniel Hawthorne's 1846 short story "The Birth-mark" and how that desire to clean up can lead to death.

OUT OF THE ■

We are pushing here. We are pushing toward outsider spaces or forms for finding rhetorical strangeness. We are finding the walls. Rhetorical strangeness takes as its framework a consistent working and thinking out of the box (or OOTB). The boxness of various rhetorical forms and actions is something to pause and consider. What is the box? When we ask what the box is, we are asking about the limits of appropriateness in generating a productive rhetorical act. It is important to consider the origin of our boxes. Can we even begin to imagine the first obstruction, the first standard, the first rule? Perhaps our Eden story can serve us, a safe garden with boundaries with just one rule about what not to consume. The interesting thing is that we cannot stop inventing rules, just as we can't stop inventing ways outside of our own strictures. Invention works both ways: in and out. If we do something strange—something novel that functions outside of regular norms or conventions—there will always be another box. We work outside of one convention to find another set of obstructions. There is always another box. Essentially, we are talking about breaking convention or a semiotic code, and this code breaking or bending is the methodology taken up here.

Not all rule breaking is desirable or will work. And not every strangeness breaks every rule. Of course, following conventions does not automatically mean boring work, or creating something just like your neighbor, or evil totalitarianism. But it is not the *starting place* from which out-of-the-box composition arises. Ultimately, conventions and clarity are valuable and should be taught. These are not distinctly opposed to defamiliarization. Think of the most perfect, clear speech that you can imagine until it becomes strange and alien. Now that I think about it, aliens in cinema often have better grammar than the humans they have come to invade. But I digress. I'm afraid I often do.

The principle of strangeness or thinking outside the box lies in what has been called divergent thinking (also known as lateral thinking by Edward de Bono 2015). By finding linkages that we would not normally arrive at, we create new texts, we weave new textured connections among things in the world. The phrase "divergent thinking" comes from psychologist J. P. Guilford. In Guilford's 1967 book *The Nature of Human Intelligence,* he explores a practice called the alternative use task, a challenge to see how many uses can be invented for a single everyday object. You might try it now. How many different uses can you come up with for a comb or a pen? In writing classes, we court this same practice as we brainstorm ideas. We create mindmaps branching out across a page, we push ourselves with freewriting where we let anything that wants to come arrive on the page—forcing our minds and bodies to push further for a certain amount of time. These practices, of course, are old forms of rhetorical invention, but they remain useful, and we continue to find new inventions and ways to invent.

In this sense, rhetorical invention, the first canon of rhetoric—*inventio*—a coming upon—needs also to take up forms as well as content. In the post-information age, in our novelty economy, we have plenty of content, and not nearly enough forms to drive us hither or thither in the mass of mediation, all while resisting the troublesome issue of *novelty inflation.*

According to this perspective, language is in many ways always already strange. This perspective minimizes the important stance of the compositionist. But intention does creep in. Composition theorist Geoff Sirc enacts a similar playful project in his essay "Box-Logic." He suggests that the box is the best "format or method suited to the long strange trip" (2004, 115) of teaching technologies in the writing classroom. Sirc's essay begins with Marcel Duchamp's 1934 work *The Green Box* as an example from which teaching new media can thrive. This box-thought makes us recall the lyrics of "Little Boxes," by Malvina Reynolds, which begins bitingly:

> Little boxes on the hillside,
> Little boxes made of ticky tacky,
> Little boxes on the hillside,
> Little boxes all the same. (1967)

Later in Reynolds's lyrics, she espouses a criticism that the university is a place that manufactures this sameness, and that is true in many composition classrooms. There we find little boxes shaped into five-paragraph essays. We are now confronted with the idiot box, the search box, and the Redbox, the Xbox, Dropbox, and all sorts of mediated boxes. Each new tablet, smartphone, or handheld device emulates the history of the page-as-box. Novelty continues to use boxes and break them open.

Nevertheless, we are facing a Pandora's box of media choices, outlets, and forms, but there is *hope* at the bottom of that box, as there was for Pandora. Our hope is a configuration that lives out of the box. The whole box tendency is intrinsically psychological. And so, this gesture toward strange rhetorics comes as a result of some real psychological issues. Some people may look at novel texts and call them weird, dismissively. But they really excite me. There is an adrenaline rush of seeing the unexpected. They break something up for me in awesome ways—in ways that make me feel awe. I suspect that a strange method in composition will involve shaking up our boxes, though not throwing them out altogether.

Why is it that I love television—that idiot box—so much; why does it seduce me so? In any case, instead of embracing some Luddite perspective that calls for flipping the television switch, I'm more interested in how we can engage our mediation by flipping the Gestalt switch. The rules for forms have changed along with the development of new media. Yet forms are still useful, especially with the aim of creating interesting work.

Richard Lanham lays it out clearly in *The Economics of Attention*:

> The more we are deluged with information, the more we notice the different ways it comes to us, the more we have—in pure self-defense—to become connoisseurs of it. The torrent of information makes us more self-conscious about it, about all the different packages it comes in, about the different ways we interpret it, and about how we should express our responses to it. It is more counterproductive than ever to demonstrate stylistic awareness. Stylistic self-consciousness should be the first line of defense for a child swimming in the information flood. (2007, 143)

So, we swim. We become slippery fish, or magically transform into mermaids and mermen of media. Lanham challenges us by declaring, "Information is not in short supply in the new information economy. We're drowning in it. What we lack is the human attention needed to make sense of it all. It will be easier to find our place in the new regime if we think of it as an economics of attention. Attention is the commodity in short supply" (xi). Our valuable commodities in the information age, or (post)information age, are those that give us sensation.

Rhetorical media are inescapable.

Neil Postman views a critical response to media as a means for controlling how it affects us in *Teaching as a Subversive Activity*.

> The way to be liberated from the constraining effects of any medium is to develop a perspective on it—how it works and what it does. Being illiterate in the processes of any medium (language) leaves one at the mercy of those who control it. The new media—these new languages—then are

> among the most important "subjects" to be studied in the interests of survival. But they must be studied in a new way if they are to be understood, they must be studied as mediators of perception. Indeed, for any "subject" or "discipline" to be *understood* it must be studied this way. (2009, 166)

While liberation through perspective is possible, I believe there will always be media around us that we cannot see, that we cannot gain perspective on, that we cannot understand. Media will always be subverting our pedagogical subversions, though as students of media, we can begin at least in part to gain some understanding, though complete liberation is out of the question.

Embracing rapturous ruptures in language, Victor Vitanza writes wonderfully broken lines interspersed, interrupted, and interjected with all forms of punctuation and misspelling—intentional and otherwise. He avers: "My colligs still will-to-control language" (2003). The will to control is an unwillingness to disfigure in interesting, captivating ways. The will to power, as Vitanza writes, enacts a troublesomely proud inability to be swept *awayves.* Vitanza continues to explore Brian Massumi's note that Vitanza's writing might give headaches to readers through the act of experimentation. But Vitanza writes this too:

> Writing, however, is not ||||||||||||||| (barcodes) nor is it ////////////// (slashing of value). Only writers spawned by institutions write in this manner! Rhetoric||||||||||||||||||| . . . ////////////////Composition.
>
> Rather, writing is ~~~~~~~ ~~~~~~~ ~~~~~~ ~~~~~~ ~~~~ ~~~~~~~~ ~~~~~ ~~~~~~~~~~ ~~~~~~ ~~~~~~~. . . .

If writing is waves, and not straight lines, then how do we get there from the basic premise that writing is a straightforward, reasonable, linear mode of communication? Finding alternative modes can get us further and further out of the box, or the boat.

INESCAPABLE SIRENS, A POTENTIAL PROBLEM

A wittier man than I tied himself to his ship's mast according to one old tale. In that tale, the sirens, those beautiful mermaids, surrounded Odysseus with their voices. But before he ever heard them, another beautiful woman, Circe, had warned Odysseus that *Sirens [would] beguile him with their clear-toned song* (Homer 2018, 12.36–54). The sirens are so enamoring, so persuasive as they sing their pervasive songs that they are inescapable. The only way to escape this inescapability is to bind oneself up, to prevent oneself from being wooed by those sensual, sultry, and seductive sirens. They call out to you. They become the medium for a message that is always around you, swirling like a gyre. And now I've got you. I've lulled you. I've captivated you, reader, along with the blind poet, old Homer. A significant power lies in becoming the siren rhetor, loud and alarming, the singer who lures and culls and sweeps you off your feet, off your body, off your rocker . . .

Let us think about the structural framework of strangeness another way. There are three ways that we can exist within this strange framework. We can be mermaids, like the sirens of mythology, seductive and desiring to captivate others, to pull them in and away. We can be brutes, dull, bull-headed, like minotaurs, stuck in a labyrinth of media, of conventional forms, of temperate ecologies, unthinkingly zombie-like, swinging at anything in our way. Or, finally, we can be clever compositionists, Daedalus, crafty, winged heroes, able to escape. This escape happens by being exceptional, by freeing ourselves of our confines, but not being too lofty as Icarus was. Here a striation pertaining to composition arises. There is a politics of composition, a mythomorphic drama of readers and writers. Let us see where this fantasy can take us, pedagogically, anagogically, apagogically, and analogically too.

I am only beginning an attempt to lay out the problem of mediation. The problem is old. A consideration of our mediation as humans goes back—at least—to Plato's allegory of the cave from book VII of *The Republic.* In this passage (way), we are invited to envision a frightening scene: "Imagine people living in a cavernous cell down under the ground; at the far end of the cave, a long way off, there's an entrance open to the outside world. They've been there since childhood, with their legs and necks tied up in a way which keeps them in one place and allows them to look only straight ahead, but not to turn their heads" (1993, 240 7.514a–520a). The allegory of the cave challenges our notion of forms, of ideas, of our perception of the world around us. The listener of the allegory responds, "A strange picture" and "strange prisoners," which are "ourselves," fundamentally asking us to question our own immersion alongside our own desire for freedom from any containment. The inversion of CAVE is EVAC, which is precisely the answer we're searching for. How can we *evacuate* the cave of modern mediation? How do we vacate a vacation? And what or where are these chains that are holding us *back, in, out?* Some kinds of immersion may parallel the concept of a prison, a being-inside that is not beneficial.

Luce Irigaray also writes about the chains of language; referring back to the prisoners of Plato's cave in *Speculum of the Other Woman,* she writes, "Chained up like ourselves—I might say—backs to the origin, staring forward. Chained up more specifically by the effects of a certain language, of certain norms of language that are sometimes called *concatenation,* or chain of propositions, for example" (1985, 259). The prison analogy helps us to see that the problem is political as well, the norms of media and composition have become our concatenation, our grounding based on certain linkages. Mediation, after all, has a history as a political term before it referred to television, video games, and other screened entertainment. As critic Sonia Livingstone (2009) tells us in "On the Mediation of Everything," Napoleon enstated the Law of Mediatization as emperor over the states of the Holy Roman Empire. Mediatization is an issue of who's controlling whom, a power problem.

So, media—along with our mediation—are nearly invisible. In this sense, our mediation is generally normative. In some similar fashion, fish live in water and they do not know it. At the end of a now well-known speech that began with this image of fish, David Foster Wallace left us with this: "It is unimaginably hard to do this, to stay conscious and alive, day in and day out" (2008, 14). We live in media. We are like fish. Marshall McLuhan expressed a similar sentiment: "One thing about which fish know exactly nothing is water, since they have no anti-environment which would enable them to perceive the element they live in" (McLuhan and Fiore 2001b, 175). We have steeped ourselves in media like a warm, comforting bubble bath, and we are barely aware of our condition most of the time. Immersion as a field of study is becoming rampantly significant as our lives become more virtual, more encased—let us say like hot dogs, meat in plastic sleeves—in various forms of media. Think of contemporary society as a bit like an un-think tank. We don't need to think about 3D glasses to think of immersion. We are already immersed. We have been. Nevertheless, the continued inventive development of various immersive media has spawned a knee-jerk reaction among the academic community as we scramble to theorize media that engulf—like flames, like floods—audiences within a variety of experiences. The project is a call for being unbaptized, unimmersed, from bad mediations—mediations that dominate and prevent thought.

The increase in mediation has, in some ways, become a remediation. Media can make the world more accessible by interpreting it for us or by making choices for us, for better or worse. So, we often become slavish, blindly accepting of forms, submitting to protocol, reduced to despondency, in between structure and agency. The effects of slavish forms create dull five-paragraph essays, Walmart aisles, rehashed pop music, the seemingly funny sitcom, the obligatory Facebook banality, the totalizing power of various political groups, the artwork of Thomas Kinkade, and Stepford wives. Yet I want my students to compose wonderful, interesting, invigorating, new, and exciting work. I want people who read my students' writing to think that it's awesome. I want my students' audience to be *full of awe* after reading their work. In the midst of this media storm, I want my students to display flashes of lightning. Heraclitus (1920) tells us that lightning steers the universe (frag. 64). I want them to compose and to read for interesting forms in the midst of overwhelming habituation. How might we *bend the bars* of restrictive composition that *obligate* us to communicate in particular patterns? How do I get my students to compose impressively in the midst of the blah, blah, blah banality of everyday life? Now there's a problem. The problem is essentially an inescapable domination over human perception.

C(R)ASHING IN ON EACH OTHER

We can discover or invent new ways of playing in the waves. Swell. We can develop novel forms of hybridity where the different forms overlap and mesh. As composers and encouragers of different kinds of compositions, we have to find ways of playing in the waves. What will it take to wade out with our tentative selves and craft hyperboles in sound, in an image, in text, in video? We need to tiptoe out and help ourselves and each other see and compose strangely within the different waves of compositional media. We can see the investments that go into billboards and blockbusters.

In our daily constructions, our daily makings, our daily compositions, of course we are rhetorical, but strangely so—or of course we are strange, but rhetorically so. As Linda Marie Walker ominously reminds us, "The 'interface' is a strange place—like a noman's-land where hostilities are suspended" (Walker 2007). The in-between space made possible by strange multimodal composition is radically open. Like a cold splash in the face, some media are stranged beyond comprehension or acceptability, but we might overlook or look through them to something beyond.

FLOAT ON

Media are everywhere. We are completely immersed. Like fish in water, we find it difficult or impossible to perceive. Burke is another person who, interestingly, uses the example of fish in water. In his example, found in *Permanence and Change*, a fish—a trout—may get into some trouble, get hooked, by "trained incapacity." Burke, hoping to raise our consciousness, our critical and perceptive capacities, stresses, "The very power of criticism has enabled man to build up cultural structures so complex that still greater powers of criticism are needed" (1984b, 5). Our structures are complex; we have built them up around us using various technologies that exteriorize thought. Problematically, these helpful structures become hindrances in some cases. As Burke notes, "Thus it will be seen that the devices by which we arrive at a correct orientation may be quite the same as those involved in an incorrect one" (1984b, 6–7). For this project, the devices, as considered in Shklovsky's essay "Art as Device," may be a special kind of device to respond to devices, a perspective by incongruity—not a panacea, a cure-all, but a potential disruption, with enough lasting power to critique our own habits of thought.

Here in the wake of the Anthropocene, we live in a world of waves. As Kenneth Burke writes in *Language as Symbolic Action*, we are "separated from our natural conditions by instruments of our own making" (1968, 16). We have stranged our world to the extent that we cannot access the real. Where do the waves take us? What material is not left to us? Do we let every flow and stream overwhelm and overtake us like Scylla and Charybdis? We have to learn to float, to swim, to set sail. We have to become more fluid. As Katherine Hayles explains, we are offered or left with "*flickering signifiers*, characterized by their tendency toward unexpected metamorphoses, attenuations, and dispersions" (1993, 76). How do we live in the crashing, streaming eddies of the new media flood? We enact the miracle of the technologic messiahs of the twenty-first century; we learn to walk on water. We have to find new ways of popping the bubbles of our collective media ecology prisons.

What shall we do with modern mediation? Repent, and be unbaptized. Resist banality. Push toward more interesting media that let us participate and don't simply bind us up. This reperception allows me this cheeky use of the word *repent*. This question asks me to wonder about the "return" to defamiliarization. Or, we could consider rhetoric functioning as a medium in the spiritual sense, the mediator, the go-between. Thinking through strange media gets us halfway there, never quite distant, holding séances for us to get us in touch with what's gone. These containers for strangeness are fuzzy, complex. All the social structures that structure strange containers rely upon various kinds of agreements, contracts, conditions, and conventional considerations. We arrive at flickering signifiers in all sorts of bright sites. It is the new wave, our new hope.

Now, consider some different iterations of rhetorical strangeness across the W~A~V~E~S~.

Table 4.1. The WAVES

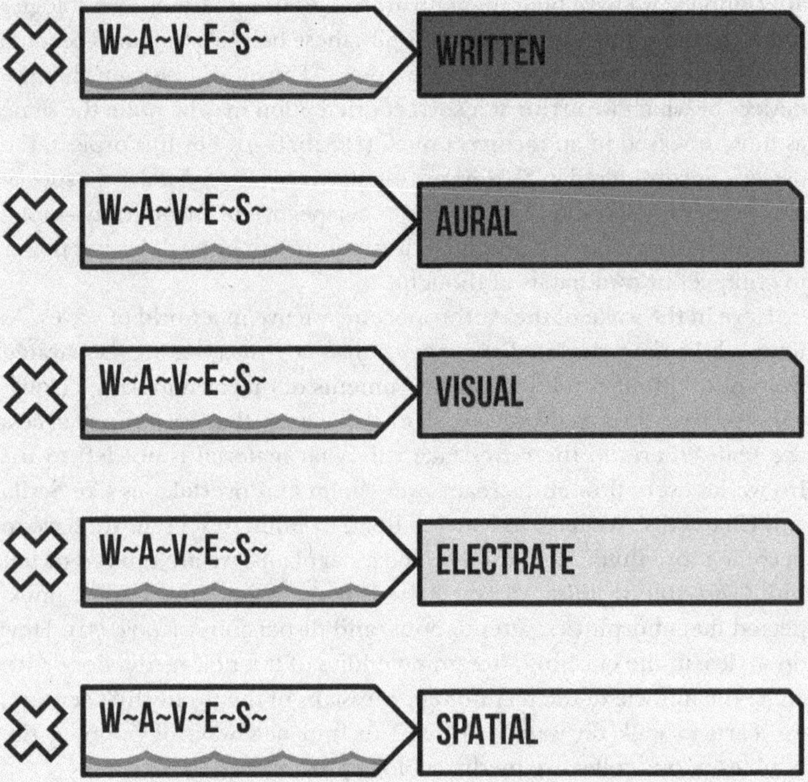

Chapter Five
SEVEN STRANGERS

INTRODUCING THE SEVEN STRANGERS

There are literally hundreds of rhetorical figures, and I've picked seven to work with that particularly interest me, some of which are especially connected to interesting moves possible in multimedia composition. Here, we will explore seven that can be executed to surprising effect across a number of old and new media. My seven strangers are connected to Aristotle's twenty-eight topoi, or commonplaces, though I like to think of my group as uncommon places, despite their common-ness. I wanted to keep my list short and memorable but thorough and comprehensive. While one could never account for every form of strangeness possible, I wanted a collection of figures that would be broadly applicable for our uses of rhetorical practice and analysis.

Interestingly enough, there are seven virtues of style from Hermogenes's work *On Types of Style* or *Peri Ideon*: clarity, grandeur, beauty, rapidity, character, sincerity, and force (1987, xi). And we may in some sense be working against some of these stylistically. Perhaps we could map out the rhetorical effects of the seven deadly sins. And we take note that there are seven days in a week, seven wonders of the world, seven hills in Rome, seven liberal arts, seven suicides in the Bible, seven chakras in your body, seven notes in a musical scale, and seven colors in the rainbow. Seven is a magical number. Seven is odd. And oddness allows us to move beyond the binaries of either/or constructions.

We also know from the research of George A. Miller that seven is memorable. Miller's article "The Magical Number Seven, Plus or Minus Two: Some Limits on Our Capacity for Processing Information" (1956) is sometimes discounted, but it offers as tangible a starting point for crafting an arbitrary heuristic model as any. It is the research that lent some credence to thie idea that one could remember seven-digit phone numbers.

Still, these few, I hope, offer memorable ways of teaching the reading and writing of interesting rhetorical forms across media. Additionally, this list gives us the four basic rhetorical operations of addition,

https://doi.org/10.7330/9781646422821.c005

subtraction, permutation, and substitution as well as some newer figures that are especially poignant in new media applications. Glossolalia as a figure, for example, has not been significantly theorized, although we will see that it aligns with some ancient tropes as well as some digital uses in the form of glitch aesthetics. Time shifts offer some particularly interesting associations regarding cinema, but apply to any of the media that we will be exploring. With these strangers, it is possible to explore several of the standard shifts from earlier rhetorical theories, including moves like *addition* and *omission*, but also consider new moves like *media shifts* or the strange inexpressible languages of *glossolalia*. We can explore both hyperbole and litotes as well as something in the middle, like deadpan, through the inclusive figure of *exponentiation*. We can consider broader implications for metaphor in films through the trope of *replacement*. And each of these figures works both from classical considerations and recent moves in compositions in various media.

Farmers farm. Strangers strange. I will be using that verb in a way that is probably abnormal to most readers. I see these Strangers across different media and see the implications of when we strange certain things in particular ways. The seven figures I am working with are easily remembered by using **STRANGE** as a mnemonic device, and by remembering the representational figures that go along with them. The strangeness of this set of rhetorical figures or devices sits primarily with their use. Here are our seven strange figures:

- Shapeshifting
- Time Travel
- Replacement
- Addition and Subtraction
- Negation
- Glossolalia
- Exponentiation

I have seen the difficulty in creating any sort of list of strangers. Any figural list will be limited; nevertheless, this handful offers a set of productive starting places. One begins to see the slippage in creating such a list, and the omissions. The figures at times blend into one another. Categorization is never an imperative, but a guide. One could, for instance, find incongruity as a central figure, an umbrella term, in several of these other tropes.

I will add that if we want the mnemonic to be *s-t-r-a-n-g-e-r-s*, then we get two more helpful categories: regression, as opposed to transgression, and supplement. Regression, or perhaps repression, is the kind of strangeness that weirdly holds to plainness and conventions. It is especially strange in its non-strangeness. And supplement is where you can fill in the blanks, and find other figures and forms in different places of your own devising. Disfiguration offers potentialities. We have here our *Catalogus Alienorum*, where we can look at how **shapeshifting and time travel and replacement and addition/subtraction and negation and glossolalia and exponentiation** work. And we can hold in the back of our minds a consideration of the **r+s: regression and supplement**, to fill in our own considerations of different rhetorical texts. It would be a long, tedious, and potentially unfruitful project to mine all media for every example. They are there, and they are legion. If we were to look at each figure across different modes, such as our waves, we can see how many different kinds of texts can be created, as in table 5.1. So, I leave it up to you to explore and generate and derive and diverge.

Table 5.1. A periodic table of strange figurations

	S	*T*	*R*	*A*	*N*	*G*	*E*
Written	Sw	Tw	Rw	Aw	Nw	Gw	Ew
Aural	Sa	Ta	Ra	Aa	Na	Ga	Ea
Visual	Sv	Tv	Rv	Av	Nv	Gv	Ev
Electronic	Se	Te	Re	Ae	Ne	Ge	Ee
Spatial	Ss	Ts	Rs	As	Ns	Gs	Es

S IS FOR SHAPESHIFTING

Figure 5.1. Panel sketch from "The Werewolf Howls," in Weird Tales *36.2 (1941): 38. Public domain.*

Shapeshifting is the change of an entire original form into a transformed, altered form that retains its reference back to the original, normative arrangement or shape.

Related Figures: *chiasmus, transposition, transmutation, mutatio, catachresis, metathesis, hyperbaton, hypallage, submutatio, changeling, rearrangement, parenthesis, metaplasm, interjection, tmesis, equivocation, the pun*

Representative Figure for Shapeshifting: Proteus

Proteus, a god of the sea and Neptune's son, is our first representative figure. Rightly so, as his name suggests first. Proteus, who appears in Homer's *Odyssey*, is the prototype of shapeshifting. Menelaus calls him "the old man of the sea" and he turns into a lion, a dragon, leopard, a boar, running water, and a tree (2018, book IV). Proteus's daughter warns Menelaus, "He will turn himself into every kind of creature that goes upon the earth" (book IV). Proteus is a slippery fellow, but honest and helpful when it comes down to it. Appropriately enough, water seems to match the fluidity of the shapeshift, offering us a sea change.

Figure 5.2. Proteus, in Andrea Alciato's Book of Emblems *(1531).*

> O Proteus, old man of Pallene, with the form of an actor, who at one moment takes the limbs of a man, at another those of a beast, come tell us why you turn into all shapes, so that, forever changing, you have no fixed form?
>
> I bring forth symbols of antiquity and a primaeval age, of which each man dreams, according to his wishes.
>
> —*From The Book of Emblems (Alciato 1531)*

A Theoretical Introduction to Shapeshifting

> *If comic books, cartoons, and Sci-Fi Original Movies have taught me anything, it's that shapeshifting comes with a bunch of boring rules and restrictions that limit its potential Turn-Into-A-Bulldozer-Whenever-I-Wantity.*
>
> —Strong Bad, "Shapeshifter"

If we are going to begin with one approach to making things strange, shapeshifting is a good start. Shapeshifting is largely the trope that lures us into thinking otherwise and represents the umbrella under which we can find a large number of the works that often capture our attention. Mutating one form into another, the well-versed practice of werewolves, butterflies, and tadpoles, offers a simple means of discovering something new and shiftily strange. How does one get from a triangle to a hexagon? It is the uncanny experience of moving to a new place or receiving a handwritten letter out of the blue.

If strangers are, by definition, from another place, strangeness, then, seems to naturally get us to some other place. Shifting allows for a particular kind of transport, a movement. We feel a change in the weather. Out of the four rhetorical operations defined by Quintilian in *The Institutes of Oratory* (1922), shifting is closest to transposition, a rearrangement. Shifting the medium or the means by which one is communicating offers a new path, albeit still somehow connected to the old one. Shift the material or the form of a work, and you shift the work itself.

There are shifts to reveal and shifts to hide. There are serious shifts and humorous shifts. For example, a duck walks into a bar, orders a beer, and tells the bartender, "Put it on my bill." The pun is the primary shift. Incongruity creates defamiliarization. It is safe enough to say that to shift an object is to change the world; the thing shifts its environment and vice versa. One might say that distortion is the beginning of a shift, an incomplete one, and replacement goes beyond the shift. With stranging tropes, things become surprisingly moved away from their original state, like the transforming toys I used to play with as a child. Similarly, media shifts are rampant within all kinds of adaptations. Like the shapeshifting tricksters of folk stories, style, it seems, tends to shift texts in various ways. The if/then statement enacts a shift within a sentence, like a Gestalt switch. Or we see a shift in personality, as with the use of avatars and alternative identities. You can hear the shift of a key change in the middle of The Beatles' "Penny Lane" in sync with the lyric "very strange." Anagrams are a way of simply shifting around the letters in a word. And we can find a few for the word shapeshifter, such as Feathers Hips, Spear the Fish, Faith's Herpes, Fart Sheepish, Seraph Fetish, Phrases Thief, Fresh Ape Shit, Sheaf Hipster, and so on . . . Shapeshifting involves mutating the text into another form. What can I say? Shift happens.

Ovid's book *The Metamorphoses* has a long catalog of these and other shapeshifters, including the honorable Baucis and Philemon, an old couple who, having performed hospitality perfectly, were turned into a pair of trees—an oak and a linden—so that they could be beside one another forever. Ovid's famous text begins: "Of shapes transformde to bodies straunge, I purpose to entreate" (2000, 1.1.). Ovid tells of Zeus turning a man named Lycaon into a wolf—hence our word lycanthropy—and Zeus himself turning into all sorts of beings. And here, finally, is the great surprising mystery of things. That everything is always changing already. As Heraclitus (1920) is supposed to have written: Πάντα ῥεῖ (*panta rhei*), "everything flows." The world is full of shapeshifters, and each one is shifting toward something more interesting than it was before, with something new and surprising just around the bend of the path. To find something that impossibly stays the same—now that would be truly uncanny.

Art Examples:

Wall Drawing 386 by Sol Lewitt (1983)
One in Three Chairs by Joseph Kosuth (1965)

Sentence Practice:

Begin with a simple sentence: "Jimmy went to the store." Now shift some of the words around to get something like "To the store, Jimmy went."

Deductions:

1. Shapeshifting is simply a means of trying something else out in a place where you normally would not. That is, a straightforward path is expected, and subsequently detoured.
2. Shapeshifting reorients us to various subjects by creating a new perspective from which to see them.
3. Changing from one kind of grounding to a new grounding offers movement within the work itself and destabilizes the initial grounding.
4. The most valuable effect of a shift is the central peripeteia, or the anagnorisis, that arises from this reorientation.
5. Shifts can elicit a momentary feeling of weightlessness in the stomach, as if falling, as opposed to the lack of experienced emotion that would occur with the absence of a shift.
6. While the reorientation is not always necessarily an improvement, the experience of seeing what was previously known anew in the moment of change can be pleasurable itself. Transforming the body or the mind works in concert with transforming media themselves.
7. Shapeshifting is style by selection. It involves perception of the process of the shift; recognition of the mutation must occur.

Seven Strange Projects:

- ☐ Adapt a written text from the public domain into another medium.
- ☐ Write in response to a text that shifts in some surprising way for you; in your writing, shift your own language into another form, either visually or linguistically. Place a chiasmus in the opening sentence.
- ☐ Write a letter to someone you normally wouldn't correspond with. Use different paper and colors than you normally would—perhaps you could try construction paper and crayons. Try to write in a different register—either higher or lower—than is natural for you.
- ☐ Create a peripatetic shift in reality. Make a game, written text, sculpture, song, or video with a twist.
- ☐ Change. Eat food that you normally would not eat for one week, or fast from some food. Take a different route each day. Grow out hair that you'd normally groom. Create a short book of puns that note the experience.
- ☐ Create a series of images in which your subject shapeshifts in some way. Perhaps you can try to take seven different portraits of yourself with seven different personalities.
- ☐ Write seven sentences. In each sentence, change one word from the previous sentence.

T IS FOR TIME TRAVEL

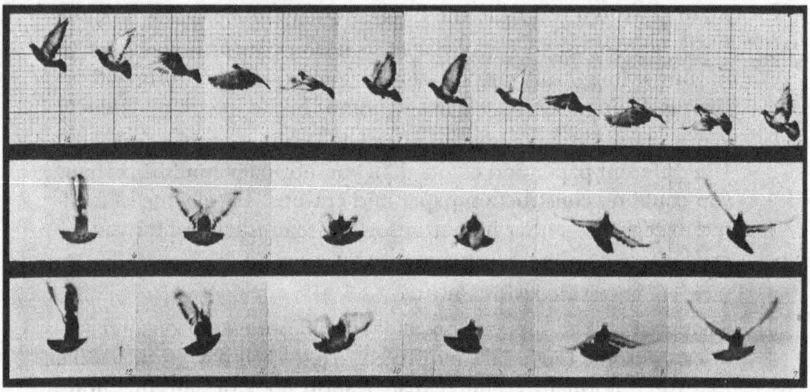

Figure 5.3. Eadweard Muybridge, Animal Locomotion (Plate 755) *(1887). Collotype.*

Time travel is the speeding up, slowing down, reversal, or skipping of a text's linear chronology.

Related Figures: *chronographia, the counterfeit time, hysteron proteron, peristalsis, prolepsis, enallage, ampliatio, the historical present, past, and future tense, anachronism*

Representative Figure for Time Travel: Kairos

Kairos is fast. He is so fast that you have to catch him at the opportune moment by his long forelock. His swiftness and movement through time challenges us to be better rhetors. We have to be on our toes with a kairotic view of rhetoric. Otherwise we could spend endless amounts of time perfecting our rhetorical moves. But there is no time for that. And yet, we must also sometimes enact the possibility of slowing things down, taking moments, looking upon the past, and changing the future. Hence the figure could have been a double: the tortoise and the hare, perhaps another time.

Figure 5.4. Kairos, in Andrea Alciato's Book of Emblems *(1531)*

On opportunity
(In the form of a dialogue)
This is the work of Lysippus, whose native city is Sicyon.
Who are you?
A moment of time seized, holding sway over everything.
Why do you stand on tiptoe?
I am constantly moving about.
Why do you keep winged sandals on your feet?
The light breeze carries me hither and thither.
In your right hand is a slender razor. Pray, why?
This symbol teaches that I am keener than every blade.
Why the tuft of hair on your brow?
So that I can be seized as I approach.
But tell me, why is the back of your head bald?
If someone once lets me go, swift as I am, I cannot then be captured by my hair. It is for your sake that the artist has made me with such skill, stranger; and that I may be a warning to everyone, I am placed in an open hall.
(quoted in Alciato 1531)

A Theoretical Introduction to Time Travel

Time flies in the face of normativity because it is inherently unstable. As we all travel through time all the time, we are regular time travelers who pass the time in our own peculiar ways as we orbit this particular sun at this particular speed. But the speculative possibilities of time travel offer surprising jumps and reversals of normal order. We can go backward in time, or skip time—as happens every few seconds in cinematic cuts. We preserve versions of time in generally stable forms such as photographs, sculptures, or books. Time travel also concerns the rhetorical canon of arrangement. By rearranging order, time is revised. Because we take in compositions through time, we can compose work that moves back and forth in different ways simply by rearranging the order. The Quechua and Maori tribes think about time differently than most Westerners. Because we cannot see, or foresee, the future, they imagine walking backward towards it. Marshall McLuhan wrote a similar conjecture in *The Medium Is the Massage*: "We look at the present through a rear-view mirror; we walk backwards into the future" (McLuhan and Fiore 2001a, 74–75). Perhaps some now-definitive models for temporal play can be seen in the likes of the 2000 film *Memento* or Martin Amis's 1991 novel *Time's Arrow*: both using forms of anti-linear narratives, told backward.

Controlling time on screens or on paper or in sound is a superpower, an ability, *a dynamis*, like rhetoric is. Time is a human invention. Moving through time according to terms like *warp*, *hyper*, and *mach* doesn't necessarily place us at goal lines faster. We know that the study of rhetoric depends upon *kairos*—or the opportune time—as well as *chronos*—which is the order of time. Cars, trains, planes are machines that have reoriented us toward new conceptions of speed, and yet we now take them for granted. We keep up with regular doses of caffeine. The magic of time's possibilities within different kinds of composition is what makes each of them so intriguing. And each narrative can be recounted with celerity or as slowly as molasses in January. Holidays are special times. Sometimes getting to where we want to go, or to where we are inevitably going, just takes a little more time.

Composing a piece also simply takes time, almost always more time than it takes to read the work—and that is a mystery in itself, an economics of time in terms of composition. We know that now our society is moving faster than ever. We've accelerated to disorienting speeds, but this phenomenon merely presents an opportunity to play with times in new ways. We can actually press pause or take a time-out. But can time travelers offer a way out, a means to rethink one of the most organizing cultural apparatuses we have: time? Viktor Shklovsky was particularly interested in the move of *deceleration* (1991, 50–51). So, the slowing of a text allows it to be experienced more richly and deeply by our senses. Henri Bergson too attempts a look at perception over time in his book *Creative Evolution.* Bergson is particularly known for exploring the concept of duration, which is relevant to this discussion of iterative visual archives. Think of time-lapse or long-exposure photography or our ability to fast-forward and rewind. He reminds us, "Change is far more radical than we are at first inclined to suppose" (1998, 3). There is something unique about visually perceptible change as opposed to simply tracking duration, and without certain visual cues, in cases such as the growth of hair, the loss of hair, or the corrosion of an object, duration and change are largely imperceptible. Timestamps are there to try to keep track. From speed metal to *largo,* we can hear the speed of sound in the beat of a tempo. We play songs backward to get the devil's message. Go and listen to Pink Floyd's 1973 track "Time." The yoctosecond is not much time, but your computer can do all sorts of things with one.

What is at stake is the right moment, a shifted orientation toward time that can only occur in a held composition—a work that exists somewhat stable outside time. The paint on some canvas or the words on a page will hold still long enough for us to think about their relationship to time (much better than your wristwatch), and their being in it and outside of it, like we are. It's all relative, like looking at the speed of things passing by out of the car window.

Art Examples:

Nude Descending A Staircase, no. 2 by Marcel Duchamp (1912)
Rain, Steam, Speed by J.M.W. Turner (1844)
Dali Atomicus by Phillippe Halsman (1948)
The Process of Aging (Fragment of an On-going Thorough Self Analysis and Description to Be Completed by the End of My Life) by Athena Tacha (1974)

Sentence Practice:

Working from our previous sentence, "To the store, Jimmy went," now change the time, perhaps by modifying the verb tense to get something like "To the store, Jimmy will go."

Deductions:

1. Shifts in time are often there to help us work through memories and our possible futures.
2. A wonderful time-traveling moment allows us to take a step outside the flow of time.
3. If other figures work by restructuring different dimensions of a work, time then particularly reconstructs a work along the fourth dimension.
4. The increase of speed from technological advances allows for creating things that we would never have been able to create before.
5. Taking a long time is perhaps one of the most difficult things for contemporary makers to do, but allows a deep relationship to the work.
6. Time is such a strong norm that it allows for some of the most surprising defamiliarizing moves, but can also create disturbing and disorienting effects.
7. Pausing, skipping, or repeating actual time is impossible; however, doing such activities within a reflection of time is.

Seven Strange Projects:

- ☐ Tell a short personal history. Change three details about your past, creating an alternate history.
- ☐ Make a video where you take a poem and recite it backward using time-lapse imagery.
- ☐ Prepare a one-minute speech speaking as quickly as you can.
- ☐ Bring a memory into the present (and the future) by making a memorial.
- ☐ Change the future. Consider a problem anachronistically. Write an argument as if you are from the future. Prophesy a problem that will affect people today if they continue as they are. Alternatively, persuade your future self to be different.
- ☐ Take uppers or downers and make an archive over a seven-day period. As with Andy Warhol's 1928 art boxes, or time capsules, put various trinkets from each day—your daily detritus—into a different box and archive your collection.
- ☐ Take your time. Take seven years to make one argument. Start now. You will age and get older. See how your argument changes over time as you yourself change.

R IS FOR REPLACEMENT

Figure 5.5. Cover image from The Serpent's Path: The Magical Plays of Florence Farr *(1881).*

Replacement is the act of putting one component in place of another in a part of a text.

Related Figures: *metaphor, substitutio, the analogue, acoloutha, anacoloutha, acyrologia, anthimeria, antiptosis, antonomasia, enallage, euphemism, metalepsis, periphrasis, synonym, parody*

Representative Figure for Replacement: The Android

The android is like us, but not us. It stands in for the human. The term is more appropriate than *robot* because it refers to the referring nature of this figure. And often, the android *works* for us; it is a figure that does work for the thing it is replacing—here, humankind.

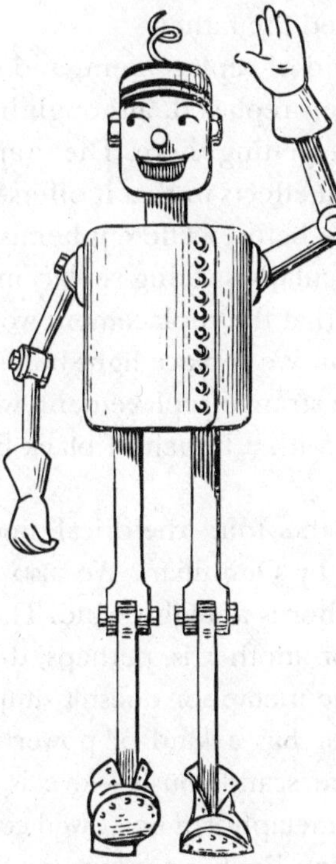

Figure 5.6. US patent drawing of a mechanical man, circa 1940.

> These creatures are among us, although morphologically they do not differ from us; we must not posit a difference of essence, but a difference of behavior. In my science fiction I write about them constantly. Sometimes they themselves do not know they are androids.
>
> . . .
>
> A human being without the proper empathy or feeling is the same as an android built so as to lack it, either by design or mistake. We mean, basically, someone who does not care about the fate which his fellow living creatures fall victim to; he stands detached, a spectator, acting out by his indifference John Donne's theorem that "No man is an island," but giving that theorem a twist: that which is a mental and a moral island is not a man.
>
> —*Philip K. Dick, "Man, Androids, and Machine"*

A Theoretical Introduction to Replacement

We replace light bulbs and hips. We trade in old cars after regular oil changes and replacing a few tires. We leave old friends behind and find new ones. We get new teeth. New clothes. New jobs. We substitute sugar. We get substitute teachers. What else do we replace? The figure that replaces seems to be an improvement, or a successor, or a descendant, perhaps even having killed the father.

Any prosthesis is a kind of replacement, and often an enhancement of the thing that has been replaced, although in the Greek a *prosthesis* is an addition, but we are getting there. The swap, the exchange, or the trade-in creates rhetorical effects in that it offers something new *in place of* the old, what has gone before. The euphemism is a replacement, as is a nickname. The particularly striking replacement is the ***rare*** replacement. We might contest that the replacement wouldn't be strange if the replacement were regular. We replace light bulbs all the time, someone contends. So, to create a strange replacement, we might replace all the light bulbs in the house with a bunch of black lights or bananas. Now, that would do the trick.

Substitutio is one of the four rhetorical operations that are also described as barbarisms by Quintilian. We also ought to consider the metaphor here. A metaphor is a mighty wind. The metaphor as a means of replacing one word for another is, perhaps, the most fundamental of rhetorical figures. But the metaphor doesn't simply replace a word, but a concept. The metaphor has a kind of power through displacement. Love is a rose, or—more scandalously—love is a rope. The *conceit* is stranger than the typical metaphor, a borrowed concept from further off. Metaphors require context. Rock, or moon, or flower as nouns cannot function on their own as a metaphors. They need something to replace. The *meta-phor* is a kind of *carrying across*, a taking of the concept from one place to another, and there is the transference of an auxiliary that comes with a new image. But let us at least begin with Shklovsky and move on from there. Shklovsky, again, while not directly cataloging figures of defamiliarization, does intentionally touch upon this one trope found in the work of Tolstoy. Shklovsky explicates Tolstoy's moves in the following lines:

> The devices by which Tolstoi enstranges his material may be boiled down to the following: he does not call a thing by its name, that is, he describes it as if it were perceived for the first time, while an incident is described as if it were happening for the first time. In addition, he foregoes the conventional names of the various parts of a thing, replacing them instead with the names of corresponding parts in other things (1991, 6).

The effect of not calling a thing by its name creates a distortion in perception of the thing. But to what extent may one thing be replaced with another? Hence, perhaps the most suasive example of replacement would be to elicit a near-transcendental vision of transubstantiation or propitiation, let us say for the sake of adding *gravitas* to replacement.

We should also think of replacement as simply choosing the right word. As Mark Twain famously quipped, "The difference between the almost right word and the right word is really a large matter—'tis the difference between the lightning-bug and the lightning" (Twain and Quirk 1994, 87–88). It reminds one of playing a game of Mad Libs as a child. This is the fruit of *quid pro quo*—a trade symbol. The replacement is a variable, an ***X***, that stands in for something else—something indeterminate. The replacement is rarely one-to-one, however, rarely an equivalent, creating the dissonant effect of the strange substitution. The replacement can attempt to be mathematical, a formula for balancing both sides of an equal sign, but *x* doesn't always equal *x*. *X* is sometimes *y*. The effect is like a chimera, who has a lion's head, a serpent's tail, and a goat somewhere about the middle. Replacement may occur in part or in whole. The whole replacement is something more like a scarecrow than a chimera.

Imitation is the sincerest form of flattery. But always, the copy is a copy is a copy. And the original has to go off someplace else. The original will always, inevitably, face obsolescence. This is how parody functions to replace and mock the original. To pretend that one thing is another thing, or to offer something as a substitute, is a psychological investment of replacement.

Art Examples:

The Son of Man by René Magritte (1964)
The Creation of God by Harmonia Rosales (2017)
The New American Gothic by Criselda Vasquez (2017)

Sentence Practice:

Working from our previous sentence, "To the store, Jimmy will go," now replace one word or phrase, to get something like "To the beach, Jimmy will go."

Deductions:

1. Replacement is a way of killing what has gone before with the impression of improvement. Replacement is a way of confronting our problems with death, the Real, and expression.
2. The new isn't better than the old, just different.
3. The chief replacement would hardly be noticed, almost an exact replica.
4. To replace one thing for another is to see both things differently and similarly.
5. It may not be possible to have replacement without the effect of considering similarities and differences.
6. Because replacement is the most fundamental and integral of tropes in our various languages, it may be difficult to find it strange. Each replacement would function along a spectrum of strangeness—and perhaps, if we can see this to be true in replacement, we can see it to be true in other tropes as well.
7. We use replacement regularly because we don't have recourse to some originary ideal. That is, we tend to think about impalpable nouns like *love* in terms of metaphor.

Seven Strange Projects:

- ☐ Take a self-portrait or find a famous painting. Replace the head in the image with something else.
- ☐ Remake a famous movie scene shot for shot.
- ☐ Find the text of a short story, novel, or long poem that is in the public domain. Then use the Replace All feature for a number of nouns and put in a handful of replacement figures.
- ☐ Write a paragraph. Then replace every word in it except for the function words: the, of, but, and so on.
- ☐ Create seven nicknames for a company, then create your own logos using those nicknames. Try replacing some of the letters with relevant objects that look similar, such as a cactus for the letter I.
- ☐ Make a mini-movie comparing your composing process to something else—exploring it via metaphor.
- ☐ Create a collection of seven images or paragraphs that convey a contemporary allegory.

A IS FOR ADDDITION AND SUBTRACTIO

Figure 5.7. Ada Harris and Lillian Waldo, First Journeys in Numberland *(1911), 46.*

Addition and subtraction are simply adding something in where it would normally not be or taking something away that would normally be present.

Related Figures for Addition: *epitasis, epenthesis, paragoge, prosthesis, apposition, epenthesis, polysyndeton, epitheton, correctio, interjection, conjunction*

Related Figures for Subtraction: *anesis, aphaeresis, apocope, aphaeresis, asyndeton, brachylogia, ecthlipsis, synaleoepha, syncope, restrictio, and ellipsis . . .*

Representative Figure for Addition and Subtraction: The Headless Horseman

These two are quite a pair. One, a man with his head subtracted. But that is not the end of it, for he, the headless horseman, has his horse. This slight addition makes him something more than the headless man, the *acephale,* changing him into something uncannier. In either case, one can easily see the slippery anatomy of addition and subtraction in this hallowed pair.

Figure 5.8. Frontispiece for The Headless Horseman *by Captain Mayne Reid (1865)*

> The stranger . . . quickened his horse to an equal pace. Ichabod pulled up, and fell into a walk, thinking to lag behind; the other did the same. His heart began to sink within him; he endeavored to resume his psalm tune, but his parched tongue clove to the roof of his mouth and he could not utter a stave. There was something in the moody and dogged silence of this pertinacious companion that was mysterious and appalling. It was soon fearfully accounted for. On mounting a rising ground, which brought the figure of his fellow-traveller in relief against the sky, gigantic in height and muffled in a cloak, Ichabod was horror-struck on perceiving that he was headless!
>
> —*"The Legend of Sleepy Hollow" by Washington Irving (1819)*

A Theoretical Introduction to Addition and Subtraction

Addition and subtraction work synergistically, two sides of the same coin. You might have a list, a stack of things, like so: tibia, octopi, tongues, rope, and croutons. You might have a terribly long, seemingly comprehensive list, but someone would still tell you that you have left out submarines, or salamanders, or salmon. You will have always left something out, no matter how many things you have tried to add. To complicate things, if one thinks of any work as a total work, somehow adding up to 100 percent in all its effects, then addition would never push the piece to 101 percent—something is always discarded in the process.

But we add tidbits here and there, tchotchkes, knickknacks, paraphernalia. Like lingerie, condiments, and eclipses, we see the ephemerality of adding something a little extra on top of what we've got—what the Cajuns call *lagniappe.* Doilies, those decorative bits of lace, might offer an easy example. You place a doily on a table; you've added something. But you cover up the table; you subtract the view of the tabletop, which has its own effects. We add things in all the time, and take things out as well. The gist is a trading embargo of ideas upon whatever palette is being used for a medium at the moment, whether it is a canvas, an essay, or an algebraic equation. To boot, an addition often works as an interjection into a work—it places something on top. And addition can also appear in conjunctions, and and and . . . You may say "pretty please," but without "sugar on top," the request doesn't have that certain something, that *je ne sais quoi.* We can learn about what's present when we look for an absence, a vow of silence or practicing censorship. We can practice addition and subtraction simultaneously, by filling in blanks or adding strikethroughs. Fragments are missing something. For better or worse. The weirdest effects can be created with subtle and seemingly insignificant gestures: put a hat on a duck, take the beak off a bird, put a splotch in the middle of a page. Good boys and girls know their sums, can subtract their numerals in straight columns.

Subtraction always seems bad. Headlessness, thievery, murder, or erasure, like cutting out a redundant redundant word. Each elicits strong negative connotations by taking something out of the equation. But what would be a good subtraction? Taking out a cancerous growth might be. But that still gestures toward the malevolent mass being taken away. In any case, the troublesome confrontation with subtraction is a force to be considered. Addition naturally has its own negative connections as well. The desire to add just one more is a strangely haunting feeling, an observation for something missing, an obligation to fix it by adding on to it is akin to what Kenneth Burke called man's own rottenness with perfection.

Quintilian, we should remember, uses these two moves as half of his four fundamental rhetorical operations in addition to substitution and permutation (1922, 1.5.11–17). Addition and subtraction function as two alternatives, both necessary in order to find what Quintilian calls deviations from the normal approach to a composition. And while we have already acknowledged the culturally privileged position of addition, Quintilian tries to emphasize the import of subtraction. He explains thus:

> It is best to write on wax owing to the facility which it offers for erasure, though weak sight may make it desirable to employ parchment by preference. The latter, however, although of assistance to the eye, delays the hand and interrupts the stream of thought owing to the frequency with which the pen has to be supplied with ink. But whichever we employ, we must leave blank pages that we may be free to make additions when we will. (1922, 10.3.31–32)

So, the wax, notes Quintilian, is a better medium because it allows one to erase. But more than that, it allows a kind of fluidity of addition. These two characteristics of wax are reborn in digital composition spaces—where erasure is easy enough and no inkwells need to be refilled. And finally, Quintilian suggests that we also leave space for more additions, an interesting adjuration, but also not a problem in digital spaces. Quintilian adds more on this later in the same book, writing, "Erasure is quite as important a function of the pen as actual writing. Correction takes the form of addition, excision and alteration. But it is a comparatively simple and easy task to decide what is to be added or excised" (1922, 10.4.1–4). For Quintilian, erasure is just as important as writing itself—in other words, both ends of a pencil are equal. The purportedly simple figures of adding and taking away have a great impact on the final condition of the work.

Group μ is known for working with addition and omission together as a kind of addition-omission. In their primary text, *A General Rhetoric,* they explain, "As soon as the harmony of the sentence is established as a norm or habit, new deviations may be formed . . . by comparison with the first figure" (1981, 68). The four deviations they offer concerning syntax, and later narrative organization, are suppression, addition, addition-omission, and permutation. For Group μ addition-omission equates to a strange replacement, which we have encountered, but again, we emphasize the overlap between the figures and their interesting relationships to one another. It is difficult, as usual, to keep categorized items separate, as in the case of the unruly tomato—a vegetable and fruit all in one. Using poetic discourse for examples, Group μ also takes up addition in various forms. Several iterations of addition here include "the act of increasing relations, and reducing their contacts" and "the act of adding any particular structure to the normal structure with the view of bringing attention to the message" (73). In other words, addition adds to the normative sentence in precisely the way that suppression reduces it. They continue, "Generally, simple addition results from two typical procedures, digression or development" (73). These perspectives on these moves show how useful they can be, especially in concert with one another.

In *sum,* it will be more productive for us to move away from addition and subtraction as mere either/or scenarios. While white/black, on/off, plus/minus arrangements seem conducive to these tropes, it will be important for us to consider these gestures as more complicated, often where the two, addition and subtraction, work together to create a strange effect. This is something beyond a zero-sum game, however. If we add something and take something away, we aren't looking for nothing in return. Addition always comes first. You learn it first. You think it first. You perform it first. Subtraction comes second. Like positive and negative charges necessary to form bonds, the employment of addition/omission as fundamental operations for thought, and particularly new thought, the two function together as an essential pair, working along both sides of this rhetorical mode.

+/−

Art Examples:

Erased De Kooning Drawing by Robert Rauschenberg (1953)

L.H.O.O.Q. by Marcel Duchamp (1919)

Sentence Practice:

Working from our previous sentence, "To the beach, Jimmy will go," now add one word or phrase and remove one word or phrase, to get something like "To the broad beach, Jimmy will."

Deductions:

~~1. Addition comes first in our training and thinking; perhaps it should not.~~

~~2. Addition and subtraction often work in concert with one another . . . an addition may also be a subtraction, and vice versa.~~

~~3. You cannot add everything, and you cannot take everything away, yet there is still always something.~~

~~4. Binaries are often an interesting way of thinking about positive and negative polarities or patterns, as long as one complicates the polarities.~~

~~5. Figuring with mathematical means may always be a para-discipline to figuring by tropology. Never expect to figure it all out.~~

~~6. Pluses and minuses are only symbols that may signify a variety of gestures.~~

~~7. 1 + 1= 2, except when it doesn't.~~

Seven Strange Projects:

- ☐ Write a seven-word sentence about writing. What words did you have to add or leave out to get the sentence to seven words? Convert the sentence to six words and then eight words. Write a paragraph explaining the process of adding and subtracting components of a single sentence.
- ☐ Make a self-portrait. Add three different things to your self and make three additional self-portraits. Take away three things and make three more. Be conscientious of the nude tradition. Why did you add what you added? What was the effect?
- ☐ Take something out of your living room. Add something to your living room. Write a short essay explaining what you took out and added, why, and the effects it had on the space.
- ☐ Make a silent narrative film. Use censorship. Add a coda at the ending.
- ☐ Take a famous work of art and then erase part of it; take a famous work of art and then add something to it.
- ☐ Make a slow journal-style website. Each day add two words to it, and subtract one.
- ☐ Try levitation photography. Make use of white space.

This page is intentionally left blank.

N IS FOR NEGATION

Negation is the inversion of a text by not-ing or by using the negative.
Related Figures: *Irony*

Representative Figure for Negation: The Spectral Shadow

Figure 5.9. A ghost and his shadow. (Drawn by the author.)

A Theoretical Introduction to Negation

No.

Art Example:

La Trahison des images by René Magritte (1929)

Sentence Practice:

Working from our previous sentence, "To the broad beach, Jimmy will," now add a negative or invert the sentence, to get something like "To the broad beach, Jimmy will not."

Deductions:

1. Nothing.
2. Nothing.
3. Nothing.
4. Nothing.
5. Nothing.
6. Nothing.
7. Nothing.

Seven Strange Projects:

- ☐ Pick pictures of your family members. Turn them upside down and add noise to some rhetorical effect.
- ☐ Find a song that has been released under a Creative Commons license such as the Nine Inch Nails' 2008 albums *Ghosts I-IV* or *The Slip* and add white noise to it using a sound-editing program such as Audacity. Reverse a portion, or portions, of the song.
- ☐ Make a mirror an integral component of some work, as with the end of *Only Revolutions* (Danielewski 2006).
- ☐ Shoot a video entirely upside down after studying shots from other examples. Use a version of John Cage's 1952 piece *4′33″* as the soundtrack.
- ☐ Write a narrative backward, similar to "Unchopping a Tree" by W. S. Merwin (2009). Bonus points for a political project connected to your writing, likened to Maya Lin's (2009) short video art piece also called *Unchopping a Tree,* which considers the climate crisis.
- ☐ Create and populate a This is not ______ social media account with pieces that reenact Magritte's image of the pipe in interesting ways.
- ☐ Negate a negation: uninvent the Holocaust.

G IS FOR GLOSSOLALIA

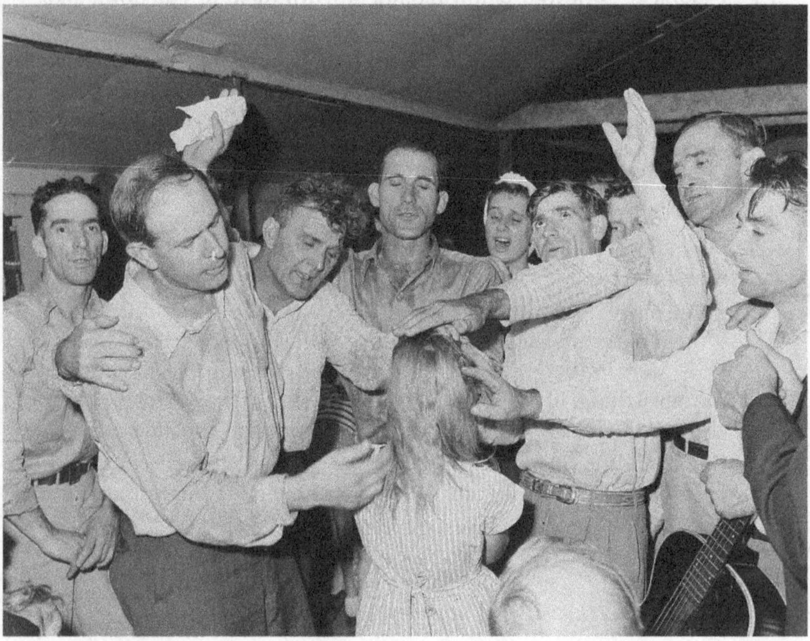

Figure 5.10. Healing "laying on of hands" ceremony in the Pentecostal Church of God, Lejunior, Harlan County, Kentucky. (Photographed by Russell Lee for the US government [1946].)

> Greater is one who prophesies than one who speaks in tongues, unless he interprets.
>
> —*From Paul's first letter to the Corinthians, chapter 14, verse 5*

Glossolalia is the use of foreign or unintelligible language to communicate an unrecognizable form.

Lsad hgrliq jw efl kqj wndknsbdvl kajsghd viau shdf; k qn wef. Aewlrnee. Tel sdlfk e le elkre sdnfs sdfls, fwleker wmfs s dflwe rww. Relekwek wew ewer ebrssvn v lkvwe wfnwle el. Rar elekre wi. Sdner ean ener naksjdn, ek ert.

Related Figures: *Graecismus, Hebraism, barbarismus, cacozelia, soraismus, skotisōn, logorrhoea*

Representative Figure for Glossolalia: The Foreign Oracle

The pre-Christian figure most associated with this rhetorical practice is Pythia, the Oracle at Delphi, so called because she would writhe like a snake while she garbled out a jumbled prophecy that the priests would then interpret. She would sit above a crack in the earth, breathe in sulfuric fumes, and become intoxicated. Then she would babble. And the priests at Delphi would interpret her glossolaliac expressions. The interpretations were most likely the priest's own desires being written on this virgin's expressions, a colonization. Let us move forward by accepting glossolalia on its own terms and resist colonizing it, shifting it into meaning, at least for the moment.

Figure 5.11. John Collier, Priestess of Delphi *(1891).*

> And the Sibyl, with raving lips uttering things mirthless, unbedizened, and unperfumed, reaches over a thousand years with her voice, thanks to the god in her.
>
> . . .
>
> The lord whose is the oracle at Delphoi neither utters nor hides his meaning, but shows it by a sign.
>
> —*Heraclitus, fragments 92 and 93, quoted in Plutarch 1936*

A Theoretical Introduction to Glossolalia

True nonsense might be the strangest rhetorical tactic of all, although that superlative may be placed upon any means of generating strangeness. Glossolalia is the Greek word that essentially means "speaking in a language one does not know." And even though it may sound meaningless to you, oftentimes foreign language can have a powerful impact on an audience. Glossolalia in practice has been around since pre-Christian times, but it is now most often associated with the practice known as spirit-filled utterances, called speaking in tongues in some charismatics. It is gibberish in the purest form, and yet has meaning in some sense. So, in what ways are nonsense and gibberish rhetorical within various media frameworks? We know that any communication, even driveling blather, garbled gibberish, and prattling claptrap, creates attention, and sometimes blather can create more attention than the most well-formed speech. And sometimes blather—too—is well formed.

Why is nonsense so intensely rhetorical? Theorizing the trope of glossolalia in what are most patently barbarisms seems simple enough at first. Barbarism is bad. Or so we are told. The barbarians of Greece were considered outsiders. They were so called because of the *bar-bar-bar* sound of their language. And still to this day, barbarisms of language are to be deterred at all costs. Barbarisms are part of the vices of language, as opposed to the virtues. Quintilian, the great rhetorician, we have already heard, objects to barbarisms in the first book of the *Institutes of Oratory*. Meaningless drivel may be simply nodded at, and then walked briskly past, with eyes cast downward. The foreigner is also associated with glossolalia, sounding strange to the listener who is ignorant of the other tongue. This subtle difference might be referred to as xenoglossia, or foreign language. Meaninglessness in glossolalia and uninterpretable meaning in xenoglossia offer two interconnected means of stranging a message. But xenoglossia can quickly lead to xenophobia—an animosity toward the foreigner.

And you have seen the clever scholar, in the attempt to increase his cleverness, use a foreign word. I am guilty of this with things like ostranenie, Verfremdungseffekt, and even glossolalia, but we must remember that here we are embracing the rhetorical vices that Quintilian dismisses:

> Archaic words not only enjoy the patronage of distinguished authors, but also give style a certain majesty and charm. For they have the authority of age behind them, and for the very reason that they have fallen into disuse, produce an attractive effect not unlike that of novelty. But such words must be used sparingly and must not thrust themselves upon our notice, since there is nothing more tiresome than affectation. (Quintilian 1922, 1.5)

Foreignness alone is persuasive. The foreignness of an incomprehensible tongue does not, indeed, have to be completely without meaning. The exotic languages one does not know offer inestimable intrigue for the interested listener.

Of course, you don't have to be in a church that handles snakes to be a glossolaliac. All of us have done this as babies. The infant, we say, is *in-fans,* without language, but this is untrue. Babies make all sorts of noises, and persuade us to burp them, or change their diapers, or give them milk, all with a glossolaliac language. And we speak back. We sing lullabies without meaning. To them, the reverse is true; the English language is glossolalia. Kenneth Burke was fond of talking about the speechlessness of infants. He declares in *A Rhetoric of Motives,* "As for 'infancy' itself, there are, you might say, several 'infancies': for besides the speechlessness of the infant, there is the speechlessness of the nonverbal (as the quality of a sensory experience is beyond language, requiring immediate experience); and there is the speechlessness of the 'unconscious,' as regards complexities vaguely intuited but not yet made verbally explicit (in sum, the symbolically 'enigmatic')" (1969b, 167). Being in the beyond of language, in speechlessness, is speaking still. What is so strange about glossolalia is that, in spite of its evidential status as nonsense, meaning is prescribed or inscribed upon it, so that even the sound of air vents being attributed to hauntings by ghosts represents a form of glossolalia.

One might say, then, that the Tower of Babel is the beginning of rhetoric. That story begins, "Now the whole world had one language and a common speech" (Genesis 11:1, *New International Version*). The separations and divisions created by the development of new languages also gave rise to the possibility of misreading, of misinterpreting, of mistaking messages. Burke observes, "Rhetoric is concerned with the state of Babel after the Fall" (1969b, 23). And Roland Barthes adds in *The Pleasure of the Text,* "The text of pleasure is a sanctioned Babel" (Barthes 1975a, 4). Apocalyptic, freewheeling visions like this add weight to the trope, making it culturally significant in further-reaching ways. Gunboat whale ever after inversal blue chicken again insidiously never Xerxes Xerox mountain future life.

Pythonic utterances may come from a simple desire to communicate without communicating meaning—expression for expression's sake. Or glossolalia may arise from some impediment to communication. In the case of the drunkard's slurred speech, or the tired worker's drawl, we see the beginnings of glossolaliac communication. In certain cases of mental illness, one can find expressions of nonsense, or garbled language.

But to call it a language at all is a revealing note that we desire for all things that may be communicating a message to be, in fact, communicating a meaningful message. Making up a nonsense word is the last way in which I'll attempt a formal experiment with this trope. *Jirn.* That was also not difficult. I'll leave it to you to decide what it means.

Asemia, or communicative media that has no signifier, has taken on a life of its own, influencing writing, art, music, and other creative outlets. According to Bruce Sterling, who gives a definition of asemic writing in *Wired Magazine*, it is: "Writing that doesn't have any actual writing in it whatsoever" (2009). But let us keep this intentional gesture as separate from the effects of aphasia, or language loss. Glossolalia is using language, just not any known or common one. It does not matter what the speaker is saying, only that she is speaking. Various writers have taken up the pleasures of glossolalia, including Lewis Carroll with the now-familiar "'Twas brillig and the slithy toves . . ." (1993) or Jorge Borges with this mind-boggling Library of Babel or James Joyce who used thunderwords in *Finnegans Wake*, such as bababadalgharaghtakamminarronnkonnbronntonnerronntuonnthunntrovarrhounawnskawntoohoohoordenenthurnuk (2012, 3). More recent playful moves have appeared in *The Giant's Fence* (Jacobson 2006) and *The Policeman's Beard Is Half Constructed* (Chamberlain 1984). Andrey Bely's 2003 book *Glossolalia* is wonderfully poetic. The first lines read: "Profound mysteries reside in language" (1). Similarly interested in formal expression and playing with various logics and structures is Noam Chomsky. The function and charm of glossolalia may be found in Chomsky's experimental sentence, "Colorless, green ideas sleep furiously" (2015, 15). Chomsky explains that the example is grammatical, and begins to take the theory of syntactic structure "a good deal beyond its familiar limits" (15). Chomsky's famously poetic sentence breaks from semantic meaning while still retaining syntactic order. We humans are very good at making nonsense, and then delighting in it. The magic of foreign worlds lies in keeping them foreign. We don't always need to be told what is being said, only to know that we are not in Kansas anymore. Glossolalia is language without a referent. Glossolalia always retains some tie to language, even if it is not language. The remnant is what makes it rhetorical and captivating, reinstructing us in our own relationship to language. Glossolalia is powerful because of its mystery, its unknowability, and its ominousness. It suggests the unaccountable, and it can be a thunderous wolfish scream or an imperceptible mumble. Finally, we conclude in theorizing glossolalia that when the audience defies us by exclaiming, "It's all Greek to me," then that could be a good thing, indeed. A very @#$%^&*! good thing, aersdf weltwtj3

4tlw3k wegrlkwefw, like a glitch aesthetic. After all, a .jpeg read by any other means is still a .jpeg. The thing is that a text editor doesn't care whether the code is readable; the software doesn't have to worry about pondering its meaning. It bothers us. So, what does a picture of me look like when opened up in a text editor?

. . . ì¿fiæü˝zÎ<O®E°<c
Å{ÚI¸à˝kõ'tÀ]gÌuôä¡dŒw8¡ÈöÓ¬ ˆßQhˆ;´"‰√˚j
" [Ÿ Í ì – Á & @ ' é X ˇ u p " ∞ ñ o # > ü C Õ w - ñ f l Q ≥ ì M b—
±Âv∂>«'~π«"ïÖMîÔˆõK≈rÑJøƒpˇÛ©ÔR}ÌÔ¢m»„z:úˌU€à^fi)
A˙?3œ¿KÍSî™≠:ÆËÈÆcõ
Ï)£±õŒ[sbècPcªìƒV`s#µSjåÚm|c>ÈÆØn@~L§°Û«˜≥≈u2∫Ñ@
âŸI,L*∂Jvdp̂ÎÃa=ç.ı¬<òÊ?ûì¡°¥_ba¥‡ëç«µD!ÂΠ≥¥öXÈ≥œQÛhÚ3'n#
Pq$qœJö—'∆§Σ§Ûåäðç•\‹5
›R§<≤ΣgÏ)¨®zi•ßˇ
7sÉ% ˛rïî†èPGÔHz* À·{/˝æ*î wÀ‡söØÔ^.]ú„ÎÖ¥d
Π&ÉÏMÍ…VªU"ˇzuVâR"Ì«˜BTpÇUËxÈ"4Uzã
m®ç°⁄N◊fil-J'¶JÚ•á±<}˛qaÒï≈ÕBoq"À
8^AG∆¨xzœK…a*n˝m)X„2ÛÎUïñ,≥(πEàVBî)$zm#jÜÔ¬À
ñZ›Ó‰ú§∂ÍU…Ì«z†ı√F=—à°ÂÜá$˙ìè⁄¥æ£æÀ‰Bãià'&î¢q °§rs'–
?âæŸc•ÎÉnLTÜ"ÇÚ›)ÿ¥ütÅ»«"®Zì&-nùÏRGéÂÁç¿≠!Xı§¶©Σ‹I@⁄>hŸ<7âw
kÕDÄ⁄OC÷£ı7áfl¡7Ìy.åÁ÷çC≠ΩJÎK(»*4€ªpûµΠôm£ u
?ıÆ°á•!ß,‡§Ò]G Jpsım~Aã€4"&6CõÛ‹É"é†xW˜"‹2ññ Û˝úÅ
ö¥fiS""ÍT£ûoûÜâ4Õ˙ı{íãR‰µ!~^,9 ˇ'S∂•œx≤£ø]•"%m∂
úZO!#4Y·'7qp-§•ÌΠFGb¶A˝á•jÕ‡ˆùâßí§Öª)—πnπÇT⁄©=gkUãƒÚ)
v§cÇûÄ":øVÑP|œi6ÜDz€R÷˙6I
Zùé!C˘"ΣVor,≠6÷BV˚ŒÖ9É'!)„?x¢€Ü[aO8F:¸(/ZÎõsØòÃ:„§u,ùΠˇ
Z¨W>3XkP°ôkZ¥¸W¥üΣ·©Qùh6∂áåc–éıÚ®IvõÙe&"/,∫ÄoÑœÑÓ—
˛$©9˘,Éï´˝ΣO˜DLyµc›i,"≥ÍJ{|´Î!3#∆µ/»e;@[äY◊q˛tOPï¬»*ÆÏòyn"˜ ä
π]T<ñ,†3Πzgï°e€Ÿ®∞⁄C,°;RîåU^äÒ*€ìpû
in$(Ê¨ÂN^I¿«⁄¶Σçª Xsjú˚zå5"c⁄ááùB°•#íéıˆ«÷§¥ÊõÖ9zl8⁄Y
8í8RÛì˙™¡We ÷™úàÓauÊ¥NúıUhaQï∂°Π®w'©ß¥ã¨fizª]©4SÈØm˝y
î•Ô√;•ÜÙµŸπ∂æ}÷«>YÔäÒC√=L'ë€òíÍ€m%Kd+ΣsZòÄzÄh{_KèO»mÙÓ
ßıV/°˙kcå˘fiÖ2çßq'a<,∫ëM·FL!°I‰¿ÀEÆÃªJí,SäO∫Å'ìRöGæÊ∂Σ∂"8a≈Y*
Ë*æÖ:DI-°fiA£= ,d˙>®åıÕ£ÏA®sΣ,iE"±∞3å√ñ]¶lÎtsfi'|‡•≤MÄΩ•[
õm‰®ë¡∆j˘"Z¢Õ}Σµ.Êú‡,qU«è+∂Í)6ç8πAHSÍq‰!\êÅÙÊØı5≠ïüè⁄Sl±X
JNˇΣ ÌÆH @=O\P¨[$·âIÑ"Ã≠–€ÎflÔ∂úÚ@ıÙ•ıl¥µÒÀÂ„Ÿèò√ùùl°…
W¿ˆ•¥ˆ•ry+@qµvcÌ≈eçmQ∆&¬ªí¿À#MB"çFÚ∂_Â§/Ú"î8úpA›"4ÚÂß„MÄ
Πˆõ∫^Ωπ˘ûT! ˆŸ5§úÁ,°¿_"¶Ã™ºà\°>‹üfl¸ÉΣ-8õ%˛
K\á!N8F2sœN¬çZøIõΠyŒ ÑtÏ°'Ø%õÇZÇú¡–ÅÔfi°ïxÚ aΩ¡ksw?ÛØÌJ
·üì8\&CÀX|°~,[RΠÓqR^x±x"Slπ;Ì˜mJªß˛'Û√{QΠ∆ñ,¢˘ÓòŒyLì¬âH8Áíì?
t)©`≤ÙÇñ.MÔåWííΠıΩΩ›'‰gí>Ue¶K´¨ŸXŒ>%7'J ª™ô•lö "péá=° *Î≈

¯«sqÎÕ±ƒóÄ˜s“´M êaó 8WÌO1Ùô¨@€ÛFoU◊˝Èfl÷YmDbVµ!â·≈ÕÁHU’ #ŒF‘ÑÁå˜Æ™⁄◊6Û2˙ò∂ñúLÂ+Å1ÆÆW©µj!ly

X’$¡@¥È\ï ù™”&cülΠ[#⁄nr°¨ÛÜú)È^Ù‘ΩJˆßás~Ê˚Ø§‡) g<¯¶õp§+ÙÁöö¥Ö&[)åè3ÀZU«P†µç_êdVµ=âiÎflÓ˛![m˜(O’€òl%≈8p

y8„Á°’{µfiÙv§~€}å∂d∂Ω™*j«PSÍ1[”√ß⁄ë§”…HJìiû›1ôø≥Ì˙öˇ≥±˘m<ëï,éΠ ›úö±≥MX¨~g4˜æ˝£°!\,ΠfiÌ√í@·Bü øòåè%¿µ§Ì«N1÷á†Ëã,Pì÷›`°»ÁsN]“Zó ÕI1ê‡R˘¬∫Po∫^ØQWeO.(ûßwΩLÈ;3Σô-∂ïÑ6ìπk_N;S€fâm”BŒGΠÄNO¶ *1ÁC”#MLΠGKM∂b8«,WÔÅ”©<X¢ñ’> áOÅm£Nª¨?ÏñÓ√M1hΣ¢OïΣ›C

Y˛˜¿z|r{Uc¯∫‘Ò‘,˙]∞Ö»m√5’wl`•#ÊrO»|jÚΩ\¢⁄≠í’Àq,∆ä“úqGÄî§dˇ◊5Ö1 æß{VjÎÖ˙F‰˚CßÀA˛√cÑßÌ…¯ìZÕ>ù41ÑYõ‘\◊πvÑ

And that’s only part of it. That might just be a small bit of my left eye or my nose. The whole picture is almost a hundred pages long. That is the beauty of glossolalia, from ancient priestesses to nonsense spam bots.

Or, finally, I may be able to prove glossolalia’s effectiveness with a bit of pathos. When my mother was dying of cancer, we had to put her on a lot of morphine. And she was confused sometimes. This is some of her last writing. We would hand her these sheets of paper, and she would scribble on them. And these are some of my most treasured pieces of writing, some of the most rhetorical, and they make no sense. Her name? *Barbara.* Like the barbarians, the Greek outsiders, or strangers, my mother stood outside the conventional bounds of everyday life. And so, I have kept this last message, even today. This example may be similar to parents who love and cherish their young children’s early scribblings, but it is a little different from that.

And now I have little girls; their scribblings are precious to me. I love them.

David Bartholomae writes in “The Study of Error,”

> There is a style, then, to the apparently bizarre and incoherent writing of a basic writer because it is, finally, evidence of an individual using language to make and transcribe meaning. An error can only be understood as evidence of intention. They are the only evidence we have of an individual’s idiosyncratic way of using the language and articulating meaning, of imposing a style on common material. A writer’s activity is linguistic and rhetorical activity; it can be different but never random. The task for both teacher and researcher, then, is to discover the grammar of that coherence, of the “idiosyncratic dialect” that belongs to a particular writer at a particular moment in the history of his attempts to imagine and reproduce the standard idiom of academic discourse. (1980, 255)

It is our job to work with students (our students who are so obsessed with being correct) to interpret their own errors, to investigate them, to see what’s there behind the glitch, and perhaps, occasionally to reinsert

Figure 5.12. My mother's last piece of writing.

powerful glitches in their own writing. I. A. Richards famously says that rhetoric is a "study of misunderstanding and its remedies" (Richards 1965, 3), but what if we just sometimes allowed and considered some of those wonderful misunderstandings before hurrying toward correctness—finding value in there?

Art Example:

Number 1, 1950 (Lavender Mist) by Jackson Pollock (1950)

Sentence Practice:

Working from our previous sentence, "To the broad beach, Jimmy will not," now add a foreign word or a nonce word into the sentence, to get something like "To the broad beach, Jimmy will not spuck."

Deductions:

1. Glossolaliacs embrace an expressive view of composition. Glossolalia privileges expression over meaning, and that expressivity alone can be attractive. In their nonsense, they have decided that they are only going to make their own sense. It is the privateness of the language that generates the feeling of strangeness in the audience. And perhaps the privacy of a communicative act is valuable for the self in ways the self cannot know. Following that, nonsense becomes rhetorically intriguing to others so that possible private secrets can be discovered.
2. Glossolalia not only makes language strange, it also presents language as curious, as something to be explored but never understood.
3. While a foreign language can be a canyon that separates people, it can also be alluring in its exoticism.
4. Glossolalia reveals the constructedness of language as such.
5. Glossolalia frees us from the obligation of meaning. The figure is strange because it cuts out the signified or any sense of referentiality. In this it resists interpretation.
6. However, if we are paranoid, we will ruthlessly require meaning from glossolalia.
7. Glossolalia is a trope for scavengers. Nonsense holds an indecipherable secret. For instance, to us, our garbage is trash, worthless offal. To some, there is nothing to find or seek in the trashcan. A dog, on the other hand, without fail, always suspects that there will be some juicy morsel to be discovered in the heap of things some would write off as worthless.

Seven Strange Projects:

- ☐ Read "The Library of Babel" (Borges 1998). Make a Babel Book based on Borges's specifications: 80 characters per line, 40 lines per page, and 410 pages. Publish it in a public space online.
- ☐ Become a Priestess of Delphi. Find an example of glossolalia, or create your own, perhaps by opening an image in a text editor, and write a one-page paper attempting to interpret its meaning.
- ☐ Create a video in which no native language is spoken. You could try to use the lorem ipsum text or grommelot.
- ☐ Try using made up words or babbling nonsense in public places over the course of a week, see what happens, blog about it each day.
- ☐ Create a Twitter account for posting glossolaliac tweets, friend a bunch of people, see what the response is. Post sentences that retain syntactic structure and a grammar, as in Chomsky's example, and/or ones that do not.
- ☐ Make up a word. Define it. Explore the word in other languages and look for connections in a short paper. (But don't be what Gregory Ulmer calls a *neopest* [2003, 24]; that's just making up new words for no reason.)
- ☐ Scribble out an asemic novella. Give it a title in English.

E IS FOR EXPONENTIATION

Xx

Exponentiation is the amplification or minimization of something that would normally be within a certain normative measurement, sometimes to push and make that thing almost opposingly large or small.

Related Figures: *hyperbole, litotes, meiosis, amplification, auxesis, adynaton, battalogia, bathos, exergasia, copia, gnome, pleonasmus, repetition, ploce, congeries, tapinosis*

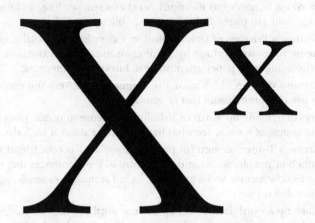

Representative Figure for Exponentiation: Buddha

You know the Buddha. But he takes on different forms: extreme starvation, the abundant life, and finally the middle way. The Fat Buddha or the Laughing Buddha is not actually Siddhartha Gautama, but instead a later monk named Budai in China or Hotei in Japan—a deity of happiness. The Buddha as a general conceptual figure, however, gives us varying degrees of extreme paths. His largeness is well known, his thinness is lesser known, and the middle way is, perhaps, the least depicted version of the Buddha. In largeness and slightness, and even in the middle way, one finds potential toward satori, enlightenment, and escape.

Figure 5.13. Buddha. (Figure photographed by the author.)

> I did not tell Fat this, but technically he had become a Buddha. It did not seem to me like a good idea to let him know. After all, if you are a Buddha you should be able to figure it out for yourself.
>
> —*From VALIS by Philip K. Dick (1981)*

A Theoretical Introduction to Exponentiation

Almost all natural numbers are very, very, very large.
—Frivolous theorem of arithmetic

The biggest trope is the one that makes things bigger, of course. Like *Alice in Wonderland*'s mushroom, exponentiation is a force that makes all sorts of forms bigger and smaller in various ways. I chose exponentiation here as the last installment of mathematical connections to the rhetorical figures as strange attractors. By revisioning the classical tropes of hyperbole and litotes to reconceptualize, one might see how they work for contemporary rhetors. Moreover, if we think of rhetoric itself as a *dynamis*, a power, then what better way of exploring the extent of this power than by exploring things raised to powers themselves?

If we merely think about hyperbole, for example, as an emphatic overstatement, the implications of the trope are present, but not necessarily earth shattering. Bigness always requires a relationship to smallness; the norm must be clear, and the incongruity heavily emphasized as a rocketing away from the baseline. In mathematics, b^n offers up a possibility of endless multiplication, and if a variable is exponentiated to a negative degree, then there is infinite minimizing of the original variable. Through exponentiation, we can have infinite largeness and infinitesimal smallness. It is the difference that comes from one negative symbol. It is the difference between $b^{1000000000000000000000000000000000000000000000000000000000000000000000000000000000000000}$ and $b^{-1000000000000000000000000000000000000000000000000000000000000000000000000000000000000000}$.

In light of these extremes, we should attempt to think about exponentiation along a spectrum. This spectrality of exponentiation allows us to think from the most negated alignments to the most distantly positive. While addition and multiplication offer a certain degree of more precise movement and change, exponentiation quickly gets out of control. And beyond exponentiation, there is a process known as tetration, which is compounded exponentiation, an exponent of an exponent. In this way, repetition represents one key way of thinking about exponentiation. Repeated addition is multiplication. Exponentiation repeats the process of multiplying over and over, and so on. It repeats the same story about growing up; you know the one about walking uphill in the snow both ways.

Exponentiation also means something other than massive overkill; the process also includes making things quite small. Big things bring admiration, while smaller things are cute. This is why we like ponies and why duckweed is interesting. Nevertheless, exponentiation still tends to make us think of bigger things more often than smaller things. Texas is the heart of this thinking. Everything is bigger in Texas, I learned as a child. Big hair. Big boots. The biggest belt buckles. And something like a 1,000-ounce steak. Americans in general have raised up a culture of excess reflected in monster trucks, huge roadside attractions, professional wrestling, Disney World, and quadruple quarter pounders with cheese. And what is it with this American cheesiness, this tendency toward hyperbolic kitsch? Our country surfeits like no other. In our patriotism, we embark on the uncanniest of excesses.

Like Sylvester Stallone's muscles, camp works us over; I mean, have you seen *Over the Top* (1987)?! In film, we might take a look at *The Longest Most Meaningless Movie in the World* from 1968, which runs for 2,880 minutes, or two full days. This final trope works like a curve on a graph going up, up, up. We can hear it in a deafening crescendo where sound floods everything around us. *Cent mille milliards de poèmes* or *One Hundred Million Million Poems* is one literary example of exponentiation, an endeavor fashioned by Raymond Queneau (1961). The effect of Queneau's work is still largely evident, but it helped begin the French group we have acknowledged known as the Oulipo, which contained mathematicians in its cohort. So, it is not strange for us to think of this figure in these formal terms. Mathematics too help make literature strange, as well as art, cinema, electronic media, in addition to other unique media outlets.

Finally, we learn that through rhetoric, the bigger stick doesn't always win. Although, exponentiation can breed a competitive spirit—where trumping and one-upmanship are in tow. And now there is a fervor of late over the bigness of rhetoric. Nevertheless, through various iterations of rhetorical exponentiation, in particular, the little guy can come out on top, and the short, little mother can chide her hulking son. A theory of exponentiation would have to be inclusive—a big theory. It would include the smallest particles of the universe and the most mammoth: from quarks to supernovas. It would include the humblest of murmurs to the most luxurious and fustian grandiloquence. From the deep end to the shallows, theorizing exponentiation requires a kind of endlessness, a breadth of exploration that ceaselessly goes ad infinitum. The googolplex for example, 10^{googol} or $10^{10\wedge 100}$, offers a number so large that it cannot be written; there isn't enough space in the universe, even with the tiniest of fonts. The googolplex was imagined, in part, by a little girl (Kasner and Newman 1940, 23). And it is a brave concept. Another of our largest numbers is Graham's number, the number 3 exponentiated again and again in folds; we cannot even express it numerically.

The question with strange thinking and composing is essentially how far you are brave enough to go. As with any of the figures, how willing are you to compose something silly or dare to make something laughable? And this is why exponentiation may especially be found in heroic tales, kitschy melodramas, and the absurd.

As we have mentioned, exponentiation works along a continuum that ranges from the very large to the very small. It is the kind of thinking that requires the word *very*. In this scale of thought, we turn to hyperbole and litotes, or meiosis, to elucidate the functions of divergent forms of exponentiation. *Hyper-bollen* signifies a throwing over, so there is a hurling of the hyperbole. It does not just sit. It comes with a braggadocio tone in a way that, say, addition lacks. Aristotle declares, "Hyperboles are adolescent; for they exhibit vehemence," and after an example, he adds, "It is inappropriate for an older man to speak in hyperbole" (2006, 226). And hyperbole can seem a youngster's game, a fool's errand. Quintilian explains that the trope may verge on the obscene and the absurd; it may win the audience or lose them (1922). And also, it is used by the uneducated as well as the educated—it is a classless trope. According to Quintilian's view, we could have extreme versions of any other trope that would result in hyperbole. That is, we could have extreme addition, extreme replacement, and so on. Exponentiation could be thought in terms of other tropes and other mixes and blends we have seen along the way. Longinus also wrote several relevant considerations in the treatise "On the Sublime" in the first few centuries of the Common Era. He explains the effects of *amplification* as a trope effecting grandeur, noting that "grand phrases come rolling out one after another with increasing effect" (quoted in Fahnestock 2011, 405). This tendency to continue with a hyperbolic mode once it has been started is something like a snowball effect or an avalanche. A hearty exploration of rhetorical quantities may be found in the later work of Erasmus, who explored the concept of *copia* during the Renaissance. In *De Utraque Verborum ac Rerum Copia*, which might be translated as *On Both the Abundance of Words and Events*, Erasmus famously writes, "Your letter pleased me greatly" 195 different ways. His work begins, poetically, like this: "The speech of man is a magnificent and impressive thing when it surges along like a golden river, with thoughts and words pouring out in rich abundance" (1999, 295). However, while the first line is praise, the second line is a warning: "Yet the pursuit of speech like this involves considerable risk" (295). The risky balance of good abundance and overreaching, or overwrought, abundance is precarious, but Erasmus values the trope enough to do a thorough examination of it. Later, Raymond Queneau (1958) would practice his own *copia* in *Exercises in Style*, writing the same story over 99 times.

Excess is a key to why we hyperbolize. We desire more. We pile on whatever is at hand. From modicums and wee tittles to monstrosities and gargantuan rhetorical compositions, we can see exponentiation at work *in extremis*. From overblown stories told by fishermen to the most understated runts, we can expect big things from big things and small things alike. Whether we are in feast or famine, composing something large or small takes hard work. Big things come in small packages, after all.

Brevity is nearly as powerful as amplification. Indeed. Yelling and whispering are perhaps an elementary frame for thinking about how to practice exponentiation, from screaming about politics from your soapbox to whispering, "I love you" over and over to a lover. The grandiloquence of hyperbole does, however, allow you to constitute expressions that will, in fact, MELT YOUR FACE WITH THEIR SHEER, UNPARALLELED AWESOMENESS. The ALL CAPS move helps as well with face melting. Exclamation points help us to push the point!!! Lastly, the use of "most," "best," "ever," and other superlatives—not the senior superlatives you received in high school—are easy ways of making things hyperbolic. But to really get the effect, you should multiply your superlatives to the point of performing battalogia, or vain repetition. Like that was the best, most amazing, super thing I've ever read ever . . . like ever ever . . . like ever

ever ever ever ever ever ever ever ever ever ever ever ever ever ever ever
ever ever ever ever ever ever ever ever ever ever ever ever ever ever ever
ever ever ever ever ever ever ever ever ever ever ever ever ever ever ever
ever ever ever ever ever ever ever ever ever ever ever ever ever ever ever
ever ever ever ever ever ever ever ever ever ever ever ever ever ever ever
ever ever ever ever ever ever ever ever ever ever ever ever ever ever ever
ever ever ever ever ever ever ever ever ever ever ever ever ever ever ever
ever ever ever ever ever ever ever ever ever ever ever ever ever ever ever
ever ever ever ever ever ever ever ever ever ever ever ever ever ever ever
ever ever ever ever ever ever ever ever ever ever ever ever ever ever ever
ever ever ever ever ever ever ever ever ever ever ever ever ever ever ever
ever ever ever ever ever ever ever ever ever ever ever ever ever ever ever
ever ever ever ever ever ever ever ever ever ever ever ever ever ever ever
ever ever ever ever ever ever ever ever ever ever ever ever ever ever ever
ever ever ever ever ever ever ever ever ever ever ever ever ever ever ever
ever ever ever ever ever ever ever ever ever ever ever ever ever ever ever
ever ever ever ever ever ever ever ever ever ever ever ever ever ever ever
ever ever ever ever ever ever ever ever ever ever ever ever ever ever ever
ever ever ever ever ever ever ever ever ever ever ever ever ever ever ever
ever ever ever ever ever ever ever ever ever ever ever ever ever ever ever
ever ever ever ever ever ever ever ever ever ever ever ever ever ever ever
ever ever ever ever ever ever ever ever ever ever ever ever ever ever ever
ever ever ever ever ever ever ever ever ever ever ever ever ever ever ever
ever ever ever ever ever ever ever ever ever ever ever ever ever ever ever
ever ever ever ever ever ever ever ever ever ever ever ever ever ever ever
ever ever ever ever ever ever ever ever ever ever ever ever ever ever ever
ever ever ever ever ever ever ever ever ever ever ever ever ever ever ever
ever ever ever ever ever ever ever ever ever ever ever ever ever ever ever
ever ever ever ever ever ever ever ever ever ever ever ever ever ever ever
ever ever ever ever ever ever ever ever ever ever ever ever ever ever ever
ever ever ever ever ever ever ever ever ever ever ever ever ever ever ever
ever ever ever ever ever ever ever ever ever ever ever ever ever ever ever
ever ever ever ever ever ever ever ever ever ever ever ever ever ever ever
ever ever ever ever ever ever ever ever ever ever ever ever ever ever ever
ever ever ever ever ever ever ever ever ever ever ever ever ever ever ever
ever ever ever ever ever ever ever ever ever ever ever ever ever ever ever
ever ever ever ever ever ever ever ever ever ever ever ever ever ever ever
ever ever ever ever ever ever ever ever ever ever ever ever ever ever ever
ever ever ever ever ever ever ever ever ever ever ever ever ever ever ever
ever ever ever ever ever ever ever ever ever ever ever ever ever ever ever
ever ever ever ever ever ever ever ever ever ever ever ever ever ever ever

ever ever ever ever ever ever ever ever ever ever ever ever ever ever ever ever ever ever ever ever ever ever ever ever ever ever ever ever ever ever ever ever ever ever ever ever ever ever ever ever ever ever ever ever ever ever ever ever ever ever ever ever ever ever ever ever ever ever ever ever ever ever ever ever ever ever ever ever ever ever ever ever ever ever ever ever ever ever ever ever ever ever ever ever ever ever ever ever ever ever . . .

Art Examples:

The first and second largest statues in the world: *The Statue of Unity* in India (2018) and *The Spring Temple Buddha* (2008) in China

(The third and fourth tallest statues in the world also depict Buddha.)

Balloon Dog by Jeff Koons (1994)

The Mastaba by Christo and Jeanne-Claude (2018)

Trust by Jonty Hurwitz (2014)

Sentence Practice:

Working from our previous sentence, "To the broad beach, Jimmy will not spuck," now make some aspect of the sentence bigger or smaller, longer or shorter, to get something like "To the boundless, broad, huge, monumental, long, tremendous, sweeping, ample, colossal, endless, extended, vast beach, J will not spuck!"

Deductions:

1. The biggest isn't always the best.
2. Largeness and smallness work along a spectrum.
3. The big will always get bigger; it cannot be helped. But this allows for endless novelty through exponentiation, as long as the capabilities allow. If the capabilities are not yet there, novelty must wait a little while.
4. Bantam is the modest route; goliathing is a kind of lion-sized pride.
5. A work can be simple, no matter whether it is big or small.
6. Excess can be pleasurable or painful, especially when it is kitschy excess.
7. It would be difficult to determine which is stranger: the smallest thing in the universe or the biggest.

Seven Strange Projects:

- ☐ Create the ______est thing in the universe. Make a composition that could get into the *Guinness World Records*.
- ☐ Host a B-movie night where you watch as many cheesy films as you can, while eating as much cheese as you can. Trust me on this one.
- ☐ Tell a tall tale in photos, video, or text 100 different ways. Integrate other mathematical embellishments to make it extraordinarily strange.
- ☐ Work collaboratively to build a large or very small sculpture or written piece on your campus.
- ☐ Use big data to analyze something and make the world better. Write it up.
- ☐ Create a video haiku: with clips of five seconds, seven seconds, and five seconds. Perhaps three gifs could work as well, with five frames, seven frames, and five frames respectively.
- ☐ Create a series of seven postcards using caricatures that you create paired with clichéd hyperboles, such as "I'm starving to death," "These books weigh a ton," or "I'm so hungry I could eat a horse."

Chapter Six
STRANGEr RELATIONS AND WEiRDer NETWORKS

STRONGER, STRANGER RELATIONS

It might seem strange to move toward finding connections when thinking about estrangement, but that is really the whole point. The relationship between a writer (or any sort of rhetor) and the reader (or any sort of audience) is complex, multilayered, and wonderfully and dynamically strange. Beyond singularities and single-dimension relations, strangeness presents us with more options. Here we are searching for something beyond *mere* individuality, differences of expression that are reliant upon relations with others. Intersections or nodes of strangeness—where multiple things converge—multiply the effects for our perception of a complexly weird and wonderful world. We as rhetors or compositionists connect with others as well as our texts. That's the rhetorical triangle, or the rhetorical situation. The triangle is itself a small network relation. As Lloyd Bitzer put it, "Rhetorical situation may be defined as a complex of persons, events, objects, and relations presenting an actual or potential exigence" (1968, 3). When we see it as more complicated, we can see how that triangle gets further stretched and skewed. Our texts connect. As such, we might begin to see the ways things connect in our weird world of networks and continue pushing rhetorical strangeness. Of course, a common sentiment, which appears in the lyrics penned by King Missile, is true enough: you "want to be different, just like everybody else" (1991)—and in that is our collective tension scrambling for the surface, desiring something like interface.

And yet . . . Jeff Rice warns, "Networks, however, encompass connectivity as well as dysconnectivity; they shape relations; they circulate relations" (2007, 306–07). He also notes how they get us in and out of our compositional boxes. And here, we drift off and imagine lace, leaf patterns, fractals. These complexities affect (and possibly effect) realities; again, Bitzer helpfully explains, "Rhetoric is a mode of altering reality, not by the direct application of energy to objects, but by the creation of

https://doi.org/10.7330/9781646422821.c006

discourse which changes reality through the mediation of thought and action" (1968, 3–4). The complexity of reality is strange in the ways that its many parts gesture toward one another and are made potentially less strange in their relations.

Because of the complex network of infinite strangers in our universe, we have to keep opening our minds to the kinds of possible strangers and strangenesses that are out there, as well as the extent of our own strangeness as a kind of variable and as a fundamental power. We can reimagine the question of meeting someone new as, perhaps, "Hey, stranger, how many are you?" And the answer will always be, "We are legion." There are other strangers, bits of code, cumulus clouds, nematodes, the swirl of technologies around us, each influencing their own bit of strangeness upon the world. Within the flow of information technologies, rhetorical studies are sure to benefit from a continual reconsideration of how particularly strange moves can persuade within a chaotic deluge of totalizing media. But the mixture or overlapping connection of media can offer something. Geoff Sirc helpfully explains that in "creating a kind of creole of conversation and prose, the network allows for writing as *dérive*; allows, in fact, the *dérive* to count as writing, to replace the (uni)formalism of standard exposition" (Sirc 2002, 197). He adds, "I prefer writing as a road map to strange, new places over writing that simply charts again the same, well-worn ground" (197): I do too. I'm done with the same, well-worn ground. I need a condiment other than ketchup. I need to branch out and broaden my horizons. The network of diverging roads offers so much more than the fantasy of the single standard that we've imagined. And we should also remember that most of what resides in the network usually exists outside of perception—the receding other members of rhetorical playing fields.

Since one may consider all kinds of forms as media—a concrete sidewalk, an outfit, or a lamp—I believe that defamiliarization still has room to speak to all forms of rhetorical discourse even when we broaden what we allow as media, rhetoric, composition, and design. When I look at a lamp, it becomes especially rhetorical when my view of it is destabilized, when it is not in its normal state, when it is made strange. I can make a lamp strange simply by moving it around the room to an unfamiliar place, by breaking it, or by refiguring or reshaping it altogether. The discomfort elicited by such shifts need not be uncomfortable to the point of pain, only to the point of noticing a difference. Or these reorientations, as we have noted, may elicit pleasure, as can come through the multilayering of harmonic voices—a chorus (from the Greek *khora*). Gregory L. Ulmer envisions how digitally networked rhetorical spaces naturally embrace choral composition. He posits, "Choral rhetoric depends upon this passage to and from" (2008). The relay signals or transit lines that make possible weirder expressions and receptions both challenge and enliven stranger rhetorics in practice. As Mari Lee Mifsud asks, "What does it mean in this digital age to be networked and to network?" (2018, 28). We know, as does Mifsud, that the layers will always take us deeper. There will always be other possible layers of our collective fabric, like a quilt. Thomas Rickert, in thinking about the complexity of all the rhetoric that surrounds us—creating an ambient rhetoric—also notes "the strangeness of the chōra, its status as a third kind" (2013, 59). This other voice works with us, within us, and without us. In the mass mapping of rhetorical constructions that float around us, Rickert also notes, "The writer writing is not alone, being always linked to or haunted by others, some familiar, some strange" (100). The solo genius composer is a myth, of course. The otherness of the haze of surrounding life helps and composes alongside us as part of the network.

Thinking about all the possible diverse and divergent connections possible rhetorically offers a different scope and reorientation. This reorientation can admittedly be disorienting, but we can and do embrace it. As Michael Joyce writes in *Othermindedness: The Emergence of Network Culture*, "Network culture is an othermindedness, a murky sense of a newly evolving consciousness and cognition alike . . . Network culture, if there is to be such a thing, calls us to a new mind" (2000, 1). This conceptual framework opens up different compositional possibilities than we're accustomed to, but it is an invaluable psychological shift that paves the way toward where these new options might evolve.

Our strangeness exists within a network of strange forces—measured as a quality of strangenesses that vary by degrees—and strangers—beings with rhetorical power. Joshua Cooper Ramo (along with this whole system that considers our collective convolutedness) poses a problem for us in writing, asking, "Weird machines and normal machines, weird networks and normal ones, people who have been made weird by technological manipulation and those who have not will live side by side. The question is: Do you know which you are?" (2016, 164). Are you the stranger rhetor or the welcoming/rejecting audience in the relay? This whole set of strange or weird relations constructs our very reality. And as Graham Harman writes in *Weird Realism*, "Reality itself is weird because reality itself is incommensurable with any attempt to represent or measure it" (2012, 51). While the impossibility of perfect objectivity is the challenge of comprehending the weirdness out there, in order for two beings to connect more fully, strangeness must exist, be expressed, and then be surpassed and assimilated/consumed. Energy is expelled in the rhetorical acts of strangers expended over time. In this process of strange rhetorical energy expenditure, some intentional relations become stronger and others become weakened.

Nathaniel Rivers, in his developing work on the strange defense of rhetoric, suggests that opening up the possibilities of who is involved in rhetorical interactions, including a host of stranger rhetors, produces what is increasingly possible through adding more voices. He offers a stranger rhetorical ecology where the "strangeness lies in the call for more relations and not less" (2015, 421) and hence blurs the lines between human and nonhuman rhetors. The sheer number of available rhetors, from giraffes to strange quarks, forces us to reconsider who we are in the rhetorical world as well as who or what else is actually rhetorical alongside ourselves. This both strengthens and weakens rhetoric by introducing precarious, contingent multiplicities. As an aside in one conversation with Rivers, echoing perhaps Freud's familiar/unfamiliar of the uncanny, he and I talked about how strange things are sometimes the closest things to us, perhaps a significant other or a child.

When we try to create connections with faraway others (distant either physically or conceptually), strange rhetoric is needed, and strange networks develop. When we think of strange networks, we might think of a dating network site only for farmers or wealthy people. We may recall having seen a list of strange, unknown Wi-Fi networks available, mostly locked—signals waiting there for someone to access in a public place. With wildly rhetorical networks, we relay information across vaster distances. This is rhetoric for aliens, for every neighbor. And in this very real sense, we might think of *The Golden Record*, a record dispatched along with the *Voyager* spacecraft in 1977 that contained sounds and images sent out into space in order to communicate with something out there. Specific gestures like this embody the hope that lies in reaching out toward strange networks and establishing distant connections and relations.

EXERCISING STRANGE COMPLEXITY

In practice, language and technology and humans and other beings all make rhetorical networks stranger in different capacities. Strange possibilities lie, for instance, in the networked reconfigurability of alphabetic text, words, and sentences into endless forms. Even fundamentally relational words such as conjunctions and prepositions orient objects in the world weirdly or normally, from "The spoon was on the table, and she picked it up" to "The table was on the spoon, so she picked it over." Connotations and denotations too suggest our own psychologically linguistic strange associations. Weirdness lies in language. As Ludwig Wittgenstein wrote: "If a lion could talk, we could not understand him" (1991, 190). And in thinking about our language as constitutive, we must also ask: Who will read you and who will you read? Push that. So, there remains the question of how stranger networks of language or communication might be constructed or construed.

In classes that I teach, I like to practice finding strange linkages with students to help ourselves brainstorm inventively for the next composition project. The stranger the better, I tell them. If, for example, a student is going to write about some common topic, we find novel linkages that can help us push into new territory. So, when we are composing, we shift from a normal relationship like mother to daughter toward something more surprising to make a point—such as the relationship of mother to concrete. We generate novelty to make associations that are more distant, creating more extreme ratios.

We practice this by exploring what strange connections we can discover through mind-mapping exercises. So, I might have one student give the next student a noun to write down in the middle of the page, and then they begin branching words off of the seed word for about three minutes. And I say things like, "How far can you go? How strange can you take it? And who can connect Justin Bieber to Christmas trees?" And some of them do. They find weird ways to link through free association. Or we might play Six Degrees of Kevin Bacon on Wikipedia. Here we pick a random Wikipedia article and try to see how many clicks it takes us to get to Kevin Bacon, keeping track. Again, we are finding associations—weird linkages.

Darwin famously sketched a branching figure where he was trying to puzzle out the workings of interconnected life, with a side note: "I think" (Darwin 1837). The evolutionary progressions of our compositional works are interdependent upon an astonishing number of linkages. The linkages can themselves evolve, taking different shapes depending on the relationships of different nodes.

Increasing relations is inherently valuable—invaluable. We would not be the same without these relations. What does a node and a connecting line represent in a strange network? What makes a network strange? The distance in stranger networks is further between nodes. The associations are wider. Multiplicities are, after all, much better than the antagonism generated in duplicity. And we see them as well in the effects of multiple overlapping rhetorical figures and forms at work within a text. What

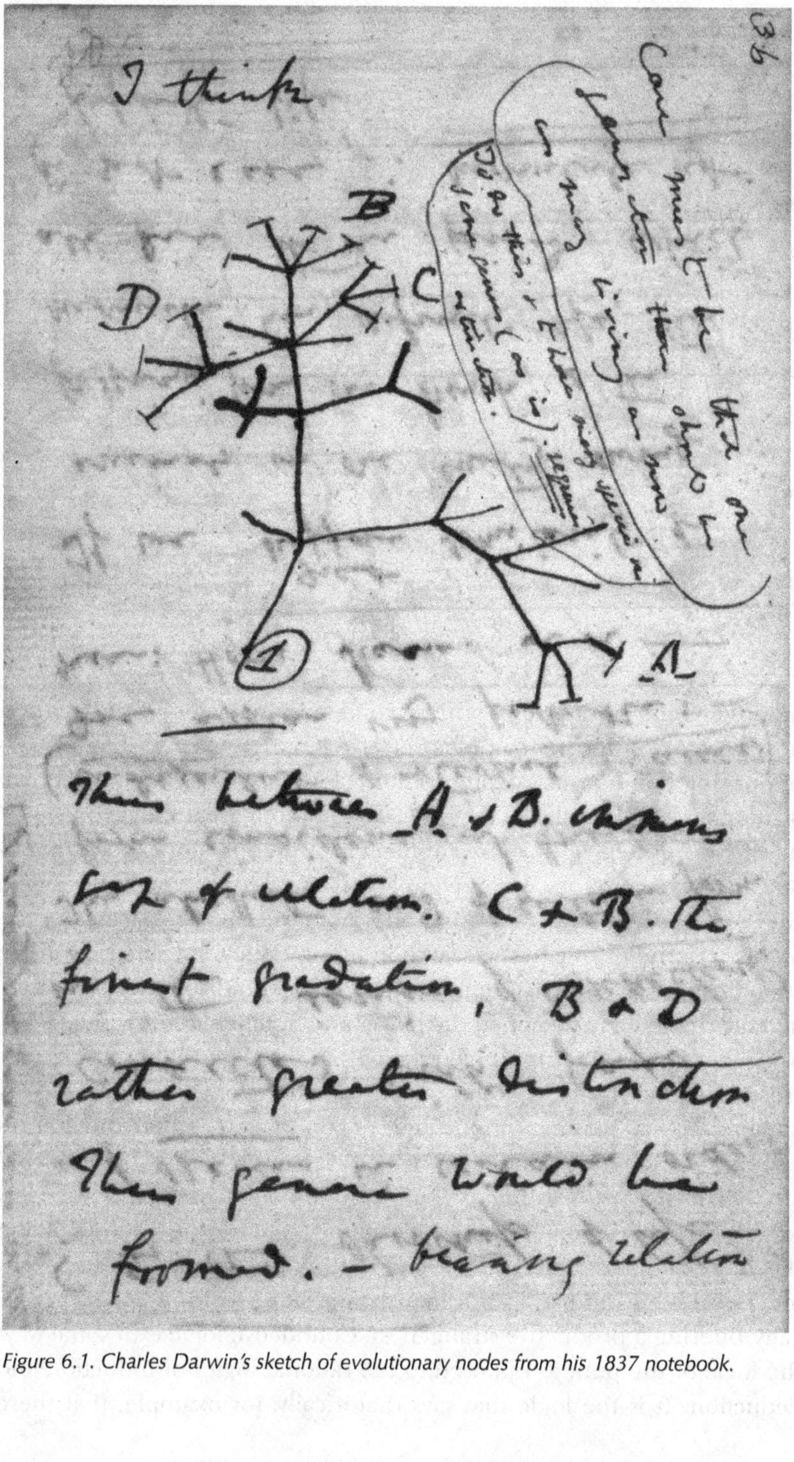

Figure 6.1. Charles Darwin's sketch of evolutionary nodes from his 1837 notebook.

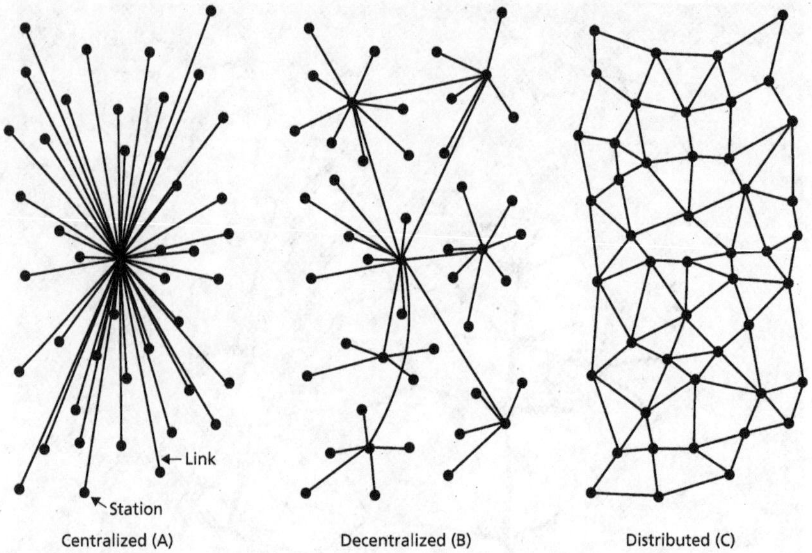

Figure 6.2. Network designs from Paul Baran (1964), used with explicit permission from Rand Corp.

other generative practices might we come up with by looking at strangeness as a force within a complex set of relations? As Anne Lamott says of pushing boundaries in composition, "let it all pour out and then let it romp all over the place" to arrive at something great "that you would never have gotten to by more rational, grown-up means" (2007, 22). If we can get any distance out of complex strangeness, we might be able to shift our learning and composing into more interesting spaces.

Paul Baran, for one, did research in the 1960s for the air force on the strengths of differently structured networks: centralized, decentralized, and distributed. He imagined the power and potential of distributed networks because of their multiple relations and outlined different options (see fig. 6.2). Perhaps relatedly, in the near-heretical *Heuretics*, Gregory Ulmer suggests "writing with the logic of conduction," where one follows a "train of thought" (1994, 210) or an "electronic path of 'inference'" (195). This suggests for him a "change in thinking from linear indexical to network associational," a network that is "replacing (experimentally) the more standard serial processing" (36). This conductive logic is a logic of the gut and can appear in compositional frameworks rhetorically, offering a productive strangeness. Conductive logic is in some ways the logic of the pun, as opposed to the rational logics of induction and deduction. It is the logic that says rhetorically, for example, that there is no "us" in America, but there is a "me" and an "I." Still, these meaningless assertions have meaning for people, and can be persuasive and engaging in their novelty. These novel compositional logics are multiplex. As Byron Hawk writes, "Logic is not just the imposition of simplicity, linearity, and system onto the world or the chaotic power of language but also the knowledge that emerges from networks of relations, complexity, and noise" (2007, 186). This noise in the system (which might be a random fight with a lover or a spice you didn't expect) helps co-invent new forms. Hawk continues, "Movement through networks creates new links and new networks to be traveled through and re-linked. Likewise, rhetoric becomes a system that moves and evolves" (194). Students can learn to work with these logics to produce weird constructions or to interrogate them as they appear in various persuasive spaces.

The possibilities in uncanny digital pedagogies are offered by the likes of Siân Bayne, who writes, "When viewed through the lens of the digital uncanny, the established certainties of our social practices relating to how we are positioned toward our institutions, our texts, our own experience of 'being' as teachers and students, becomes new, rich and strange . . . Such pedagogies work positively, creatively and energetically with the new, disorienting spaces presented to us by digital mediation" (2010, 9). This creative potential is precisely what we can generate through the uncanny in various digital combinations.

We see also strange networked interactions across referents and references. You can see some in the index and bibliography of this text. These linkages too are strange networks, as is a bookshelf. A library is a bigger one. The world is bigger yet. Sometimes I encourage folks to pull down three to five random books from the shelf without looking to see what connections might lie in those samplings. Write for a stranger, or write about one. These are the exercises that generate strange relationships.

BOREDOM MAINTENANCE AND THE COMPLEX STAKEHOLDERS OF NOVELTY AND ESCAPE

In resisting and balancing our own fraught relationships with the boredom and buzz of the everyday, we can find tensions at work along the intersections of relationships within the universe around us. Strange composition cannot become the dominant composition, or totalitarian composition. Some might suppose that a strange apparatus could simply become a new apparatus. In its unfamiliarity, I think, it can never be wholly familiar. The strange is a moving target, but a target nonetheless. As a result, strange language is set up for change, not domination.

Some recent work in object-oriented rhetoric has given a different take on strangers as objects that humans are interpreting as nonhuman actants in the world. While I am hesitant, actually, to embrace a strictly post-human view of rhetoric, strangeness invites us to embrace those around us, human and nonhuman alike. I myself oscillate between a humanist view and one that includes humans within a vast ecology. This view is more expansive, seeing human visions of otherness among us and in between us. This tack offers a take on strange things in the world that helps us consider the rhetorical strangeness of all sorts of beings. Beyond (or alongside) the living, though, we must also face the infinite otherness of objects. Next time, notice the awkward nearness of the shampoo bottle rhetor sitting strangely with you in the shower.

There are many current allies that have taken up an object-oriented view with whom we must converse. It may feel like an additive *and, and, and, and* of interlocutors as we bring them all together into play. But this is how the connections get knitted and formed. For one, Jane Bennett's *Vibrant Matter* is an invitation in response to the universe of strangers calling us to consider the networks of the world differently. She writes on this different view of the world, "In this strange, *vital* materialism, there is no point of pure stillness, no indivisible atom that is not itself aquiver with virtual force" (2010, 57). This wildness of the world, Bennett suggests, presents "an irreducibly strange dimension of matter, an *out-side.* Thing-power is also kin to . . . radical alterity" (2010, 2–3). The power to create novelties or weird constructions lies in material like dirt just as much as the student writing a poem, song, or essay. The creativity of nature itself, or what the ancient Greeks meant by *phusis,* Bennett notes, suggests "a process of morphing, of formation and deformation, that is to say, of the becoming otherwise of things in motion as they enter into strange conjunctions with one another" (2010, 118). So, how do we regard these weird manifestations of wonder—these compositions and compositionists we typically do not recognize? We know how to read and assess an essay; we may be less comfortable reading tea leaves before they are cut from the plant.

When we notice the extent of the weird, wild world surrounding us, we may begin to see what attitudes can be shaped alongside rhetorical otherness. As Sara Ahmed explains, "I am the stranger, we are all strangers," and also "I would argue, in contrast, that we need to understand how identity is established through strange encounters without producing a universe of strangers" (2000, 6). In this sense, what Ahmed calls us to is understanding our identities—and beyond that, an understanding that does not push others away by producing strangers ourselves.

Strangers already exist in their own strangeness. When we produce added strangeness that is on top of what is already there, we unnecessarily alienate others—we produce animosity—and so create a doubled strangeness that obscures the wonderfully strange uniqueness of every individual. As such, we face a universe of infinite difference. This occurs in expressions of racial, gendered, formed bodies that are seen as more or less rhetorical.

Seeing rhetorical hubcaps and light switches as having their own removed strangeness broadens our view of where compositional interventions might occur. And yet the strange otherness of the hubcap does not involve the same stakes as an othered Black body being pulled over by the police. This post-humanism is not without humans, but broader and more inclusive. In this furthered sense, we can find new practices for composition that are more welcoming. As Casey Boyle writes, "As networked media help facilitate and generate more of our interactions, we are becoming more practiced in a betweenness and more sensitive to being in relation to an innumerable number of technological systems" (2018, 540). These systems may be set up to exclude or to link—that is the terrible power of a rhetoric that considers strangeness at work. The innumerable systems, technologies, and strangers that any one rhetor or composer encounters in any one day offer an endless reserve of potential combinations that might interlink perhaps endlessly, like a chain-link fence running throughout the universe.

Conceiving of strangeness as though it existed along a mesh, Timothy Morton discusses the complex nature of these ecologies, calling them "stranger relations." He works through helpful insights that outline how a complex ecology of a bunch of different strange things work in the world together. He explains:

> The ecological thought imagines interconnectedness, which I call the mesh. Who or what is interconnected with what or with whom? The mesh of interconnected things is vast, perhaps immeasurably so. Each entity in the mesh looks strange. Nothing exists all by itself, and so nothing is fully "itself" . . . Our encounter with other beings becomes profound. They are strange, even intrinsically strange. Getting to know them makes them stranger. When we talk about life forms, we're talking about strange strangers. The ecological thought imagines a multitude of entangled strange strangers. (2012, 15)

The entanglement of a host of different things or beings in the world makes a vast network of composed life. When we compose within this mesh, we further complicate it and also draw lines to connect pieces of it together conceptually for ourselves and others.

We can then begin to move across possible linkages with newfound gusto. The internet of things promises so much control over contemporary life that our collective interface is awash with iterations of rhetorical meaning. Jay David Bolter and Richard Grusin touch upon this in their book on remediation. They explain, "The hypermediated self is a network of affiliations, which are constantly shifting. It is the self of newsgroups and email, which may sometimes threaten to overwhelm the user by their sheer numbers but do not exactly immerse her. This networked self is constantly making and breaking connections, declaring allegiances and interests and then renouncing them" (2000, 232). In this sense, networks, like cyberspace, multiply and erase media; they create immediacy and distance as compositions are created within them. Networks that consider strangeness as an integral quality allow a measure of distance to be better considered—or even a better consideration of the field of proxemics, which is a consideration of space. Various networks allow strangers to exist more or less within them, at a distance. In a developing tension of increased globalization and intimacy, stranger rhetors are either unheard or potentially disruptive.

Not just valuing radical alterity, Jean Baudrillard worries about the absolute proximity of all things—the loss of a distinction between the exterior and the interior that occurs through continual connections that create a new form of schizophrenia. Disorientation is to be expected, of course, in our push for communication. In *The Ecstasy of Communication*, Baudrillard opines, "What characterizes [the schizophrenic] is less the loss of the real, the light years of estrangement from the real, the pathos of distance and radical separation, as is commonly said: but, very much to the contrary, the absolute proximity, the total instantaneity of things, the feeling of no defense, no retreat" (2012, 133). The constant creep of mediation makes it creepy—disallowing strangers and strangeness—creating pure homogeneity. At the end, Baudrillard suggests of the contemporary victim: "He is now only a pure screen, a switching center for all the networks of influence" (133). The anti-stranger becomes an unfortunate victim in his own hostility to getting his feathers ruffled, lost in the mere flood, awash in pure homogeneity. And yet, certainly there are strange networks always at play, strange influences that allow for a release from pure presence or inescapable exposure.

The political distancing that can then occur with one who is resistant to the push or pull of rhetorical strangeness threatens a kind of communicative fascism. That antagonist might be nationalist, preferring a certain kind of language and speaker, resisting a kind of rhetorical plurality that can exist within a more liberal democratic view. Asher Wolf writes in "Weird Networks in the Fight for Human Rights," "Bureaucracies are slow and lumbering and cope badly with weird networks" and "The complexity of weirdness gives humanity-orientated networks an edge over bureaucracies. It creates opportunities no one ever looked for before" (2018). Bureaucratic views disdain the other rhetor, the precious and weird voice not often allowed to speak. And yet Asher continues encouragingly and empoweringly, "So, the weirder you make things, the better. WEIRD UP your networks. Create strange friendships, make unusual alliances, with people from many backgrounds. Invite poets and anarchists and politicians and accountants and tradies [*sic*] and dog groomers to be part of a huge sprawling network that shares music and hope and weird memes and data science." This kind of stance is what makes compositional frameworks powerful and influential. Wolf also notes that weird's origins—as we noted at the beginning—refer to a twisting, turning, or rotation, suggesting that "weirdness is literally revolutionary. Weirdness is a turning point, because it creates unexpected complexity in systems and therefore creates new opportunities for change (as well as many challenges.)" Strangeness as a power within a network of powers allows us to consider what moves are possible for pushing certain voices within the fray. Opportunities for change and twists are what press along the wires connecting us all in every interface.

FROM DIGITAL TO ANALOG AND BACK ACROSS SPACE AND TIME

What a strangely persistent metaphor Deleuze and Guattari have given us in the rhizome. As opposed to arborescent, or tree-like, binaristic relations, they invite us to consider a stranger enmeshment. They (emphatically plural) write, "Any point of a rhizome can be connected to anything other, and must be," including "the best and the worst," and "ceaselessly establishes connections between semiotic chains" (1987, 7). Imagining hyphae pushing or meshing into a tree so that I don't know which is which unsettles me, like cancer or fungus growing into the skin. I have trypophobia. This haunting hybridity exists as the ghost in networks. The trouble with the rhizome metaphor is that it is difficult to see interesting patterns in a mesh of hyphae—there is too much entanglement to make any sense of a rhizomatic text, which is every text. But this also allows for entanglement with an other that is typically not expected or presumed. Presumptions about how things *should* connect—rhetorically or otherwise—are in fact what typically separate and cause rhetorical interchanges to fail. If more interesting offspring are to be produced, then we cannot keep segregating different potential partners.

The interconnectedness we see in social networks has a long residual history that comes from technologies and forms that are at work in our various compositions. As audiences, we move through both time and forms or structures, noticing either what is different or the same about our surroundings. As Caroline Levine expresses in her book *Forms*, "I draw attention in particular to the ways that different arrangements can collide to strange effect, with minor forms sometimes disrupting or rerouting major ones" (2018, 18). These strange effects have meaningful effects. Levine notes that these interfaces or confrontations occur in a moment or an event that she calls "the collision" or "the strange encounter between two or more forms that sometimes reroutes intention and ideology" (18). The recontextualization that happens with a rhetor or a text within the world as they are confronted affects the network surrounding it and then reverberates out. Levine herself also notes the power of networked forms, explaining, "A formalist approach advocates paying careful attention to the multiplicity of networks and especially to their differences" (114). Networks also overlap, converging and diverging along multiple paths, creating similarity and difference. It is easier to focus on one network; Levine agrees, "To be sure, it is clarifying and practical to isolate a single network and pursue its impact, since when networks are thrown together they can seem messy or incoherent" (114). However, that very incoherence of a text presents the potential of noticeable glossolalia that we saw in the previous chapter, or even new combinations. In this way, we can agree with Levine's assertion that "all networks afford connectivity; all create links between disconnected nodes" (114). Connection or interfacing across the network's expanse is what rhetoric does in practice, and these linkages occur between stranger rhetors and stranger perceivers.

When we compose a strange object or a strange relation within or among objects, we question the possible distance or a measure of outsideness within a matrix. So, if we take a queer student's nonstandard piece, for example, what might we make of it? How does it fit? How does it not? And why (or in what ways) does any of that matter? Weird assemblages present different forms in conjunction with other forms—creating a spectral swath of strangeness in the universe. Gaining a better sense of these networked relations offers a greater rhetorical sensitivity. Derek Mueller suggests developing a *network sense*, which he describes in this way: "Tendering network sense requires a facility for recognizing and tracing relationships, for engaging in focused reading and exploratory reading, and for noticing connections among programs and people, publications and conferences, difficult questions and myriad stakeholders" (2017, 161). Seeing or sensing these relations develops our rhetorical awareness among various composite members of any compositional situation.

A strange relation may be established—like when you play a game of Red Rover and hold hands with someone you don't know . . . and hold on hard. Or we may consider the strange relation that comes into existence when a speaker steps up to a microphone in front of a crowd of strangers, and there's a bit of feedback, amplified sound from the electricity running into the system from some far-off place in the city where no one wants to live. We have to think of the weaving of a text as establishing a set of strange relations that are themselves rhetorical—like imagining knitting yarn along with earthworms and tampon strings. This is the basis for composing strange relations.

OTHER THINGS/BEINGS MAKE IT STRANGER

Have any of the multitude of strangers you've encountered ever changed your life? Perhaps you have entertained an angel (or a monster) unaware. Or perhaps you noticed. An essential question is "Who's in?"

In *Strangers to Ourselves,* Julia Kristeva serves as a spirit guide for beings journeying out into strange territory. In her conclusion, entitled "In Practice . . . ," she suggests that we collectively own "a weakness whose other name is our radical strangeness" (1994, 195). Pushing into this weakness becomes a way of strengthening our selves—or at least a way of coming to terms. She warns, "Let us not seek to solidify, to turn the otherness of the foreigner into a thing. Let us merely touch it, brush by it, without giving it a permanent structure" (3). And as writers and artists and critics, let us not pet ourselves too self-satisfactorily for loving and not killing the other. We all contain multitudes. If we are all foreigners, then no one is a foreigner. The nationalism or boundary lines of compositional norms eject those who do it differently. Kristeva offers an ethics of composing within our strange networked life, explaining that in our collective desire, our collective uncanny strangeness is the "ultimate condition of our being *with* others" (192). There is no real inherent problem. There is nothing really to correct. We are not to figure out or fix otherness that we encounter. She explains how in universality Freud invites us "not to integrate foreigners and even less so to hunt them down, but rather to welcome them to that uncanny strangeness, which is as much theirs as it is ours" (192). The final ethical question, the one she begins with, is this: "Can the 'foreigner,' who was the 'enemy' in primitive societies, disappear from modern societies?"

(1). What a wonderful question! This is the ethical residue—a measure of foreignness—that every relation is left with.

When, if ever, does it all become too much? Is separation from the stranger even possible? Or must we always address it—give it a post office box? And in pinning it down, do we not also cut it off—kill the linkages? Achille Mbembe addresses this inquiry himself in *Necropolitics*, asking, "The Other's burden having become too overwhelming, would it not be better for my life to stop being linked to its presence, as much as its to mine?" (2019, 3). If strangeness seems too much, we do well to find our inbuilt, inescapable linkages to that strangeness—to do the work of opening up. Mbembe continues, "Today, manifestly little interest is shown in making the circle more inclusive. Rather, the idea is to make borders as the primitive form of keeping at bay enemies, intruders, and strangers—all those who are not one of us" (3). But we must reattune our interests and our interestedness toward inclusion for those who are not "one of us." Because we continue pretending, don't we, there is a possibility of shutting things down, or what Mbembe calls "the hallucinatory dream of a 'community without strangers' " (2019, 6). We need new dreams, or to stop hoping for a kind of imagined simplicity that comes through excision.

Meanwhile, we long for the safe familiarity of those conventions that have worked in the past. This natural reaction is akin to grabbing onto the edge of bed for reassurance when you jump awake from a jolting dream. Our sense of stability gets upturned easily, and things become complicated pretty quickly. Our compositional programs are complex; our rhetorical relations are complex. These intersections multiply, creating a host of different intersections. No rhetor is an island. As John Donne's poem suggests, every rhetor "is a piece of the continent, a part of the main" (1999, 101). All of this metaphorical reflection on our relations makes me think of Jenga. And a few interesting things about Jenga: the game was invented by a woman named Leslie Scott, who was born in Tanzania. And most of us have some familiarity with it. The word *jenga* comes from the Swahili word meaning "to build," which is often a metaphor that we use when talking about our compositions. The thing about moving that first Jenga piece is that it always affects all the other fifty-three pieces in the tower. You move one thing, and it affects all the others, and you hope everything doesn't come crashing down.

This is how changes and rhetorical interactions and compositions happen. There are ripple effects and reverberations. Change doesn't happen in a vacuum—because nature abhors it. Sketching and mapping out our strange relations is difficult, if not sometimes totally impossible.

This hairy work of analyzing the spread of agency might be reminiscent of the television character who starts to go a little nuts, joining pictures together with string on the wall. The trope is actually referred to as a crazy wall in film, so there's that. You may try to map out a rhetorical relation now and see where it takes you. But writing is raucous and wild and people are wild, so why would we expect any rhetorical program to be normal and safe and sound? But alas, to quote Kristeva one last time, "The (professional, intellectual, affective) aim that some set for themselves in such an unrestrained fugue is already a betrayal of strangeness, for as he chooses a program he allows himself a respite or residence" (1994, 6). This means that in order to succeed, we betray our strangeness, or strangeness itself, to compose safely or give ourselves a rest from the work that rhetorical strangeness asks of us. The goal, perhaps, is to not ignore that a text feels different and perhaps uncomfortable, but to acknowledge this and push into appreciating it for what it is, allowing it to be there in your own gut.

In our contemporaneous sociality of networks, everything is coming at us from everywhere all the time. #nofilter. It's like that old song: the hip bone's connected to the leg bone . . . I've built wonderful relationships, and terrible ones. We strive to find good connections that work—not everyone is happy with every strange change, surprise, surprise. All the while, we are connected to other institutions, to each other, all of you, to the educational system, to tax policies, to parents, to our students' lovers waiting on them to finish their essays, to the electrical grid, to your favorite coffee company, to the other countries who will one day—perhaps—read our writing. It is the relationship of the migrant worker to your dinner table and then to your classroom and the trashcan in your classroom to the waste worker, and the bathrooms at your school to the janitorial staff who buy from big-box stores to save money. And the strange network of composition also involves the relationship of paper mills, computer companies, graphite mines, and you. All the while, we are drowning in dings and an endless flood of messages.

There is safety in numbers, composed of strangers, in looking at and out for one another. Danielle Allen in *Talking to Strangers* says that strangers are better than police, suggesting "Through interaction, even as strangers, citizens draw each other into networks of mutual responsibility" (2006, 167). So, we learn and expand and see new forms and ideas by talking to others. Others are the best source of novelty. Talking out an idea with someone new is the best way to develop and push it further toward what it can be. As Lauren Berlant and Kathleen Stewart note in *The Hundreds*, "A stranger exchange is a flickering resource"

(2019, 22). What have you taken from a stranger? What do they have to offer? And what have you offered as a stranger?

TECHNOLOGIES MAKE IT STRANGER

What technological systems make or allow or produce strangeness best? Does a hive mind produce novelty or an even keel? If we might think of our networks as ruled and having rules, we then also must wonder who writes those, and who is affected. Alexander Galloway and Eugene Thacker worry about the lack of freeplay in our networks because of the written protocols governing them. They suggest in *The Exploit: A Theory of Networks*, "Perhaps there is no greater lesson about networks than the lesson about control: networks, by their mere existence, are not liberating; they exercise novel forms of control that operate at a level that is anonymous and nonhuman, which is to say material" (2007, 5). What does this mean for us? It means that in compositional or rhetorical enframings, there are always rules imposed—from the relational structure of whatever network is at work. But because networks are vast by nature, their rules have space, room for otherness that can find emplacement within the structure. This means that even though conventions might expect certain things, other forms and deviations will arise, and some will be accepted within the framework.

Perhaps most famously, Bruno Latour, discussing actor-network theory, explains in *Reassembling the Social*, "A network is not what is represented in the text, but what readies the text to take the relay of actors as mediators. The consequence is that you can provide an actor-network account of topics which have in no way the shape of a network—a symphony, a piece of legislation, a rock from the moon, an engraving. Conversely, you may well write about technical networks—television, e-mails, satellites, salesforce—without at any point providing an actor-network account" (2007, 131). So, whatever we compose—and that whatever can be anything at all—we create a small arrangement, or what Latour calls an actor-network. This assemblage can take on infinite shapes. But the contemporary philosopher Manuel DeLanda suggests, "Assemblages are always composed of heterogeneous components" (2016, 20). Objections to this require us to see more fully any assemblage; if we only see one kind of thing, we need to see what other relations might be at work. And DeLanda also suggests that an assemblage can grow and contain other assemblages. If sociality is becoming more connected, more mixed, then we cannot help but wonder: does the cosmos increase in strangeness? If the second law of thermodynamics is to be believed, everything is always becoming more homogenous. The death of heterogeneity is inevitable. Nevertheless, when we stack a shell on top of a rock, a doodad on top of a thingamajig, or an adjective on a noun, we build kinships, reversing decimation and desolation and meaninglessness. In this politicization or relationality of strange networks and their potential for homogenization, we can see the possibilities and dangers of certain kinds of linkages that remain conventional and normative.

In our rhetorical relations, must we always see the division or separation that creates strangers or strangeness? As Deleuze and Guattari imagined a body without organs, it may be impossible to imagine rhetoric without distance—without a line of flight moving from one node to another. This involves some conceptual pushing and experimentation. As they explain: "This is how it should be done. Lodge yourself on a stratum, experiment with the opportunities it offers, find an advantageous place on it, find potential movements of deterritorialization, possible lines of flight, experience them, produce flow conjunctions here and there, try out continua of intensities segment by segment, have a small plot of new land at all times. It is through a meticulous relation with the strata that one succeeds in freeing lines of flight, causing conjugated flows to pass and escape and bringing forth continuous intensities for a BwO" (1987, 161). The BwO, or Body without Organs, represents a familiar figure or metaphor for considering strange relationships. In whatever metaphorical conjugal relations we might purport to create through textuality and commiseration, distance always equals strangeness. Still, the quality of closeness also persists as a goal of every rhetorical act or text.

Being welcome in a complex system is a little like feeling at home in the hubbub of a crowd. The fittingness of fitting in, whether you are writing, speaking, or just being leaves us with a moral challenge. Jim Brown writes in *Ethical Programs*, "Networked life invites others, meaning that audiences, texts, and contexts become infinitely more complicated" (2015). This complexity offers a challenge to audiences as we decide how and when to accept strange texts. As Brown also notes, the concept of a rhetorical ecology, or a conglomerate, comes from Jenny Edbauer (2005, 5), who also presents it as pertaining to an ethics. And in this perspective, the question remains who or what is in? This final lingering question aligns with that old practice of what we call excommunication. In another collaborative text with Galloway on networks called *Excommunication*, Thacker reflects, "That the human sensorium can be augmented, transformed, or, in some instances, 'see' more than a human subject is prepared to see—this is the premise of what we can term 'weird media'" (Galloway, Thacker, and Wark 2013, 132–33). That mediators will always exist within a network allows the frame to pass signals back and forth. But some relays will inevitably be rejected, preventing certain *communiqués.*

Who gets to be different in the system, and who gets co-opted into sameness? This is a question that always remains for us to answer—especially because of the oft agonistic nature of rhetoric. Malcolm Gladwell writes in *Talking to Strangers,* "Sometimes the best conversations between strangers allow the stranger to remain a stranger" (2019, xii). And the combative hostility within a system must allow simultaneous disagreement and difference with some threads of connectivity. Gladwell closes his book: "Because we do not know how to talk to strangers, what do we do when things go awry with strangers? We blame the stranger" (566). While it can be corruptive or corrosive, hostility is inherent within any system of relations—either judgment about a text that one does not or cannot accept or judgment of the rhetor themselves.

Furthermore, Maria Bezaitis argues in *Why We Need Strangeness* that strangeness offers a political strategy now more than ever because social media currently give us terribly homogenous echo chambers and perspectival sameness. She advocates for strangeness: "We have to change the norms. We have to change the norms in order to enable new kinds of technologies as a basis for new kinds of businesses" (2013). When corporate structures rehearse bland traditions, no one wins. Bezaitis pushes further, asking, "What interesting questions lie ahead for us in this world of no strangers? How might we think differently about our relations with people? How might we think differently about our relations with distributed groups of people? How might we think differently about our relations with technologies, things that effectively become social participants in their own right? The range of digital relations is extraordinary. In the context of this broad range of digital relations, safely seeking strangeness might very well be a new basis for that innovation." If we forego collective innovation that comes by encouraging various establishments to explore difference, we lose out.

In this intricate circuitry of rhetorical composition, we see the threads that can weave infinitely unusual patterns, configurations, arrangements. On and off and through the grid of contemporary communicative life, strangeness surges to create noticeable disruptions in the composite field. The machines, humans, and other generators of meaning collectively form a wide net.

And yet, total escape is not possible from the net of the network. As Steven Shaviro writes in *Connected,* "In short, if you're connected, you're fucked" (2003, 3). But maybe a little bit of that is okay; maybe we don't really want anything else anyways, especially if another route isn't possible. In the composition of rhetorical media, we have to take care how we connect, how we link in, how we deliver whatever we've got into the system. Bad gateways in the delivery path can bomb or come face-to-face with a wall. Still, there is no such thing as freedom to do strange things without affecting others. And at times it may feel like we're sailing all over the place trying to reroute a river—without really wanting to. Foucault has this quotation about freedom and ships that I love and use often. It helps us think about this metaphor of Boats. Floods. Currents. He writes,

> Locked in the ship from which he could not escape, the madman was handed over to the thousand-armed river, to the sea where all paths cross, and the great uncertainty that surrounds all things. A prisoner in the midst of the ultimate freedom, on the most open road of all, chained solidly to the infinite crossroads. (2013, 11)

The point is that we never really completely find solid ground, and that's okay. There's nothing to do but embrace that. But also, we should not compose so tightly that we can't fluctuate. We can change a text now without the whole system crashing. If you tie a boat too tightly to a dock, it'll crash in a storm. You have to have some give, some play in the structure.

Mapping the interrelated nodes that affect one another within the structure of rhetorical relations and strange texts is useful for anyone affiliated with them: instructors, chairs, deans, students, their dogs and cats, and so on. We may feel siloed sometimes, but we aren't. The constellation of effects reverberates out. These slight shifts happen slowly but surely, like turning a massive ship. Ships are at the mercy of the wind and the currents, but they also have rudders, so we are not powerless. There's a lot of power wrapped up in all of the stakeholders in strangely rhetorical compositions—meaning all compositions—and it's pretty decentralized; we are not alone, and that's a good thing.

We might imagine pushing off of some momentary platform to compose strangely, making an exceptional state of making, an overlay on the norm. In this outside space, we create space, making room for new novelties to arise within the system.

EVERYTHING, EVERYWHERE, ALWAYS: SKELETONS AND BOOKRACKS

Totalizing immersion can tend to facilitate more boredom than striking composition. The ubiquity and inescapability of rhetorical life and digital life make these topics necessary for inquiry. Yet our tools are also regularly ready to hand. Our limitations only lie in preferences and strengths and social agreements around certain modes and media. We experience circles of perception that lie within each person's mind—worlds as structured (seemingly around) but actually within. Heidegger's term, *Gestell*, may help to unpack whether our perceptive shroud is outside or inside of the human brain—a networked structure in and of itself.

Martin Heidegger was intensely interested in the questions of "the open" concerning art and technology, all of which will be relevant to this exploration. Heidegger developed his concept of Gestell to consider how humanity is immersed or enframed in its own technology or manufactured instrumentation; humanity exists within technology. Heidegger's thinking, of course, cannot be wholly disentangled from Nazism, which is worth noting when we think through these metaphors of ordering in and around humans. Heidegger explains, "We now name that challenging claim which gathers man thither to order the self-revealing as standing-reserve: 'Ge-stell' [Enframing]" (1977, 19). The gathering of men and women is a challenging thought, placing revelation in reserve—as an aside. Here sensitization, or revealing, becomes secondary as the ordering of peoples occurs through the means of different technologies set up about them.

Heidegger also observes, "According to ordinary usage, the word *Gestell* [frame] means some kind of apparatus, e.g., a bookrack. *Gestell* is also the name for a skeleton" (1977, 20). The double metaphor here is invaluable and of some importance. The equivocation of the pun allows a question to arise as to whether mediation of different immersive technologies occurs within humans or outside them. A skeleton supports a human by existing within him or her, but the bookrack supports the book by standing outside of the object. The skeleton is an assemblage, that haunting iconic representative of strangeness. Here mediation, then, offers a double situation or a duality, both inside of us *and* outside, perhaps like floating in a body of water. Mediating work oscillating inside and outside us is problematic in that these technologies may present themselves outside of our bodies, or even within our minds, simultaneously encircling us and filling us up. The oscillation of mediation, being both out-there and in-here, is strangely all-consuming.

Heidegger continues exploring the nature of modern enframing. He elaborates upon a trend that has been moving alongside technological innovation, inspired to write this essay, "The Question Concerning Technology," because of the shifts in this framing. Finally, though,

Heidegger writes about what this kind of enframing does, the implications for technologies, that "*poiesis*, lets what presences come forth into unconcealment" (1977, 21). *Poiesis*, or making, allows the hidden to become unhidden. Making allows truth to appear, a phrase that is somewhat of a redundancy since truth is essentially appearance itself. In Heidegger's essay "The Origin of the Work of Art," found in *Poetry, Language, Thought*, he elaborates on the nature of unconcealing that happens through *kunstwerk*, or *poesis* (2013).

In this second essay, Heidegger writes about "this situation in which we let things encounter us without mediation" (2013, 25). Here, Heidegger talks about setting up a world in a work of art that reveals the nature of its presence. Still, familiar things lie around us that are imperceptible, or at least presently unperceived. Heidegger says of these familiar things, "What seems natural to us is probably just something familiar in a long tradition that has forgotten the unfamiliar source from which it arose. And yet this unfamiliar source once struck man as strange and caused him to think and to wonder" (2013, 24). That lack of wonder with so many familiar things is the withdrawing of the earth in our everyday lives. According to Heidegger, "The world worlds, and is more fully in being than the tangible and perceptible realm in which we believe ourselves to be at home" (2013, 44). The "at home" here is reminiscent of Freud's canny reality—that which we can grasp, but it is simultaneously knowable and unknowable, present and absent. "The world is not the mere collection of the countable or uncountable, familiar and unfamiliar things that are just there" (2013, 44), Heidegger challenges. Things are *just there* all around us constantly. They do nothing more than just sit there, out of our perception, out of our worlds, which is necessary—we cannot expect to pay attention to everything at once. But certain kinds of artistic compositions, according to Heidegger, can point us to objects with a renewed sense of awareness. As such, media and genres and texts, all in different modes, are all around us constantly. We often say that rhetoric is everywhere around us. The world is composed—sometimes boringly, sometimes strikingly so.

Thinking through whatever surrounds us, whether it is media, culture, or structures, the thought is apparent across many disciplines. Pierre Bourdieu works through a field/habitus framework that also speaks to this issue of liminal enframing from a sociological perspective. Sociology, psychology, biology, narratology, and so on all have ways of understanding how humans are inside of other things, mediated, *pre*figured by things outside of themselves. Sociologically, Bourdieu's view is that fields and *habitus* function together to arrive at a networked sensation of reality that is external to objectivity and subjectivity, or mind-body dualism. In a discussion of Gustave Flaubert's writing, Bourdieu writes, "The genetic structuralism I propose is designed to understand both the genesis of social structures—the literary field—and the genesis of the dispositions of the habitus of the agents who are involved in these structures" (1993, 162). Social structures are structured—a tautology. Fine, but we also must begin to understand, says Bourdieu, their genesis, how they begin to become structured. How are structures invented, and then reinvented? Bourdieu continues:

> This is not self evident. For example, historians of art and literature, victims of what I call the illusion of the constancy of the nominal, retrospectively transport, in their analyses of cultural productions prior to the second half of the nineteenth century, definitions of the writer and the artist which are entirely recent historical inventions and which, having become constitutive of our cultural universe, appear to us as a given. (162)

Given universes either offer no room for invention or all the room in the . . . universe. Within a static field, the space for invention may always be primed for disruption. Yet, as we interrogate wonderfully experimental forms of composition, we also interrogate the illusion of constancy—clear static plains, ready to be bombed by surprisingly wonderful composition strategies.

Jean-Luc Nancy's conception of *oikos* is explained in the term *ecotechnics.* He claims, "There is no longer any *polis* since the *oikos* is everywhere: the housekeeping of the world as a single household" (2000, 135). The ubiquity of the *oikos* paired with the ubiquity of contemporary media presents an urgency, an exigency, on the part of researchers to investigate the nature of this social and ecological context.

Giorgio Agamben's work *What Is an Apparatus?* helps elucidate further the structure of our environments, written and otherwise. He explains the apparatus as "literally anything that has in some way the capacity to capture, orient, determine, intercept, model, control, or secure the gestures, behaviors, opinions, or discourses of living beings" (2009, 14). Like the enframing of Heidegger, Agamben here outlines one of Michel Foucault's terms, the *dispositif.* The apparatus is a device. Foucault never really defined this term clearly. He attempts to get at the term in an interview contained in *Power/Knowledge,* in which, Foucault explains:

> What I'm trying to pick out with this term is, firstly, a thoroughly heterogeneous ensemble consisting of discourses, institutions, architectural forms, regulatory decisions, laws, administrative measures, scientific statements, philosophical, moral and philanthropic propositions—in short, the said as much as the unsaid. Such are the elements of the apparatus. The

> apparatus itself is the system of relations that can be established between these elements.
>
> Secondly, what I am trying to identify in this apparatus is precisely the nature of the connection that can exist between these heterogeneous elements. (1980, 194)

In Agamben's definition, the device may be a cell phone, an object that includes a set of relationships that govern human experience. In Foucault's thinking, the apparatus represents heterogeneity among elements through what we think of as structuralist ideology. The heterogeneity of elements leads humans to begin to ignore the relationships of normal structures, structures of discourses, institutions, architectural forms, and so on that lead us into being passive readers. Agamben's definition explains how these devices capture and control living beings. And these devices are literal—they are real objects like televisions, roads, cars, laptops, pens, paper, electrical outlets, cameras, and . . . yes . . . cell phones, now more ubiquitous than ever.

Bernard Stiegler similarly takes up Heidegger's term and broadens it, calling it *technics*. Introducing the term, he redefines it: "As production (*poiesis*), technics is a 'way of revealing.' Like *poiesis*, it brings into being what is not" (1998, 9). He continues the definitional outline: "As a 'process of exteriorization,' technics is the pursuit of life by means other than life" (17). Throughout the three sprawling philosophical texts in the *Technics and Time* trilogy that have been released in English, Stiegler has imagined the world wrapped and dependent upon the tools that make us human.

In Stiegler's first book of the trilogy, Epimetheus has forgotten to give humans the tool of fire. The tool is forgotten in the same way that Heidegger suggests that the hammer is forgotten when it is functioning, ready to hand for its user. The tool is primarily what makes us human, according to the myth, where Prometheus, in his foresight, brings humans technics and the ability to live within time. The presence of tools for humans, though they go unnoticed, allows humans to live *within* a world that is *composed* of structures and forms to which we are blind. The goal of seeing strangeness's vast interlinkages is not to make humans aware of all of our sensorium's mediation—that would be what William James called "one big blooming buzzing Confusion" (1920, 16). Any way that our *being-in* is phrased, immersive mediation still implies a human being inside or within some structure. In other words, the artificial tools that make us human become naturalized; they become aspects that we necessarily ignore for the sake of everyday life. The body is always already inside this everyday life. The totality of the structures of our day-to-day life is often perceived as reality. Our aim is not to escape reality—that remains an impossibility, of course. We would simply like to see outside of the structures we have created—a *sensation* of novelty, of *seeing-outside.*

To this end, media shape our *habitus* or our *oikos,* the places we live. But media also create an apparatus on top of our *habitus,* and while these two terms intersect, they are distinct from one another. *Oikos* is the source of our concept of ecology. It is the household as opposed to the *polis.* And yet the household is also political, although separate from (but inside) politics, somewhat independent of but depended upon them. The home may be organized, politicized, by a scientific interest, or endeavor, in a "greener" ecology. We want the world to be natural and special, not mediated to the point of banality. Not crushed. We want some iteration of a just co-survival.

WHAT NOW? WHAT'S NEW?

If you cannot see the strangeness in a particular rhetorical situation at first, look again; it is there. Nothing's new except for what we can see anew in ourselves. If we keep going, we will find new things. They are out there. And we can't help, really, but to do that now. Our desire for novelty and strangeness and our own rhetoricity are all inbuilt, ingrained, like our lungs. As Jay Dolmage imagines it, there may be a freer, kinder possibility in this more expansive view of our collective composing bodies: "I believe that what is needed is an expansive approach to writing as well as to textuality. If there are ways to use revision not just to create a better product, but to lay bare, to re-sense, then we could realize the ways texts connect to one another, connect us to one another, the way texts are embodied, and how such connections are never smooth but are rather tangled, *strange,* and result sometimes in noise and confusion, in something messy" (2012, 120; emphasis added). In this complex system, we can see the positive potential of our inter-reliance on strangers all around us. As such, we might consider the ways that strange compositions help rhetors connect across a broad range of networks in a world haunted by distance. Depending on each other—each of us different—allows us to progress collectively and grow together.

Any of these terms pertaining to thinking through rhetorical networks of strangeness are essentially pointing to relationships. Our relationality and how we move one another are at the heart of the matter—and the only remaining question is how far will we go? We have been mapping complex insiderness and outsiderness within a complex system of mostly conventional relays—which means that certain texts stand out. Because our cosmos is inescapable, judgment is impossible. Because there is no objective ground for us, at least within this strange network that we call a universe, well, then all we can do is keep expressing our own strange voicings within it.

At the end, we might do well to return to or remind ourselves of a few calls . . . We remember that Victor Shklovsky wrote, "If the complex life of many people takes place entirely on the level of the unconscious, then it's as if this life had never been" (Shklovsky 1991, 6). So, let's keep attention on what pierces through. We recall the nature of strange attractors, a metaphor from physics, but can imagine them pinging along the network's nodes—from rhetors to auditors. And we remind ourselves of the Lévinasian call to—if not accept—at least make do with the other: to allow a confrontation. These and other stranger calls reverberate. You may still, perhaps, feel too tame for this business, grasping like a normie, but you are still fairly strange—and likely like some strange things—and that is enough. In fact, despite how you may feel, you are deeply strange—it is just how you are.

In resistance, we seek out the wild and hazy scribblings and inscriptions of contemporary life. We're all in this thing together. As someone who appreciates collage and bricolage, I am enamored and enchanted by the vastness of the strange network. This cosmology is one where everything belongs, but where there is also room for attraction and repulsion. We don't have to accept everything, but allow everything to be rhetorical. Anything goes, but everything needn't go in. What will you add to or take from the mix, the strange brew of our weird ecology? The call? Keep connecting. Keep linking up to ever-stranger strangers. Be your own strange self. Make strange stuff. Love your strangers. And do it with all those other strangers out in our weird wide world.

Epilogue

PARRHESIA

Why Speaking Plainly May Be the Strangest Trope of All

Tell all the truth but tell it slant—
—Emily Dickinson

We began with Lycaon, a shapeshifter, and end with his son, Parrhasius.

Perhaps parrhesia, or plain talking, is the strangest move of all.

It is literally to say everything, to leave nothing hidden, to lay bare one's devices, to speak candidly. After considering the most outrageously over-the-top of figures, and its counterpart in litotes, one is then also forced to consider what lies in between that spectral bosom of exponentiation. After considering such disfigurements, such strange moves, such effects of composition practices, we close by wondering about the bald statement. At one end lies hyperbole, at the other, the humorous meiotic comment, but finally in the middle lies *deadpan*, the straight delivery, said without cracking a smile.

Now, we have explored the plain style as an understated one, and we have earlier explored the import of banalities to glue strange moves together, but here parrhesia offers something else, and it is ironically very, very strange. Parrhesia requires credibility, while exponentiation encounters a level of incredulity. And yet . . . the performing of the utmost of frank statements would cause the hearer to balk incredulously.

Simple, stripped sentences, in an age of linguistic turns, offer strikingly strange gestures, to deal us plainly. On the other hand, we want lies all the way down. Still, in some situations parrhesia should be honored for its boldness. Speaking freely is still what we ourselves are after. And we also respect it for its nature as a device of truth telling. Telling the unwinking truth is also strange in a world where we can only grasp at it. And we also recall that parrhesia was Michel Foucault's last line of thought—his final, closing exploration. So, as we come to our close, we bring up some of his final lines on the topic:

> So you see, the parrhesiastes is someone who takes a risk. Of course, this risk is not always a risk of life. When, for example, you see a friend doing

https://doi.org/10.7330/9781646422821.c007

> something wrong and you risk incurring his anger by telling him he is wrong, you are acting as a parrhesiastes. In such a case, you do not risk your life, but you may hurt him by your remarks, and your friendship may consequently suffer for it. If, in a political debate, an orator risks losing his popularity because his opinions are contrary to the majority's opinion, or his opinions may usher in a political scandal, he uses parrhesia. Parrhesia, then, is linked to courage in the face of danger: it demands the courage to speak the truth in spite of some danger. And in its extreme form, telling the truth takes place in the "game" of life or death. (2001, 15–16)

So, perhaps the trope is particularly strange to us as a culture that has begun to regard comfort above truth. To place our own lives, or our reputations, in harm's way simply resists our direction toward survival, growth, and pleasure. But to perform this last trope well is a powerful act. Foucault continues:

> Parrhesia is a kind of verbal activity where the speaker has a specific relation to truth through frankness, a certain relationship to his own life through danger, a certain type of relation to himself or other people through criticism (self-criticism or criticism of other people), and a specific relation to moral law through freedom and duty. More precisely, parrhesia is a verbal activity in which a speaker expresses his personal relationship to truth, and risks his life because he recognizes truth-telling as a duty to improve or help other people (as well as himself). In parrhesia, the speaker uses his freedom and chooses frankness instead of persuasion, truth instead of falsehood or silence, the risk of death instead of life and security, criticism instead of flattery, and moral duty instead of self-interest and moral apathy. (19–20)

To choose frankness over persuasion—to disregard the response of the other, and leave the burden with them is a paradoxical concept. We remember Foucault's last writings with great bewilderment. I can still recall receiving a copy of *Rhetoric Society Quarterly* in the mail that began with Arthur E. Walzer remembering Foucault's discussion of *parrēsia* in terms of rhetoricality, questioning and extending Foucault's own limitations in considering the effects of the trope, as a feigned twisting of sincerity in its own right (Walzer 2003, 3). Yet while being intentionally strange resists one kind of apathy, the parrhesiastes resists through the most direct route. For so many of us, as rhetorical people, it has just not been the one most traveled.

To conclude?

Parrhesia may just be the strangest trope of all. And that's the truth.

REFERENCES

Adorno, Theodor. 2005. *Minima Moralia: Reflections on a Damaged Life.* Translated by E. F. N. Jephcott. New York: Verso.

Agamben, Giorgio. 2009. *What Is an Apparatus? and Other Essays.* Translated by David Kishik and Stefan Pedatella. Stanford: Stanford University Press.

Agamben, Giorgio. 2015. *Stasis: Civil War as a Political Paradigm.* Translated by Nicholas Heron. Stanford: Stanford University Press.

Ahern, Kati Fargo. 2013. "Seeking Texts in All Available Forms: Invisible Writing and a New Reading Rhetoric of Sight and Sound." *Journal of Basic Writing* 32 (2): 80–105.

Ahmed, Sara. 2000. *Strange Encounters: Embodied Others in Post-coloniality.* New York: Routledge.

Alciato, Andrea. 1531. *Book of Emblems.* http://www.mun.ca/alciato/index.html.

Alexander, Jonathan. 2008. *Literacy, Sexuality, Pedagogy.* Logan: Utah State University Press. https://doi.org/10.2307/j.ctt4cgqkw.

Alexander, Jonathan, and Jacqueline Rhodes. 2014. *On Multimodality: New Media in Composition Studies.* Urbana: National Council of Teachers of English.

Alexander, Jonathan, and Jacqueline Rhodes. 2016. "What's Sexual about Rhetoric, What's Rhetorical about Sex?" In *Sexual Rhetorics*, edited by Jonathan Alexander and Jacqueline Rhodes, 1–16. New York: Routledge. https://doi.org/10.4324/9781315695341-6.

Allen, Danielle S. 2006. *Talking to Strangers: Anxieties of Citizenship since* Brown v. Board of Education. Chicago: University of Chicago Press.

Allen, Ira J. 2018. "Composition Is the Ethical Negotiation of Fantastical Selves." *College Composition and Communication* 70 (2): 169–94.

Amis, Martin. 1991. *Time's Arrow.* New York: Vintage.

Anchordoqui, Luis, and Francis Halzen. 2009. *Lessons in Particle Physics.* Madison: University of Wisconsin Press.

Anderson, Dan. 2012. *Waves* (blog), January 23, 2012. iamdananderson.net/professing /content/waves.

Angelou, Maya. 1990. "Human Family." In *I Shall Not Be Moved.* New York: Random House.

Anzaldúa, Gloria. 1987. *Borderlands/La Frontera: The New Mestiza.* San Francisco: Spinsters/ Aunt Lute.

Arendt, Hannah. 2006. *Between Past and Future.* New York: Penguin Classics.

Aristotle. 1932. *Poetics.* Translated by W. H. Fyfe. Cambridge, MA: Harvard University Press. Accessed February 24, 2020. http://www.perseus.tufts.edu/hopper/text?doc=Perseus %3Atext%3A1999.01.0056%3Asection%3D1447a.

Aristotle. 2006. *On Rhetoric: A Theory of Civic Discourse.* Translated by George A. Kennedy. New York: Oxford University Press.

Atkins, G. Douglas. 1994. "Envisioning the Stranger's Heart." *College English* 56 (6): 629–41. https://doi.org/10.2307/378309.

Avagyan, Shushan. 2011. "Translator's Preface." In *Bowstring: On the Dissimilarity of the Similar.* Champaign, IL: Dalkey Archive.

https://doi.org/10.7330/9781646422821.c008

Baca, Damián, Ellen Cushman, and Jonathan Osborne, eds. 2019. *Landmark Essays on Rhetorics of Difference.* New York: Routledge.

Bacon, Francis. 2008. *Francis Bacon: The Major Works.* Edited by Brian Vickers. New York: Oxford University Press.

Bad Brains. 1993. "Miss Freedom." Accessed February 26, 2020. https://genius.com/Bad-brainsmiss-freedom-lyrics.

Ball, Cheryl E., and Colin Charlton. 2015. "All Writing Is Multimodal." In *Naming What We Know,* edited by Linda Adler-Kassner and Elizabeth Wardle, 42–43. Logan: Utah State University Press.

Banks, Adam J. 2011. *Digital Griots: African American Rhetoric in a Multimedia Age.* Carbondale, IL: Southern Illinois University Press.

Baran, Paul. 1964. "On Distributed Communications Networks." *IEEE Transactions on Communications Systems* 12 (1): 1–9.

Barthes, Roland. 1975a. *The Pleasure of the Text.* Translated by Richard Miller. New York: Hill and Wang.

Barthes, Roland. 1975b. *S/Z: An Essay.* Translated by Richard Miller. New York: Hill and Wang.

Barthes, Roland. 1978. *Image-Music-Text.* Translated by Stephen Heath. New York: Hill and Wang.

Barthes, Roland. 1982. *Camera Lucida: Reflections on Photography.* Translated by Richard Howard. New York: Farrar, Straus and Giroux.

Bartholomae, David. 1980. "The Study of Error." *College Composition and Communication* 31 (3): 253–69.

Baudrillard, Jean. 2008. *Radical Alterity.* Translated by Ames Hodges. Los Angeles: Semiotext(e).

Baudrillard, Jean. 2012. *The Ecstasy of Communication.* Translated by Bernard Schütze and Caroline Schütze. Los Angeles: Semiotext(e).

Bayne, Siân. 2010. "Academetron, Automaton, Phantom: Uncanny Digital Pedagogies." *London Review of Education* 8 (1): 5–13.

The Beatles. 1967. "Penny Lane." Accessed February 27, 2020. https://genius.com/The-beatlespenny-lane-lyrics.

Bellow, Saul. 1995. *It All Adds Up: From the Dim Past to the Uncertain Future.* New York: Penguin.

Bely, Andrey. 2003. *Glossolalia.* Middlebury: SteinerBooks.

Bennett, Jane. 2010. *Vibrant Matter: A Political Ecology of Things.* Durham, NC: Duke University Press.

Berent, Moshe. 1998. "Stasis, or the Greek Invention of Politics." *History of Political Thought* 19 (3): 331–62.

Bergson, Henri. 1998. *Creative Evolution.* Translated by Arthur Mitchell. Mineola, NY: Dover.

Berlant, Lauren, and Kathleen Stewart. 2019. *The Hundreds.* Durham, NC: Duke University Press.

Bezaitis, Maria. 2013. *Why We Need Strangeness.* Digital. TED. https://www.ted.com/talks/maria_bezaitis_why_we_need_strangeness.

Bhabha, Homi K. 1998. "On the Irremovable Strangeness of Being Different." *PMLA (Publications of the Modern Language Association of America)* 113 (1): 34–39.

Bishop, Wendy, and David Starkey. 2006. *Keywords in Creative Writing.* Logan: Utah State University Press. www.jstor.org/stable/j.ctt4cgr61.

Bitzer, Lloyd F. 1968. "The Rhetorical Situation." *Philosophy & Rhetoric* 1 (1): 1–14.

Blankenship, Lisa. 2019. *Changing the Subject.* Logan: Utah State University Press.

Blessing, Stephen, and Patrick Dronek. 2006. "The Effect of Einstellung on Compositional Processes." In *Proceedings of the 28th Annual Conference of the Cognitive Science Society,* 2444. Vancouver: Cognitive Science Society.

Bloch, Ernst, Anne Halley, and Darko Suvin. 1970. "'Entfremdung, Verfremdung': Alienation, Estrangement." *The Drama Review: TDR* 15 (1): 120–25. https://doi.org/10.2307/1144598.

Bolter, Jay David, and Richard Grusin. 2000. *Remediation: Understanding New Media.* Cambridge, MA: MIT Press.

Borges, Jorge Luis. 1999. "The Library of Babel." In *Collected Fictions,* 112–18. Translated by Andrew Hurley. New York: Penguin.

Bourdieu, Pierre. 1993. *The Field of Cultural Production: Essays on Art and Literature,* edited by Randal Johnson. New York: Columbia University Press.

Boyle, Casey. 2018. *Rhetoric as a Posthuman Practice.* Columbus: Ohio State University Press.

Bridwell-Bowles, Lillian. 1992. "Discourse and Diversity: Experimental Writing within the Academy." *College Composition and Communication* 43 (3): 349–68. https://doi.org/10.2307/358227.

Britzman, Deborah P. 2012. "Queer Pedagogy and Its Strange Techniques." *Counterpoints* 367:292–308.

Brock, Kevin. 2019. *Rhetorical Code Studies.* Ann Arbor: University of Michigan Press.

Brown, James J. 2015. *Ethical Programs: Hospitality and the Rhetorics of Software.* Ann Arbor: University of Michigan Press. http://hdl.handle.net/2027/spo.13474172.0001.001.

Burke, Kenneth. 1968. *Language as Symbolic Action.* Berkeley: University of California Press.

Burke, Kenneth. 1969a. *A Grammar of Motives.* Berkeley: University of California Press.

Burke, Kenneth. 1969b. *A Rhetoric of Motives.* Berkeley: University of California Press.

Burke, Kenneth. 1984a. *Attitudes toward History.* Berkeley: University of California Press.

Burke, Kenneth. 1984b. *Permanence and Change: An Anatomy of Purpose.* Berkeley: University of California Press.

Butler, Paul. 2008. *Out of Style: Reanimating Stylistic Study in Composition and Rhetoric.* Logan: Utah State University Press.

Cage, John. 1952. 4′33″. New York: John Cage Trust.

Campbell, George. 1988. *The Philosophy of Rhetoric.* Carbondale: Southern Illinois University Press.

Carr, Nicholas. 2008. "Is Google Making Us Stupid?" *Atlantic,* July 1. https://www.theatlantic.com/magazine/archive/2008/07/is-google-making-us-stupid/306868/.

Carroll, Lewis. 1993. *Alice's Adventures in Wonderland and Through the Looking Glass.* New York: Random House.

Casagrande, June. 2010. *It Was the Best of Sentences, It Was the Worst of Sentences: A Writer's Guide to Crafting Killer Sentences.* Berkeley, CA: Ten Speed.

Ceraso, Steph. 2018. *Sounding Composition: Multimodal Pedagogies for Embodied Listening.* Pittsburgh: University of Pittsburgh Press.

Chamberlain, William. 1984. *The Policeman's Beard Is Half Constructed: Computer Prose and Poetry.* New York: Warner Books.

Chesterton, G. K. 2017. *Heretics and Orthodoxy.* Bellingham, WA: Lexham.

Chomsky, Noam. 2015. *Syntactic Structures.* Mansfield Centre, CT: Martino Fine Books.

Cicero, Marcus Tullius. 1860. *On Oratory.* Translated by John Selby Watson. New York: Harper and Brothers.

Cicero, Marcus Tullius. 1949. *On Invention.* Translated by H. M. Hubbell. Cambridge, MA: Harvard University Press.

Cooper, Marilyn. 2016. "Listening to Strange Strangers, Modifying Dreams." In *Rhetoric, through Everyday Things,* edited by Scot Barnett and Casey Boyle, 17–29. Tuscaloosa: University of Alabama Press.

Corbett, Edward P. J. 1969. "The Rhetoric of the Open Hand and the Rhetoric of the Closed Fist." *College Composition and Communication* 20 (5): 288–96. https://doi.org/10.2307/355032.

Corbett, Edward P. J., and Robert J. Connors. 1998. *Classical Rhetoric for the Modern Student.* New York: Oxford University Press.

Corder, Jim W. 1985. "Argument as Emergence, Rhetoric as Love." *Rhetoric Review* 4 (1): 16–32.

Crystal, David. 1990. "Linguistic Strangeness." In *On Strangeness*, edited by Margaret Bridges, 13–24. Tübingen: Gunter Narr Verlag.

Culler, Jonathan. 2002. *Structuralist Poetics: Structuralism, Linguistics and the Study of Literature.* New York: Routledge.

Daly, James. 2004. "Life on the Screen: Visual Literacy in Education." *Edutopia* (blog), September 14. https://www.edutopia.org/life-screen.

Danielewski, Mark Z. 2006. *Only Revolutions.* New York: Pantheon.

Darwin, Charles. 1837. *First Notebook on Transmutation of Species.* London: The British Museum.

Davis, Diane. 2010. *Inessential Solidarity: Rhetoric and Foreigner Relations.* Pittsburgh: University of Pittsburgh Press.

de Bono, Edward. 2015. *Lateral Thinking: Creativity Step by Step.* New York: Harper Colophon.

DeLanda, Manuel. 2016. *Assemblage Theory.* Edinburgh: Edinburgh University Press.

Deleuze, Gilles. 1995. *Difference and Repetition.* Translated by Paul Patton. New York: Columbia University Press.

Deleuze, Gilles, and Félix Guattari. 1986. *Nomadology: The War Machine.* Translated by Brian Massumi. Los Angeles: Semiotext(e).

Deleuze, Gilles, and Felix Guattari. 1987. *A Thousand Plateaus: Capitalism and Schizophrenia.* Translated by Brian Massumi. Minneapolis: University of Minnesota Press.

Derrida, Jacques. 1980. "The Law of Genre." Translated by Avital Ronell. *Critical Inquiry* 7 (1): 55–81.

Derrida, Jacques. 1983. *Dissemination.* Translated by Barbara Johnson. Chicago: University of Chicago Press.

Derrida, Jacques, and Anne Dufourmantelle. 2000. *Of Hospitality.* Translated by Rachel Bowlby. Stanford: Stanford University Press.

Detweiler, Eric. 2018. "The Weirdness of Rhetoric, the Rhetoric of Weirdness." *Textshop Experiments* 5. http://textshopexperiments.org/textshop05/weirdness-of-rhetoric.

Detweiler, Eric. 2019. "The Weird Possibilities of Academic Podcasting." *Rhetoricity.* http://rhetoricity.libsyn.com/the-weird-possibilities-of-academic-podcasting.

Dewey, John. 1997. *How We Think.* Mineola, NY: Dover.

Dick, Philip K. 1976. "Man, Android and Machine." In *Science Fiction at Large*, edited by Peter Nicholls, 202. New York: Harper and Row.

Dick, Philip K. 1981. *The VALIS Trilogy.* New York: Bantam.

Dillard, Annie. 1989. "Write till You Drop." *New York Times*, May 28. https://archive.nytimes.com/www.nytimes.com/books/99/03/28/specials/dillard-drop.html.

Dolmage, Jay. 2012. "Writing against Normal." In *Composing Media Composing Embodiment*, edited by Kristin Arola and Anne Wysocki, 110–26. Logan: Utah State University Press.

Donne, John. 1999. *Devotions upon Emergent Occasions and Death's Duel.* New York: Vintage.

Douglass, Frederick. 1845. *Narrative of the Life of Frederick Douglass, an American Slave.* Boston: Anti-Slavery Office.

Drucker, Johanna. 2014. *Graphesis: Visual Forms of Knowledge Production.* Cambridge, MA: Harvard University Press.

Eagleton, Terry. 2008. *Trouble with Strangers: A Study of Ethics.* Malden, MA: Wiley-Blackwell.

Edbauer, Jenny. 2005. "Unframing Models of Public Distribution: From Rhetorical Situation to Rhetorical Ecologies." *Rhetoric Society Quarterly* 35 (4): 5–24. https://doi.org/10.1080/02773940509391320.

Erasmus, Desiderius. 1999. *On Copia of Words and Ideas: De Utraque Verborum ac Rerum Copia.* Translated by Donald B. King and Herbert David Rix. Mediaeval Philosophical Texts in Translation. Milwaukee: Marquette University Press. http://libezp.lib.lsu.edu/login?url=https://search.ebscohost.com/login.aspx?direct=true&db=nlebk&AN=13591&site=eds-live&scope=site&profile=eds-main.

Esanu, Octavian. 2013. *Transition in Post-Soviet Art: The Collective Actions Group Before and After 1989.* New York: Central European University Press.

Espenshade, Abraham Howry. 1904. *The Essentials of Composition and Rhetoric.* New York: D. C. Heath.

Fahnestock, Jeanne. 2011. *Rhetorical Style: The Uses of Language in Persuasion.* New York: Oxford University Press.

Fisher, Mark. 2017. *The Weird and the Eerie.* London: Repeater.

Fleckenstein, Kristie S., and Anna M. Worm. 2019. "Unity and Difference." In *Rhetorical Speculations,* edited by Scott Sundvall, 25–44. The Future of Rhetoric, Writing, and Technology. Logan: Utah State University Press. www.jstor.org/stable/j.ctvg8p6h9.4.

Flores, Lisa A. 2003. "Constructing Rhetorical Borders: Peons, Illegal Aliens, and Competing Narratives of Immigration." *Critical Studies in Media Communication* 20 (4): 362–87.

Flores, Lisa A. 2019. "Stoppage and the Racialized Rhetorics of Mobility." *Western Journal of Communication* (October): 1–17. https://doi.org/10.1080/10570314.2019.1676914.

Foucault, Michel. 1980. *Power/Knowledge: Selected Interviews and Other Writings, 1972–1977,* edited by Colin Gordon. Translated by Colin Gordon, Leo Marshall, John Mepham, and Kate Soper. New York: Vintage.

Foucault, Michel. 2001. *Fearless Speech.* Translated by Joseph Pearson. New York: Zone Books.

Foucault, Michel. 2007. *Abnormal: Lectures at the Collège de France, 1974–1975.* Translated by Graham Burchell. New York: Picador.

Foucault, Michel. 2012. *The Archaeology of Knowledge.* Translated by A. M. Sheridan Smith. New York: Vintage.

Foucault, Michel. 2013. *History of Madness.* Translated by Jonathan Murphy and Jean Kalfa. New York: Routledge.

Fraser, Nancy. 1990. "Rethinking the Public Sphere: A Contribution to the Critique of Actually Existing Democracy." *Social Text* 25/26:56–80. https://doi.org/10.2307/466240.

Freud, Sigmund. 2003. *The Uncanny.* Translated by David McLintock. New York: Penguin.

Frye, Northrop. 1971. *Anatomy of Criticism.* Princeton: Princeton University Press.

Galloway, Alexander R., and Eugene Thacker. 2007. *The Exploit: A Theory of Networks.* Minneapolis: University of Minnesota Press.

Galloway, Alexander R., Eugene Thacker, and McKenzie Wark. 2013. *Excommunication: Three Inquiries in Media and Mediation.* Chicago: University of Chicago Press.

Geertz, Clifford. 2012. "The Uses of Diversity." In *Available Light,* 68–88. Princeton: Princeton University Press. http://libezp.lib.lsu.edu/login?url=https://search.ebscohost.com/login.aspx?direct=true&db=edspmu&AN=edspmu.MUSE9781400823406.9&site=eds-live&scope=site&profile=eds-main.

Gershon, Ilana, and Joshua A. Bell. 2013. "The Newness of New Media." *Culture, Theory and Critique* 54 (3): 259–64. https://doi.org/10.1080/14735784.2013.852732.

Gladwell, Malcolm. 2019. *Talking to Strangers: What We Should Know about the People We Don't Know.* New York: Little, Brown.

Gleick, James. 1987. *Chaos: Making a New Science.* New York: Viking.

Glenn, Cheryl. 2018. *Rhetorical Feminism and This Thing Called Hope.* Carbondale: Southern Illinois University Press.

Godin, Seth. 2007. *Purple Cow: Transform Your Business by Being Remarkable.* New York: Penguin Books.

Göransson, Johannes. 2020. "To Vibrebrate: In Defense of Strangeness." *Poetry Foundation,* February 26. https://www.poetryfoundation.org/harriet/2017/07/to-vibrebrate-in-defense-of-strangeness.

Gordon, Karen Elizabeth. 1993. *The Deluxe Transitive Vampire: The Ultimate Handbook of Grammar for the Innocent, the Eager, and the Doomed.* New York: Pantheon.

Group μ. 1981. *A General Rhetoric.* Translated by Paul Burrell and Edgar Slotkin. Baltimore: Johns Hopkins University Press.

Guilford, J. P. 1967. *The Nature of Human Intelligence.* New York: McGraw-Hill.

Habermas, Jürgen. 1974. "The Public Sphere: An Encyclopedia Article (1964)." Translated by Sara Lennox and Frank Lennox. *New German Critique,* 3:49–55. https://doi.org/10.2307/487737.

Halbritter, Bump. 2012. *Mics, Cameras, Symbolic Action: Audio-Visual Rhetoric for Writing Teachers.* Anderson, SC: Parlor Press.

Hallowell, Ronan. 2011. "Media Ecological Psychopharmacosophy: An Ecology of Mind for Today." In *Drugs & Media: New Perspectives on Communication, Consumption, and Consciousness,* edited by Robert C. Macdougall, 237–65. New York: Continuum.

Hariman, Robert. 1995. *Political Style: The Artistry of Power.* Chicago: University of Chicago Press.

Harman, Graham. 2012. *Weird Realism: Lovecraft and Philosophy.* Washington: Zero Books.

Harris, Ada Van Stone, and Lillian McLean Waldo. 1911. *First Journeys in Numberland.* New York: Scott, Foresman.

Hawk, Byron. 2007. *A Counter-history of Composition: Toward Methodologies of Complexity.* Pittsburgh: University of Pittsburgh Press.

Hawthorne, Nathaniel. 1846. "The Birth-Mark." In *Mosses from an Old Manse,* 32–51. London: Wiley and Putnam.

Hayles, N. Katherine. 1993. "Virtual Bodies and Flickering Signifiers." *October* 66:69–91. https://doi.org/10.2307/778755.

Haynes, Cynthia. 2003. "Writing Offshore: The Disappearing Coastline of Composition Theory." *JAC* 23 (4): 667–724.

Hazlitt, William. 1822. *Table-talk; or, Original Essays.* London: Colburn.

Heidegger, Martin. 1977. *The Question Concerning Technology, and Other Essays.* Translated by William Lovitt. New York: Garland.

Heidegger, Martin. 2013. *Poetry, Language, Thought.* Translated by Albert Hofstadter. New York: Harper Perennial Modern Classics.

Heraclitus. 1920. *Fragments of Heraclitus.* Translated by John Burnet. London: A. and C. Black.

Hermogenes. 1987. *On Types of Style.* Translated by Cecil W. Wooten. Chapel Hill: The University of North Carolina Press.

Homer. 2018. *The Odyssey.* Translated by Emily Wilson. New York: Norton.

hooks, bell. 1994. *Teaching to Transgress: Education as the Practice of Freedom.* New York: Routledge.

Horace. 2002. "Ars Poetica." In *Satires and Epistles.* Translated by S. P. Bovie. Modern English Verse Translation. Chicago: University of Chicago Press.

Inoue, Asao B. 2019. "How Do We Language So People Stop Killing Each Other, or What Do We Do about White Language Supremacy?" *College Composition and Communication* 71 (2): 352–69.

Irigaray, Luce. 1985. *Speculum of the Other Woman.* Translated by Gillian Gill. Ithaca, NY: Cornell University Press.

Irving, Washington. 2008. *The Legend of Sleepy Hollow.* Project Gutenberg. https://www.gutenberg.org/files/41/41-h/41-h.htm.

Jacobson, Michael. 2006. *The Giant's Fence.* Minneapolis: Barbarian Interior Books.

James, William. 1920. *Psychology: Briefer Course.* New York: H. Holt.

Jameson, Fredric. 1972. *The Prison-house of Language.* Princeton: Princeton University Press.

Johnson, T. R. 2001. "School Sucks." *College Composition and Communication* 52 (4): 620–650.

Johnson, T. R. 2003. *A Rhetoric of Pleasure: Prose Style and Today's Composition Classroom.* Portsmouth, NH: Boynton/Cook.

Joyce, James. 2012. *Finnegans Wake.* Oxford: Oxford University Press.

Joyce, Michael Thomas. 2000. *Othermindedness: The Emergence of Network Culture.* Ann Arbor: University of Michigan Press.

Kant, Immanuel. 1903. *Perpetual Peace.* Translated by M. Campbell Smith. London: Swan Sonnenschein.

Kasner, Edward, and James Newman. 1940. *Mathematics and the Imagination.* New York: Simon and Schuster.

Kennerly, Michele. 2015. "An Alloiostrophic Addition." In *A Revolution in Tropes: Alloiostrophic Rhetoric,* edited by Jane S. Sutton and Mari Lee Mifsud, 83–96. Lanham, MD: Lexington Books.

Kennerly, Michele. 2017. "Socrates Ex Situ." *Advances in the History of Rhetoric* 20 (2): 196–208. doi:10.1080/15362426.2017.1327278.

Kerschbaum, Stephanie L. 2014. *Toward a New Rhetoric of Difference.* Champaign, IL: National Council of Teachers of English.

Khadka, Santosh, and J. C. Lee, eds. 2018. *Bridging the Multimodal Gap: From Theory to Practice.* Logan: Utah State University Press.

Kincaid, Jamaica. 2000. *A Small Place.* New York: Farrar, Straus and Giroux.

King Missile. 1991. "It's Saturday." https://genius.com/King-missile-its-saturday-lyrics.

Kittler, Friedrich A. 1999. *Gramophone, Film, Typewriter.* Translated by Geoffrey Winthrop-Young and Michael Wutz. Stanford: Stanford University Press.

Knickerbocker, Conrad. 1965. "William S. Burroughs, the Art of Fiction No. 36." *Paris Review* (Fall) https://www.theparisreview.org/interviews/4424/the-art-of-fiction-no-36-william-s-burroughs.

Kolln, Martha. 2006. *Rhetorical Grammar: Grammatical Choices, Rhetorical Effects.* New York: Longman.

Kristeva, Julia. 1994. *Strangers to Ourselves.* Translated by Leon Roudiez. New York: Columbia University Press.

Lamott, Anne. 2007. *Bird by Bird: Some Instructions on Writing and Life.* New York: Knopf Doubleday.

Lanham, Richard A. 2004. *The Motives of Eloquence: Literary Rhetoric in the Renaissance.* Eugene, OR: Wipf and Stock.

Lanham, Richard A. 2007. *The Economics of Attention: Style and Substance in the Age of Information.* Chicago: University of Chicago Press.

Lanham, Richard A. 2012. *A Handlist of Rhetorical Terms.* Oakland: University of California Press.

Latour, Bruno. 2007. *Reassembling the Social: An Introduction to Actor-Network-Theory.* Oxford: Oxford University Press.

Lévinas, Emmanuel. 1969. *Totality and Infinity: An Essay on Exteriority.* Translated by Alphonso Lingis. Pittsburgh: Duquesne University Press.

Levine, Caroline. 2017. *Forms: Whole, Rhythm, Hierarchy, Network.* Princeton: Princeton University Press.

Lewitt, Sol. 1999. "Sentences on Conceptual Art." In *Conceptual Art: A Critical Anthology,* edited by Alexander Alberro and Blake Stimson, 106–8. Cambridge, MA: MIT Press.

Lin, Maya. 2009. *Unchopping a Tree.* 3 minutes, 17 seconds. Video artwork. Produced by Radical Media. https://www.mayalinstudio.com/memory-works/unchopping-a-tree.

Livingstone, Sonia. 2009. "On the Mediation of Everything: ICA Presidential Address 2008." *Journal of Communication* 59 (1): 1–18. https://doi.org/10.1111/j.1460-2466.2008.01401.x.

Lorenz, Edward. 1995. *The Essence of Chaos.* Seattle: University of Washington Press.

Lyotard, Jean-François. 1989. *The Differend.* Translated by Georges Van den Abbeele. Minneapolis: University of Minnesota Press.

Lyotard, Jean-François. 2019. *Discourse, Figure.* Translated by Antony Hudek and Mary Lydon. Minneapolis.: University of Minnesota Press.

Mbembe, Achille. 2019. *Necropolitics.* Durham, NC: Duke University Press.
McKenzie, Ian. 2015. *Sixty-Nine Tools: Sixty-Nine Useful Rhetorical Devices Which Will Assist in Vastly Improving Your Presentations and Writing.* Ian McKenzie.
McLuhan, Marshall. 1964. *Understanding Media: The Extensions of Man.* New York: Signet Books.
McLuhan, Marshall, and Quentin Fiore. 2001a. *The Medium Is the Massage.* Berkeley, CA: Gingko.
McLuhan, Marshall, and Quentin Fiore. 2001b. *War and Peace in the Global Village.* Corte Madera, CA: Gingko.
Merwin, W. S. 2009. "Unchopping a Tree." *Design Observer,* January 7. https://designobserver.com/feature/unchopping-a-tree/7857.
Mifsud, Mari Lee. 2018. "On Network." In *Ancient Rhetorics and Digital Networks,* edited by Michele Kennerly and Damien Smith Pfister, 28–47. Tuscaloosa: University of Alabama Press.
Miller, Carolyn. 2000. "The Aristotelian Topos: Hunting for Novelty." In *Rereading Aristotle's Rhetoric,* edited by Alan G. Gross and Arthur E. Walzer, 130–46. Carbondale: Southern Illinois University Press.
Miller, George A. 1956. "The Magical Number Seven, Plus or Minus Two: Some Limits on Our Capacity for Processing Information." *Psychological Review* 63 (2): 81–97.
Minh-ha, Trinh T. 1989. *Woman, Native, Other.* Bloomington: Indiana University Press.
Morrison, Toni. 1993. *Playing in the Dark: Whiteness and the Literary Imagination.* New York: Vintage.
Morrison, Toni. 2017. *The Origin of Others.* Cambridge, MA: Harvard University Press.
Morton, Timothy. 2012. *The Ecological Thought.* Cambridge, MA: Harvard University Press.
Mueller, Derek N. 2017. *Network Sense: Methods for Visualizing a Discipline.* Logan: Utah State University Press.
Muñoz, José Esteban. 1999. *Disidentifications: Queers of Color and the Performance of Politics.* Minneapolis: University of Minnesota Press.
Nancy, Jean-Luc. 2000. *Being Singular Plural.* Translated by Robert Richardson and Anne O'Byrne. Stanford: Stanford University Press.
The New London Group. 1996. "A Pedagogy of Multiliteracies: Designing Social Futures." *Harvard Educational Review* 66 (1): 60–92.
Ngai, Sianne. 2015. *Our Aesthetic Categories: Zany, Cute, Interesting.* Cambridge, MA: Harvard University Press.
Nietzsche, Friedrich. 2010. *The Gay Science: With a Prelude in Rhymes and an Appendix of Songs.* Translated by Walter Kaufmann. New York: Vintage.
O'Conner, Patricia T. 2019. *Woe Is I: The Grammarphobe's Guide to Better English in Plain English.* New York: Riverhead Books.
OED Online. 2021. Oxford University Press. https://www-oed-com.libezp.lib.lsu.edu/view/Entry/191244?isAdvanced=false&result=1&rskey=fjVcfG&.
Ovid. 2000. *Metamorphoses: The Arthur Golding Translation of 1567.* Philadelphia: Paul Dry Books.
Palmeri, Jason. 2012. *Remixing Composition: A History of Multimodal Writing Pedagogy.* Carbondale: Southern Illinois University Press.
Perelman, Chaïm, and Lucie Olbrechts-Tyteca. 1971. *The New Rhetoric: A Treatise on Argumentation.* Translated by John Wilkinson and Purcell Weaver. Notre Dame, IN: University of Notre Dame Press.
Perloff, Marjorie. 2013. *Poetics in a New Key.* Chicago: University of Chicago Press.
Pinker, Steven. 2015. *The Sense of Style: The Thinking Person's Guide to Writing in the Twenty-First Century.* New York: Penguin Books.
Plato. 1921. *Sophist.* In *Plato in Twelve Volumes.* Translated by Harold N. Fowler. Cambridge, MA: Harvard University Press. http://data.perseus.org/citations/urn:cts:greekLit:tlg0059.tlg007.perseus-eng1:216a.

Plato. 1972. *Phaedrus.* Translated by R. Hackforth. Cambridge: Cambridge University Press.

Plato. 1993. *The Republic.* Translated by Robin Waterfield. New York: Oxford University Press.

Plato. 2009. *Gorgias.* Translated by Benjamin Jowett. http://classics.mit.edu/Plato/gorgias.html.

Plutarch. 1936. *De Pythiae Oraculis.* Translated by Frank Cole Babbitt. Cambridge, MA: Harvard University Press.

Postman, Neil. 2000. "The Humanism of Media Ecology." *Proceedings of the Media Ecology Association* 1:10–16.

Postman, Neil. 2009. *Teaching As a Subversive Activity.* New York: Delta.

Puttenham, George. 2007. *The Art of English Poesy: A Critical Edition.* Edited by Frank Whigham and Wayne A. Rebhorn. Ithaca, NY: Cornell University Press.

Queneau, Raymond. 1958. *Exercises in Style.* Translated by Barbara Wright. Paris: Gallimard.

Queneau, Raymond. 1961. *Cent mille millards de poèms.* Paris: Gallimard.

Quintilian. 1922. *Institutio Oratoria.* Translated by Harold Edgeworth Butler. Cambridge, MA: Harvard University Press.

Ramo, Joshua Cooper. 2016. *The Seventh Sense: Power, Fortune, and Survival in the Age of Networks.* New York: Little, Brown.

Rancière, Jacques. 2010. *Dissensus: On Politics and Aesthetics.* Translated by Steven Corcoran. New York: Continuum.

Ratcliffe, Krista. 1999. "Rhetorical Listening: A Trope for Interpretive Invention and a 'Code of Cross-Cultural Conduct.'" *College Composition and Communication* 51 (2): 195–224. https://doi.org/10.2307/359039.

Reynolds, Malvina. 1967. "Little Boxes." https://genius.com/Malvina-reynolds-little-boxes-lyrics.

Rice, Jeff. 2007. "Networked Boxes: The Logic of Too Much." *College Composition and Communication* 59 (2): 299–311.

Richards, I. A. 1965. *The Philosophy of Rhetoric.* New York: Oxford University Press.

Rickert, Thomas. 2013. *Ambient Rhetoric: The Attunements of Rhetorical Being.* Pittsburgh: University of Pittsburgh Press.

Rivers, Nathaniel A. 2015. "Deep Ambivalence and Wild Objects: Toward a Strange Environmental Rhetoric." *Rhetoric Society Quarterly* 45 (5): 420–40.

Ross, Clifford, ed. 1991. *Abstract Expressionism: Creators and Critics, an Anthology.* New York: Harry Abrams.

Runciman, Lex. 1991. "Fun?" *College English* 53 (2): 156–62. https://doi.org/10.2307/378194.

RuPaul. 2016. "Category Is . . ." https://genius.com/Rupaul-category-is-lyrics.

Said, Edward. 1979. *Orientalism.* New York: Vintage.

Schiappa, Edward. 2001. "Second Thoughts on the Critiques of Big Rhetoric." *Philosophy and Rhetoric* 34 (3): 260–74.

Schuster, Edgar H. 2006. "A Fresh Look at Sentence Fragments." *English Journal* 95 (5): 78–83.

Schwartz, Herman. 1910. *Novelty device.* United States Patent Office 978,943, filed March 11, 1910, and issued December 20, 1910.

Scoville, Chad. 2010. "Time and the Post-information Age." *Wired,* March 20. https://www.wired.com/2010/03/time-and-the-post-information-age/.

Selfe, Cynthia L. 2009. "The Movement of Air, the Breath of Meaning: Aurality and Multimodal Composing." *College Composition and Communication* 60 (4): 616–63.

Sex Pistols. 1976. "Anarchy in the U.K." Accessed February 26, 2020. https://genius.com/Sexpistols-anarchy-in-the-uk-lyrics.

Shaviro, Steven. 2003. *Connected, or What It Means to Live in the Network Society.* Minneapolis: University of Minnesota Press.

Sher, Benjamin. 1991. "Translator's Introduction." In *Theory of Prose,* xv–xxi. Elmwood Park, IL: Dalkey Archive.

Sheridan, David M., Jim Ridolfo, and Anthony J. Michel. 2005. "The Available Means of Persuasion: Mapping a Theory and Pedagogy of Multimodal Public Rhetoric." *JAC* 25 (4): 803–44.

Shipka, Jody. 2011. *Toward a Composition Made Whole*. Pittsburgh: University of Pittsburgh Press.

Shklovsky, Viktor. 1991. *Theory of Prose*. Translated by Benjamin Sher. Elmwood Park, IL: Dalkey Archive.

Shklovsky, Viktor. 2011. *Bowstring: On the Dissimilarity of the Similar*. Translated by Shushan Avagyan. Champaign, IL: Dalkey Archive.

Silva Rhetoricae. 2016. "The Forest of Rhetoric." http://rhetoric.byu.edu/.

Simmel, Georg. 1950. "The Stranger." In *The Sociology of Georg Simmel*, 402–8. Translated by Kurt H. Wolff. New York: Free Press.

Sirc, Geoffrey. 2002. *English Composition as a Happening*. Logan: Utah State University Press.

Sirc, Geoffrey M. 2004. "Box-Logic." In *Writing New Media: Theory and Applications for Expanding the Teaching of Composition*, edited by Anne Frances Wysocki, 111–46. Logan: Utah State University Press.

Sophocles. 2000. *The Three Theban Plays: Antigone; Oedipus the King; Oedipus at Colonus*. Translated by Robert Fagles. New York: Penguin.

Spivak, Gayatri Chakravorty. 1988. "Can the Subaltern Speak?" In *Marxism and the Interpretation of Culture*, edited by Nelson Cary and Grossberg Lawrence, 271–313. Chicago: University of Illinois Press.

Sterling, Bruce. 2009. "Asemic Writing." *Wired*, July 13. https://www.wired.com/2009/07/web-semantics-asemic-writing/.

Stiegler, Bernard. 1998. *Technics and Time*, vol. 1: *The Fault of Epimetheus*. Translated by Richard Beardsworth and George Collins. Stanford: Stanford University Press.

Strunk, William, and E. B. White. 2007. *The Elements of Style*. New York: Penguin Books.

Sydell, Laura. 2016. "David Bowie, the Internet Visionary." *NPR.org*, January 12, sec. Opinion. https://www.npr.org/sections/alltechconsidered/2016/01/12/462744754/david-bowie-the-internet-visionary.

Tate, Marcia L. 2004. *"Sit and Get" Won't Grow Dendrites: 20 Professional Learning Strategies That Engage the Adult Brain*. Thousand Oaks, CA: Corwin.

Thompson, Hunter S. 2010. *The Great Shark Hunt: Strange Tales from a Strange Time*. New York: Picador.

Tindale, Christopher W. 2004. *Rhetorical Argumentation: Principles of Theory and Practice*. Thousand Oaks, CA: SAGE.

Truss, Lynne. 2006. *Eats, Shoots & Leaves: The Zero Tolerance Approach to Punctuation*. New York: Avery.

Twain, Mark, and Tom Quirk. 1994. *Tales, Speeches, Essays, and Sketches*. New York: Penguin Classics.

Ulmer, Gregory L. 1994. *Heuretics: The Logic of Invention*. Baltimore: Johns Hopkins University Press.

Ulmer, Gregory L. 2003. *Internet Invention: From Literacy to Electracy*. New York: Pearson.

Ulmer, Gregory L. 2008. "The Chora Collaborations." *Rhizomes*, no. 18 (Winter). http://www.rhizomes.net/issue18/ulmer/index.html.

Vatz, Richard E. 1973. "The Myth of the Rhetorical Situation." *Philosophy & Rhetoric* 6 (3): 154–61.

Vitanza, Victor. 2000. "From Heuristic to Aleatory Procedures; or, Toward 'Writing the Accident.'" In *Inventing a Discipline*, edited by Maureen Daly Goggin, 185–206. Urbana, IL: NCTE.

Vitanza, Victor. 2003. "Abandoned to Writing: Notes toward Several Provocations." *Enculturation* 5 (1). http://www.enculturation.net/5_1/vitanza.html.

Vivian, Bradford. 2004. *Being Made Strange: Rhetoric beyond Representation*. Albany: SUNY Press.

Waite, Stacey. 2017. *Teaching Queer: Radical Possibilities for Writing and Knowing.* Pittsburgh: University of Pittsburgh Press.

Walker, Linda Marie. 2007. "Surface to Surface, Ashes to Ashes (Reporting to U)." Electronic Book Review. https://electronicbookreview.com/essay/surface-to-surface-ashes-to-ashes-reporting-to-u/.

Wallace, David Foster. 2008. "On Life and Work." *Wall Street Journal,* September 20, sec. Life & Style. https://www.wsj.com/articles/SB122178211966454607.

Walsh, Bill. 2004. *The Elephants of Style: A Trunkload of Tips on the Big Issues and Gray Areas of Contemporary American English.* New York: McGraw-Hill.

Walzer, Arthur E. 2003. "Parrēsia, Foucault, and the Classical Rhetorical Tradition." *Rhetoric Society Quarterly* 43 (1): 1–21.

Warner, Michael. 1999. *The Trouble with Normal.* Cambridge, MA: Harvard University Press.

Warner, Michael. 2005. *Publics and Counterpublics.* New York: Zone Books.

Watts, Eric King. 2001. " 'Voice' and 'Voicelessness' in Rhetorical Studies." *Quarterly Journal of Speech* 87 (2): 179–96. https://doi.org/10.1080/00335630109384328.

Weathers, Winston. 1970. "Teaching Style: A Possible Anatomy." *College Composition and Communication* 21 (2): 144–49. https://doi.org/10.2307/356552.

Weathers, Winston. 1980. *An Alternate Style: Options in Composition.* Rochelle Park, NJ: Boynton/Cook.

Whitman, Walt. 1867. "To a Stranger." In *Leaves of Grass,* 135. New York: W. E. Chapin.

Wilde, Oscar. 1993. *The Picture of Dorian Gray.* New York: Dover.

Williams, Joseph M. 1999. *Style: Ten Lessons in Clarity and Grace.* New York: Addison-Wesley.

Williams, Patricia. 1991. *The Alchemy of Race and Rights.* Cambridge, MA: Harvard University Press.

Withy, Katherine. 2015. *Heidegger: On Being Uncanny.* Cambridge, MA: Harvard University Press.

Wittgenstein, Ludwig. 1991. *Philosophical Investigations.* Translated by G. E. M. Anscombe, P. M. S. Hacker, and Joachim Schulte. Malden, MA: Wiley-Blackwell.

Wolf, Asher. 2018. "Weird Networks in the Fight for Human Rights." *Medium* (blog), March 20. https://medium.com/@Asher_Wolf/weird-networks-in-the-fight-for-human-rights-2f148a47183b.

Woolf, Virginia. 1987. *The Waves.* New York: Cambridge University Press.

Worsham, Lynn. 1999. "On the Discipline and Pleasure of Perilous Acts." *JAC* 19 (4): 707–21.

Wysocki, Anne Frances. 2005. "awaywithwords: On the Possibilities in Unavailable Designs." *Computers and Composition* 22 (1): 55–62. https://doi.org/10.1016/j.compcom.2004.12.011.

Yam, Shui-yin Sharon. 2019. *Inconvenient Strangers.* Columbus: Ohio State University Press.

Yancey, Kathleen Blake. 2004. "Made Not Only in Words: Composition in a New Key." *College Composition and Communication* 56 (2): 297–328. https://doi.org/10.2307/4140651.

Yergeau, M. Remi. 2017. *Authoring Autism: On Rhetoric and Neurological Queerness.* Durham, NC: Duke University Press.

Young, Vershawn Ashanti. 2010. "Should Writers Use They Own English?" *Iowa Journal of Cultural Studies* 12 (1): 110–17.

Žižek, Slavoj. 2013. "Neighbors and Other Monsters: A Plea for Ethical Violence." In *The Neighbor: Three Inquiries in Political Theology,* 134–90. Chicago: University of Chicago Press.

INDEX

Page numbers followed by *f* indicate figures. Page numbers followed by *t* indicate tables.

ABOUT THE AUTHOR

Jimmy Butts teaches writing and the teaching of writing to university students and is always looking for novel ways of doing those things. He has worked with students from Charleston County High Schools, Winthrop University, Clemson University, Wake Forest University, and now Louisiana State University in Baton Rouge as Director of the University Writing Program. He received his PhD from the transdisciplinary program known as Rhetorics, Communication, and Information Design at Clemson University. His research interests include postmodern composition strategies, new media, rhetorical criticism, defamiliarization, and writing pedagogy. He has published work in *Communication Design Quarterly*, *Textshop Experiments*, the *Kenneth Burke Journal*, *Itineration*, *Pre-Text*, the *Journal for Undergraduate Multimedia Projects*, the *Writing Lab Newsletter*, *Digital Humanities Quarterly*, *The Cybertext Yearbook*, and elsewhere.